Springer's Forensic Laboratory Science Series

Series Editor
Ashraf Mozayani, Ph.D.

For other titles published in this series, go to
http://www.springer.com/series/8401

Jennifer Bayuk
Editor

CyberForensics

Understanding Information Security Investigations

Foreword by Amit Yoran

Editor
Jennifer Bayuk
Cybersecurity Program Director
School of Systems and Engineering
Stevens Institute of Technology
Castle Point on Hudson
518 Babbio Center
Hoboken, NJ 07030, USA
jennifer@bayuk.com

ISBN 978-1-60761-771-6   e-ISBN 978-1-60761-772-3
DOI 10.1007/978-1-60761-772-3
Springer New York Dordrecht Heidelberg London

Library of Congress Control Number: 2010931676

© Springer Science+Business Media, LLC 2010
All rights reserved. This work may not be translated or copied in whole or in part without the written permission of the publisher (Humana Press, c/o Springer Science+Business Media, LLC, 233 Spring Street, New York, NY 10013, USA), except for brief excerpts in connection with reviews or scholarly analysis. Use in connection with any form of information storage and retrieval, electronic adaptation, computer software, or by similar or dissimilar methodology now known or hereafter developed is forbidden.
The use in this publication of trade names, trademarks, service marks, and similar terms, even if they are not identified as such, is not to be taken as an expression of opinion as to whether or not they are subject to proprietary rights.
While the advice and information in this book are believed to be true and accurate at the date of going to press, neither the authors nor the editors nor the publisher can accept any legal responsibility for any errors or omissions that may be made. The publisher makes no warranty, express or implied, with respect to the material contained herein.

Printed on acid-free paper

Humana Press is part of Springer Science+Business Media (www.springer.com)

Contents

1 **Introduction** 1
   Jennifer Bayuk

2 **The Complex World of Corporate CyberForensics Investigations** .. 7
   Gregory Leibolt

3 **Investigating Large-Scale Data Breach Cases** 29
   J. Andrew Valentine

4 **Insider Threat Investigations** 45
   Shane Sims

5 **Accounting Forensics** 53
   Tracy McBride

6 **Analyzing Malicious Software** 59
   Lenny Zeltser

7 **Network Packet Forensics** 85
   Eddie Schwartz

8 **RAM and File Systems Investigations** 103
   Rita M. Barrios and Yuri Signori

9 **One Picture is Worth a Million Bytes** 117
   Don Fergus and Anthony Agresta

10 **Cybercrime and Law Enforcement Cooperation** 129
   Art Ehuan

11 **Technology Malpractice** 141
   Paul Rohmeyer

Glossary 149

Index 153

Foreword

Cyberforensics is a fairly new word in the technology our industry, but one that nevertheless has immediately recognizable meaning. Although the word forensics may have its origins in formal debates using evidence, it is now most closely associated with investigation into evidence of crime. As the word cyber has become synonymous with the use of electronic technology, the word cyberforensics bears no mystery. It immediately conveys a serious and concentrated endeavor to identify the evidence of crimes or other attacks committed in cyberspace. Nevertheless, the full implications of the word are less well understood. Cyberforensic activities remain a mystery to most people, even those fully immersed in the design and operation of cyber technology. This book sheds light on those activities in a way that is comprehensible not only to technology professionals but also to the technology hobbyist and those simply curious about the field.

When I started contributing to the field of cybersecurity, it was an obscure field, rarely mentioned in the mainstream media. According to the FBI, by 2009 organized crime syndicates were making more money via cybercrime than in drug trafficking. In spite of the rise in cybercrime and the advance of sophisticated threat actors online, the cyber security profession continues to lag behind in its ability to investigate cybercrime and understand the root causes of cyber attacks. In the late 1990s I worked to respond to sophisticated attacks as part of the U.S. Department of Defense Computer Emergency Response Team. In that endeavor, the criticality and immeasurable value of cyberforensics became blatantly clear. As the Director of the National Cyber Security Division and US-CERT programs at the Department of Homeland Security, we continued to encourage greater cyberforensic capabilities for federal departments and agencies. I continue to testify to Congress about the need for better cyberforensic capabilities both in the government and in the private sector, where the understanding of ever more sophisticated attacks remains immature.

As CEO of a cyberforensics software company whose products are widely used by both government and industry, I am exposed to many sophisticated incidents that have infiltrated both these markets. These markets have nearly identical technology infrastructures and are increasingly targeted by the same advanced threat actors. Only through such cross-sector sharing of threat intelligence, expertise, and technology can we hope to better protect and defend the systems on which we rely. It has been gratifying to see this theme echoed by the expert authors in this book.

As in many aspects of emerging technologies, the experts in the field are not limited to those who have studied it in academia. This book describes technology investigations based on specimens identified in the wild, not those modeled in a laboratory. The chapter authors have been recruited for their ability to provide the matter-of-fact analysis that can only be attained by direct experience.

Even professional cyberforensics textbooks are largely written from a technology perspective, where the aim is for the reader to understand how cyberspace works so that they may trace activity in it. While the technology field is broad, there are relatively few with the prerequisite security experience to become proficient at end-to-end cybersecurity investigations that involve organizational and human elements as well as technology. Each chapter author in this book is a professional who plays a highly focused role in the field of cyberforensics, yet is also clearly aware of the broader field as a whole. They have differentiated their contributions in a methodical and complementary manner, allowing the reader to appreciate how they can be implemented in unison based on the requirements of any cyberforensic investigation. These contributions have the benefit of Jennifer Bayuk's vast experience in bringing cybersecurity concepts to the layman, and her skillful editing has contributed to its overall readability.

Herndon, VA   Amit Yoran

Contributors

Anthony Agresta Vice President, Centrifuge Systems, McLean, VA, USA

Rita M. Barrios Assistant Professor, University of Detroit Mercy, National Security Agency Center of Academic Excellence, Detroit, MI, USA

Jennifer Bayuk Stevens Institute of Technology, Hoboken, NJ, USA

Art Ehuan Forward Discovery, Alexandria, VA, USA

Don Fergus Vice President of IT Risk Management and Chief Security Officer Intekras, Inc., Sterling, VA, USA

Gregory Leibolt Senior Technical Director, AT&T Inc., 208 S. Akard St., Dallas, TX 75202, USA

Tracy McBride Certified Public Accountant [CPA/CFF], TMM Advisors LLC, New Jersey, USA

Paul Rohmeyer Howe School of Technology Management, Stevens Institute of Technology, Castle Point on Hudson, Hoboken, NJ 07030, USA

Eddie Schwartz Chief Security Officer, NetWitness Corporation, 500 Grove Street Herndon, VA 20170, USA

Yuri Signori President, Lead Analyst, I-PingU, LLC, Dearborn Heights, MI, USA

Shane Sims PricewaterhouseCoopers, 1800 Tysons Bouvelard, McLean, VA 22102-4261

J. Andrew Valentine Senior Investigator and Team lead, Forensics and Incident Response Team, Verizon Busines/Cybertrust Inc., Ashburn, VA, USA

Lenny Zeltser SANS Technology Institute, Bethesda, MD, USA

CyberForensics Chapter Abstracts

Introduction

The introduction was composed by Jennifer L. Bayuk, the editor of this volume. It briefly describes the history of the cyberforensics field and places the subsequent chapters into context. The last section of the introduction, *Expert Explanations*, describes the format of the following sections and also how the sections complement each other. Jennifer Bayuk is an information security management and information technology due diligence expert, experienced in virtually every aspect of the field of information security. She specializes in security roadmaps, and is engaged in a wide variety of industries with projects ranging from technical architecture requirements to security governance. She has been a Wall Street chief information security officer, a manager of information systems internal audit, a Price Waterhouse security principal consultant and auditor, and a security software engineer at AT&T Bell Laboratories. She has authored two textbooks for the Information Systems Audit and Control Association: *Stepping through the IS Audit* and *Stepping through the InfoSec Program*, and a third book on *Enterprise Security for the Executive, Setting the Tone from the Top*, published by Praeger. In addition to editing this Springer edition on *CyberForensics*, Jennifer has co-edited a collection of works on *Enterprise Information Security and Privacy* for Artech House. She is a sought-after speaker and an industry professor at Stevens Institute of Technology.

The Complex World of Corporate CyberForensics Investigations

This chapter describes the technology environment typically encountered in a very large enterprise. It provides detail on the distinguishing characteristics of forensics investigations in the enterprise environment, including a recommended approach and a case study. The chapter concludes with a discussion of the trends one may expect to encounter in large enterprise forensics investigations. The chapter is written by Gregory Leibolt, GCFA, GCIH, GREM, GPEN, C|EH, GCCF, CISSP, a Senior Technical Director at AT&T where he leads both the Digital Forensics Team and the Ethical Hacking Team. His full bio appears at the start of the chapter.

Investigating Large-Scale Data Breach Cases

This chapter describes the circumstances typically encountered during investigations of large-scale data breaches. It provides detail on the distinguishing characteristics of forensics investigations in such data breaches, including a recommended approach and a case study. The chapter concludes with a discussion of the trends one may expect to encounter in data breach investigations. The chapter is written by J. Andrew Valentine, a senior investigator and team leader for the Forensics and Incident Response Team within Verizon Business/Cybertrust Inc. His full bio appears at the start of the chapter.

Insider Threat Investigations

This chapter describes the circumstances typically encountered in cases where insiders, that is, employees or other authorized workers, commit cybercrimes. It provides detail on the techniques commonly used in forensics investigations of insider threat cases, including a recommended approach and a case study. The chapter concludes with a discussion of the trends one may expect to encounter in cyberforensics investigations of insider threat. The chapter is written by Shane Sims, at PricewaterhouseCoopers, focused on cyber investigations, insider threat assessments, and anti-cybercrime services. His full bio appears at the start of the chapter.

Accounting Forensics

This chapter describes the organizational characteristics typically encountered in cases of accounting fraud and other accounting application-enabled cybercrimes. It provides detail on the methods and procedures of forensics investigations of accounting practices, including a recommended approach and a case study. The chapter concludes with a discussion of the trends one may expect to encounter in accounting forensics investigations. The chapter is written by Tracy McBride, an independent consultant with more than 20 years of experience in the financial services industry. Her full bio appears at the start of the chapter.

Analyzing Malicious Software

This chapter describes the electronic evidence typically encountered in investigations focused on malicious software. It provides detail on the distinguishing characteristics of forensics investigations that require technical software analysis, including a recommended approach and a case study. The chapter concludes with a discussion of the trends one may expect to encounter in forensics investigations into potentially malicious software. The chapter is written by Lenny Zeltser, who leads the security consulting practice at Savvis and is a member of the Board of Directors at SANS Technology Institute. His full bio appears at the start of the chapter.

Network Packet Forensics

This chapter describes the technology of network traffic recording as well as the variety of digital evidence that may be compiled using network forensics technique. It provides detail on the distinguishing characteristics of forensics investigations in the network environment, including a recommended approach and case studies. The chapter concludes with a discussion of the trends one may expect to encounter in network forensics investigations. The chapter is written by Eddie Schwartz, the Chief Security Officer for NetWitness, a leading producer of advanced threat intelligence and network forensics software. His full bio appears at the start of the chapter.

RAM and File Systems Investigations

This chapter describes the computer operating system technology in a manner that makes it clear how digital evidence may be collected and the extent to which is may be relied upon as evidence in cyberforensics investigations. It provides detail on the distinguishing characteristics of operating system data, both in file and in transient memory, including a recommended approach to operating systems forensics and a case study. The chapter concludes with a discussion of the trends one may expect to encounter in forensics investigations involving operating systems. The chapter is written by Rita Barrios, an expert in digital forensics, access controls, and secured software development and an Assistant Professor at University of Detroit Mercy, a National Security Agency Center of Academic Excellence. The case study was provided by Yuri Signori, the President and Lead Analyst for the data forensics company, I-PingU, LLC. Full bios appear at the start of the chapter.

One Picture is Worth a Million Bytes

This chapter describes tools and techniques used to analyze digital evidence, including commercially available data repositories that are often integrated into cyberforensics data analysis. It provides detail on the distinguishing characteristics of forensics investigations that benefit from cross-platform data analysis, including a recommended approach and a case study. The chapter concludes with a discussion of the trends one may expect to encounter in large enterprise forensics investigations. The chapter is written by Don Fergus, the Vice President of IT Risk Management and Chief Security Officer at the information assurance services firm Intekras, Inc., and Anthony Agresta, a Vice President at Centrifuge Systems, a provider of next-generation interactive analytics technology. Their full bios appear at the start of the chapter.

Cybercrime and Law Enforcement Cooperation

This chapter describes the interaction with law enforcement that typically occurs in cyberforensics investigations. It provides detail on the interaction between public and private investigators, including a recommended approach and case studies. The chapter concludes with a discussion of the trends one may expect to encounter when working with law enforcement on forensics investigations. The chapter is written by Art Ehuan, a director with Forward Discovery, an information security company that provides extensive cyber training and services to law enforcement agencies in the United States and internationally. His full bio appears at the start of the chapter.

Technology Malpractice

This chapter describes the obligations of technology management in protecting certain data from loss or exposure, and the corresponding accountability for observing information security standards and best practices. It provides detail on the distinguishing characteristics of investigations into information security due diligence, including a recommended approach and a case study. The chapter concludes with a discussion of the trends one may expect to encounter in cyberforensics investigations of technology management. The chapter is written by Paul Rohmeyer, a consultant and faculty member at Stevens Institute of Technology's Howe School of Technology Management, where he teaches and conducts research on IT risk management and business resiliency. His full bio appears at the start of the chapter.

Chapter 1
Introduction

Jennifer Bayuk

1.1 A Brief History

The field of cyberforensics has a long and rich history. U.S. military and intelligence agencies in the 1970s were the first to use computer forensics techniques. It was a counterintelligence approach using mainframe systems. Although classified and not documented at the time, this type of computer investigation was sensationalized in popular literature as a best-selling book and BBC television series.[1]

There were a few sensational law enforcement investigations of cybercrime against corporations in the 1970s, most notably a notorious theft of phone service case in 1972,[2] but for the most part companies conducted and resolved their own internal cyber investigations. Digital evidence was relevant, but it was rarely robust enough to support a prosecutor's case.[3]

By the early 1980s, if criminal investigators were involved in cyberforensics at all, it was to support the investigation of physical crimes. Criminals started posting on the social networking sites of the day, which were bulletin boards reached by dial-up phone lines. This milieu is where many investigators had their beginnings in digital investigations.[4] The early cyberforensics investigators were investigating drug, murder, and child pornography crimes that were facilitated by computers. The criminals stored the plans, accounting data, and photographs on computers, and cyber investigations provided evidence that the computer user was involved in some physical crime.

Thus, the first dedicated cyberforensics professionals were law enforcement professionals who saw computers and the communications facilities supported by computers as a new criminal weapon. They studied it as they would any new attack tool, with respectful and conscientious diligence. They devised repeatable investigation techniques that they could teach each other, although, in the 1970s, this instruction did not make it into police academies. Yet most of the cases they investigated were not what we today would call cybercrime. While investigations of physical crimes were then and still are aided by cyber-investigative techniques, cybercrime today implies that there is crime using computers as weapons against computers.

It was in the corporate environment that cybercrime was the most prevalent. In the 1970s, however, corporations dealt with these issues quietly, relying on their own technology staff to provide evidence needed to take action against cybercriminals. In those days, those we now think of as cybercriminals were committing fraud by finding unobtrusive ways to steal corporate assets by faking computer inventory records in asset repositories such as bank accounts and warehouse supply records. Only a few corporations were affected to the extent that it was worth it to them to call in law enforcement and make examples of a few of the more flamboyant criminals. The most notable of these was the AT&T prosecution of *The Mentor*, a phone service thief who taught hundreds of online followers how to get free long distance.[5]

So, the field of cyberforensics matured. Side by side, the law enforcement agents who viewed computers as criminal weapons worked with the corporate security officers who viewed computers as leaky buckets. Law enforcement managed to stay a technology step ahead of the less sophisticated computer users,

J. Bayuk (✉)
Stevens Institute of Technology, Hoboken, NJ, USA

and gained inroads in successful prosecution based on a new kind of evidence: digital evidence. On the corporate side, computer audit became the corporate defense mechanism of choice, and fear of discovery kept a lid on all but the easiest of corporate fraud.

Occasionally, a corporation would decide to make an example of a particularly offensive white collar criminal, and call in law enforcement, so these two dimensions of the cyberforensics evolution would intersect. When they did, the inadequacies of each approach quickly became clear to the other. Law enforcement investigators were appalled by the cavalier attitude of corporate security toward evidence preservation, while the corporate security officers were appalled by the ignorance of law enforcement officers of the complexity of business technology platforms. Case by case, these two sides started building precedents for the successful prosecution of cybercrime. A standard body of knowledge gradually evolved for the collection and preservation of digital evidence.[6]

By the early 1980s, it had become more common for this computer-enabled fraud to be big enough to call in law enforcement, and computer crime started to make headlines.[7] Throughout the 1980s, public awareness of potential criminal activity in computer systems grew. The awareness became inescapable in 1988, when the son of an AT&T Bell Labs researcher shocked the then-small online world by bringing down a large percentage of the computers on the Internet by exploiting well-known vulnerabilities just for the sake of showing that it was possible.[8] He eventually turned himself in and was brought to justice. But was not until 1990 that there was a coordinated law enforcement crackdown on cybercrime.[9]

By 1990, there was enough systematic theft combined with enough audacity on the part of criminals to motivate corporate and law enforcement investigators to join forces and demonstrate to the online criminal community that there would be consequences for cybercriminal behavior. And, 1990 was also the year that Cliff Stoll published *The Cuckoo's Egg*, a first-hand account of a true story wherein a meticulous system administrator spent countless sleepless hours trying to find out why his computer had made an 8-cent billing error, and his investigation led to the arrest and successful prosecution of an organized cyber-espionage ring.[10] The publication of *The Cuckoo's Egg* delighted computer security professionals worldwide, who were at that time a very small and very concerned group, because it very clearly demonstrated that computers were very vulnerable and in need of protection measures that they had been advocating. The year 1991 saw the creation of the FBI's Computer Analysis and Response Teams (CART), which began to systematically provide investigators with the technical expertise necessary to obtain evidence from the computers of suspects.[11]

As more and more organizations developed dependencies on the Internet throughout the 1990s, computer-on-computer crime increased correspondingly. The range of cybercrime was no longer just fraud, theft of computer services (by then called *joy riders*), and international espionage. Cybercrimes common by then included cyber bank robbing, identity theft, defacement of websites for political reasons (by then called *hacktivism*), and corporate spying.[12] This last, the growing threat to intellectual property created by the ubiquity of online access, presented yet another dimension to cybercrime: new Internet search capability left a thin line between legal business intelligence gathering and criminal intellectual property theft.[13]

Awareness that computer criminals were a threat to intellectual property became mainstream with the case of a technically unsophisticated computer criminal who frequented the Internet sites of more experienced hackers and also regularly used social engineering techniques to fill in bits of knowledge he was missing to exploit systems. For example, he would call bank operations center and pretend to be from another branch of the same bank to get the bank's operations personnel to provide him with security codes or passwords.[14] This criminal was eventually prosecuted, not because of government and law enforcement cooperation, but because he attacked technically sophisticated security researchers. One of the researchers eventually was motivated by personal revenge to launch a crusade to track down the criminal and collect enough evidence to prosecute.[15] Both the criminal and the security researcher were widely interviewed and wrote popular accounts of their experiences throughout the investigation.

By the year 2000, reporters and pundits found fertile ground in exposing the weaknesses of the exponentially growing cybercommunity, and they published entertaining case histories on a wide variety of cybercriminal cases. The 1990s had seen cyberforensic laboratories introduced into the Federal Bureau of Investigation (FBI), the U.S. Postal Inspection Service, the Bureau of Alcohol, Tobacco and Firearms (ATF), the U.S. Customs Service, the Drug Enforcement Administration (DEA), the Immigration and Naturalization Service (INS), the Internal Revenue Service (IRS), National Aeronautics and Space Administration (NASA), and the U.S. Secret Service (USSS), as well as international law enforcement communities such as the International Organization on Computer Evidence (IOCE) and INTERPOL.[16]

As the number of types of both cybercrime and computer environments increased, it soon became evident to these organizations that applying historical standards of digital evidence to modern-day information gathering had become a major challenge.[17] It quickly became clear that no one individual could master all the tasks required to complete computer investigations in the ever-widening diversity of information system implementations. Data available for collection were no longer limited to what a police officer could gather from a suspect's apartment but encompassed corporate networks hosting thousands of machines in hundred of locations. Specialists in various technologies published detailed accounts of data-gathering techniques in various operating system environments, but at the same time warned that the appropriate level of abstraction by which to reason with evidence varies depending on the investigation.[18]

The investigative challenge of defining the scope for data gathering was further compounded by the fact that not all the gathered evidence met court standards for reliability. The decade starting in the year 2000 saw a return to the basics in deciding what constitutes digital evidence.[19] Not only technology specialists, but also lawyers and judges, had to start learning enough about computer operation to distinguish between identity and authentication, between computer-generated and computer-stored information, and between hearsay and reliability with respect to computerized business records.

1.2 A CyberForensic Framework

There are few practitioners who saw the field of cyberforensics grow from infancy. In this volume, we have managed to gather many who joined at its toddler stage. These professionals from diverse backgrounds have come to appreciate the advances in professional expertise that conceptually fall under the umbrella of "cyberforensics." Although they all actively practice cyberforensics, their work is still very diverse. Although in the 1970s a single cyber-investigator could glean all the knowledge there was to be had from a computer under investigation, today's practitioners are required to immerse themselves in a specialized type of study to be productive contributors to the field.

Moreover, there is as yet no academic consensus on the professional education required for cyberforensics specialists to practice. There is just the body of knowledge created and handed down and across by practitioners. That is why this book is composed by such practitioners. The wide variety of expertise in the following chapters illustrates just how wide and deep the field has become. The qualifications of our practitioners have been vetted in the marketplace for cyberforensic expertise. All the authors have more than 10 years experience in successful investigation of cybercrime and some of them more than 20. The book is organized to introduce the reader to the field of cybersecurity using situations encountered by investigators. We begin with the point of view of corporate investigation, and gradually progress through more and more detail and complexity surrounding the issues encountered in the cyberforensics context.

This book shows that cyberforensics blends investigative experience with technology management and oversight requirements. There is a cohesive core set of concepts that binds cybersecurity investigators to a shared vision. That vision is not yet a subject of study in computer science or systems engineering curriculums but continues to emerge as a body of knowledge that cyberforensics professionals generally agree should be a prerequisite to the professional practice of information security.

Figure 1.1 is a cognitive framework within which various specialties in the field may be understood as a coherent whole.[20] The framework begins with the investigator in the field and shows how specialized investigation techniques may be understood in the context of a comprehensive holistic investigative approach. It also shows links to technical specialization that are required to perform investigations in certain categories. By combining evidence with analytics, we find an ability to make those investigation results comprehensive to law enforcement and technology management. This capability in turn imposes requirements on technology management, legal and

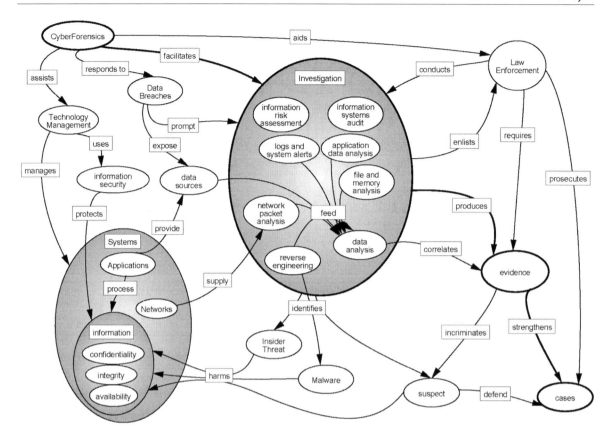

Fig. 1.1 Cyberforensics framework

regulatory expectations that in turn support generalized investigations.

Although our framework does include elements of the technological capability required to protect, defend, and recover from cyberattacks, those tools and techniques are not the focus of this book. This book picks up where the protection mechanisms fail. Although investigations may be launched when detection mechanisms provide alerts, these alerting techniques are not part of the investigation process.

1.3 Expert Explanations

The experts in the field who have been recruited to contribute to this book explain the tools and techniques used by their particular area of specialty in a manner that allows us to map their expertise into a more generic understanding of what a cybersecurity investigation really is. Each author has described what would otherwise seem an extremely esoteric specialty in four easy-to-understand sections:

1. Investigation Characteristics
2. Investigative Approach
3. Case Study
4. Issues and Trends

We begin with an overview of enterprise security investigations. Greg Leibolt, a senior technical director at AT&T, a company with decades of successful prosecution of corporate cybercrime, leads us though the investigator's experience of a typical case. Jim Valentine, a law enforcement veteran who now uses his skills in corporate support, follows with a behind-the-scenes description of the investigations underlying newspaper identity theft headlines that motivated data breach reporting laws. Shane Sims, a former Federal Bureau of Investigation Agent who made a successful transition to the corporate security realm, picking up academic credentials along the way, addresses quandaries with respect to the criminals themselves with his contribution on insider threat. Tracy McBride, a seasoned forensics accountant who has exposed technically devious practices among white collar criminals, provides insight into how those cybercriminals exploit corporate applications.

Our volume also addresses the highly technical requirements that cyberforensics demands of practitioners. Lenny Zeltser, a director of a leading security consulting practice and a senior fellow at a world-reknowned security training institute, provides an extreme example of the subject matter expertise heights to which investigators must aspire to achieve hitherto elusive goals of stalking the well-funded, well-equipped, and highly intelligent espionage agent. Eddie Schwartz, a former law enforcement and corporate investigator who now devotes full-time efforts to the development of technical investigation tools, describes just how exacting a network security investigation has to be. Rita Barrios, a software expert and successful forensics consultant, explains the arcane but critically necessary techniques of bit-level operating system memory recovery.

All these types of technical tools and techniques are being constantly refined into higher-level data analysis that enriches findings with law enforcement databases such as those described by Tony Agresta and Don Fergus, who are specialists in using interactive analytics to support cyberforensics investigations. They remind us that the evidence gathering is all about building a case, and we can never forget our key stakeholders. Law enforcement contacts and cooperation remain the key to successful prosecution. Art Ehuan, a former Special Agent with both the FBI and Air Force Office of Special Investigations (AFOSI), with considerable corporate experience as well, provides sage advice on the right way to prepare cases for and communicate with law enforcement. On the corporate side, Paul Rohmeyer, a successful management consultant and professor of technology management, shows us how corporate standards for reasonable security measures have set the bar not only for investigations of corporate networks but also for the secure management of technology that is expected by courts when defending the appropriateness of security and privacy efforts.

Through this interaction of these types of individuals throughout the decades, the field of cyberforensics, as well as the field of cybersecurity in general, has evolved. Although each chapter follows the thread of a cyberforensics approach from a different angle, the reader should appreciate that, any given investigation requires some combination of these approaches. In any actual investigation these players would be working side by side on the same investigation. Each role will have more or less focus depending on the facts of the given case. Successful conclusions to investigations such as those described in our case studies require the knowledge of all types of techniques described in the chapters that follow, as well as an ability to recognize when a given investigation meets the characteristics of one of these techniques.

It is also required that a cyber-investigator understands that, no matter how many sophisticated techniques there are to learn, the next generation of techniques may be the ones that we have yet to develop. As one of the field's most respected experts advises, "Our approach is typical of how we advocate solving problems, rely on past experience, listen to advice from others, use existing tools. But also, don't be afraid to turn common wisdom into myth, to create your own tools, and to develop your own methodology when that is needed to crack a case."[21]

Notes

1. McNeil, John, *The Consultant, A Novel of Computer Crime*, Coward, McCann, and Geoghegan, Inc., New York, 1978.
2. Schmidt, Howard, *Patrolling Cyberspace*, Larstan Publishing, 2006, pp. 13–19.
3. See Schweitzer, James, *Protecting Information in the Electronic Workplace*, Reston Publishing, a division of Prentice Hall, 1983, Chapter 9: Cases of Fraud and Deception.
4. Ibid., Schmidt, p. 23
5. Sheetz, Michael, *Computer Forensics: An Essential Guide for Accountants, Lawyers, and Managers*, Wiley, 2007, Chapter 1.
6. Icove, David, *Computer Crime, a Crimefighter's Handbook*, O'Reilley & Associates, 1995.
7. Alexander, Charles, Crackdown on Computer Capers, *Time Magazine*, Feb 8, 1982.
8. Littman, Jonathan, Shockwave Rider, *PC Computing*, June 1990.
9. Sterling, Bruce, *Hacker Crackdown*, Bantam Books, 1992.
10. Stoll, Cliff, *The Cuckoo's Egg*, Doubleday, 1990.
11. *History of the FBI*, Aug 2003, http://www.policyalmanac.org/crime/archive/fbi.shtml

12. Power, Richard, *Tangled Web,* Que, Macmillan, 2000.
13. Shorrock, Tim, *Spies for Hire*, Simon and Schuster, 2008.
14. Mitnick, Kevin, *The Art of Deception*, Wiley, 2002.
15. Shimomura, Tsutomu, John Markoff, *Takedown*, Hyperion, 1996.
16. Whitcomb, Carrie Morgan, An Historical Perspective of Digital Evidence, *International Journal of Digital Evidence*, Volume 1, Number 1, Spring 2002.
17. Paul, George, *Digital Evidence*, American Bar Association, 2008.
18. Farmer, Dan and Wietse Venema, *Forensic Discovery*, Addison Wesley, 2004, p. 37.
19. Paul, ibid.
20. Figure 1.1 is an example of a systemigram, or a way to describe systems via components and relationship. For more detail on the construct, see Boardman and Sauser, *Systems Thinking: Coping with Twenty-First Century Problems*, Taylor & Francis, 2008.
21. Ibid., Farmer and Venema, 4, p. 4.

Chapter 2
The Complex World of Corporate CyberForensics Investigations

Gregory Leibolt

Gregory Leibolt, GCFA, GCIH, GREM, GPEN, C|EH, GCCF, CISSP is a Senior Technical Director at AT&T where he leads both the Digital Forensics Team and the Ethical Hacking Team. Leibolt's extensive experience in incident response and digital forensics includes large and small cases involving intrusions, intellectual property theft, financial embezzlement, investigating employee misuse of assets, malware infestations, and others. He has spent considerable effort developing tools and techniques in support of the Linux and UNIX environments. He regularly evaluates new forensics tools and techniques to find the best solutions for this challenging field. On the ethical hacking side, Leibolt's penetration testing experience encompasses ethically exploiting websites, databases, computer systems, internal LANs, perimeter defenses, and wireless networks. He has evaluated and tested numerous network components, various critical architectures such as Communications Assistance for Law Enforcement Act (CALEA) implementations and many other unique environments. Leibolt's extensive IT experience also includes UNIX and Windows system administration, software development, project management, evaluating security tools, and advanced security research. Leibolt holds multiple GIAC certifications, including Certified Forensics Analyst (GCFA), and is a member of the GIAC Advisory Board. His other certifications include Certified Incident Handler (GCIH), Reverse Engineer Malware (GREM), Certified Penetration Tester (GPEN), Certified Ethical Hacker (C|EH), and Certified Information System Security Professional (CISSP). Leibolt has a BA from Barry University, an MA in Computer Resources and Information Management from Webster University, and a Graduate Certificate in Computer Forensics (GCCF) from the University of Central Florida.

2.1 Investigation Characteristics

This chapter addresses key points of corporate cyberforensics that are required to explain the many challenges investigators face within the corporate environment. The information technology (IT) environment of a large corporation can be daunting to characterize. Large corporations are often composed of a mixture of IT components ranging from legacy production systems to bleeding-edge laboratory systems. Additionally, business acquisitions, partnering, and nonstandard IT implementations usually bring additional variety to the mix. As a result, many corporations go for many years without ever knowing the full extent of their corporation's networks and systems. Basically, it is safe to say that, from a cyberforensics perspective, just about any type of IT environment can be encountered.

A more granular view would show that a wide variety of computer operating systems and hardware is usually deployed. The ever-popular Microsoft® Windows operating system permeates most corporate IT environments. A corporation that is predominately a Windows shop can make life easier for investigators because the forensic skill sets are similar across the different Windows platforms. In large companies one can expect to see virtually every type and version of

G. Leibolt (✉)
Senior Technical Director, AT&T Inc., 208 S. Akard St., Dallas, TX 75202, USA

Windows desktop and server operating systems. In the author's corporation, similar to many others, there is a mixed bag of operating systems (OS) to address. The investigators routinely run into Windows, Linux, Solaris, HP-UX, and AIX, plus different versions of each OS.

Not only are there different operating systems, but also they are deployed in a wide array of implementations. Some are running relatively small, self-contained servers and desktops that use native file system types. Others use large RAID, SAN, or NAS storage or employ a mixture of various file systems.[1] The environment might also be heavily integrated with many support systems, such as database, LDAP, or other component servers.[2]

Administration also comes in a variety of flavors. Systems could be accessed by either direct or virtual consoles. A single system could have one or more administrators. Authentication could be local or via domain administrative access. Two-factor authentication that is based on "something you know" such as a password and "something you have" such as an RSA SecurID® token might be required. What this means is that investigators can often find it difficult to gain administrative access because of technical issues, complex paperwork, hard-to-locate administrators, or complex access control lists (ACL). To perform incident response or remote forensics, computers often need to be accessed via the network, but sometimes this is a problem for reasons of network routing, ACLs, or firewalls. Even the environment containing the system of forensic interest is an important factor. Production, test, laboratory, and desktop environments are vastly different from each other and greatly affect the forensic approach.

The discussion so far has centered on the different types of computers and operating systems. There are also many elements supporting a network such as routers, switches, firewalls, and intrusion detection systems that are likely to be part of the investigation. Computers and network equipment can be located in very diverse physical locations. VLANs[3] can support multiple servers on one subnet, even though the actual hardware is distributed in different buildings miles from each other. Last but not least, investigators need to have some understanding of the various applications that could be related to a compromise. Aside from the technical challenges, there are legal, political, financial, geographical, cultural, time zone, resource, and skill set issues. In a word, cyberforensics in large corporate IT environments can be *complex*.

The most important aspect of successfully managing cyberforensics in a corporate environment is cooperation. Upper management must support a designated corporate forensics team working all such cases, and the corporation as a whole must be aware of the proper policies and procedures relating to incident response and digital forensics. Take, for example, intrusion cases, which have life cycles with the following phases: preparation, identification, containment, eradication, recovery, and follow-up. The complexity of the corporate IT environments means that many parties must work together to handle cases such as these. For example, legal departments, application owners, application developers, system administrators, network engineers, firewall administrators, and many others must cooperate. Early communications between members of this conglomerate team would be based around topics such as understanding the details of the incident, analyzing business risk, defining and providing appropriate access methods and controls to the investigators, coordination of legal matters with corporate attorneys, and reporting to upper management and government entities as needed. The lead investigator must provide the leadership to orchestrate the multi-team procedures and activities to ensure the integrity and preservation of the evidence. In addition, each case must be managed in specific ways to ensure that evidence is protected, properly collected, and correctly transferred, which includes documenting the chain of custody. All parties handling any evidence should take detailed notes of all activities involving that evidence. Clearly, cyberforensics professionals need a broad range of skills, both technical and managerial, especially when handling large corporate incidents.

2.2 The Investigative Approach

Cyberforensics investigators appreciate the simple cases. An example might be a straightforward desktop computer system that, because of the nature of the case, can simply be unplugged and taken to the lab. These cases provide the opportunity to follow the traditional forensics procedures that can be performed on systems that do not require live forensics: they only require imaging the drive and analyzing a static system. However, times are changing, and in the corporate world even the simplest of cases can be complex. Many user computer systems, particularly laptops, are now using full disk encryption, which requires application of appropriate decryption methods, before acquiring the necessary data. Hard drive sizes are growing in capacity each year, which also adds time to the acquisition and analysis of data. Access to user computer systems is often difficult because corporate users can be widely dispersed in remote offices or they may telecommute from their home offices. Older traditional methods are constantly being supplemented with tools and techniques that expand investigators' capabilities and help to work around many of today's complexities.

There is a growing shift in the corporate environment toward performing cyberforensics remotely. For example, the author's corporation frequently uses this approach. It has proven to be a great asset in performing cyberforensics and in the e-Discovery[4] of user systems. It also circumvents the need to decrypt encrypted hard drives and provides easy access to systems. Four often-mentioned forensics software vendors—Access Data®, Guidance Software (R), MANDIANT, and Technology Pathways—provide tools that enable remote forensics. Their software has the ability to connect to a small applet on a target computer system and perform the forensic acquisition and analysis of data.[5] The old standard forensics practice of unplugging a system and analyzing a static image is becoming less and less common as new tools and practices are emerging to support evolving technology.

Investigators will tell you that each case is different. Even though standard policies and guidelines may be in place, the investigative approach taken in each case can vary. The approach is primarily determined by the characteristics of the incident in relation to the affected environment. In other words, the type of incident (for example, an insider threat, a hacking incident, a malware infestation) is considered when the investigators think about the best way to identify, preserve, and acquire potential evidence. Naturally, many approaches are considered. A sniffer on the network might be important, capturing system memory may be critical, disconnecting from the network might be important, or monitoring activity on the system may be the best approach. In addition to the type of incident, knowledge of the attacked environment (for example, an external website, a customer database server, an employee desktop, a lab test system) is critical and may severely limit the ability to implement some of the approaches originally considered. Finally, in addition to the incident type and the environment, the final approach must take into account issues such as physical access to the system(s), network access to the system(s), login access, skill sets, software tools, and political, legal, and business/network risk factors.

The union of all these many factors ultimately determines which approach is taken by the investigators. Because of these many complexities, the ultimate goals of an investigation sometimes lean toward identifying, containing, and remediating the problem rather than obtaining useful evidence for legal action. As such, investigators can find themselves in situations in which they can only apply "best forensics practices" in certain areas, but not all; these are usually cases where the company is not likely to go to court. Regardless of the type of case, the investigators should be sure to document why certain investigative steps took place. This ensures that all the actions can be explained should the need arise.

To provide multiple examples of investigative approach, the following discussion raises issues relating to a theoretical intrusion incident of a complex environment, such as a web portal. Whether the investigator is dealing with a small or large case, the investigative approach always starts with obtaining information. Especially in larger cases, it is not unusual to go back and ask for the same information several times. The first time that investigators receive information, it is often incomplete, and it can be inaccurate. This problem happens for many different reasons. One reason is that it is human nature for people to think that their network or system has not really been compromised. Investigators are often told that the problem is probably something a system administrator did, or an application programming issue, or maybe just a minor script kiddie[6] attack. Additionally, people may be afraid that they could be in trouble and are not likely to provide any self-incriminating information. Another reason is that the needed information is not always at someone's fingertips. It may take some time for people to find the most recent network diagram or application description document. Or, it may not exist. And, of course, key people who must be consulted may not be available. It is necessary for investigators to start the investigation with what they have, but keep going back for more accurate and detailed information.

Using all the information related to the incident, investigators must try to identify, preserve, and acquire all possible sources of potential evidence. The following steps are important:

- Ensure that system administrators do not start their own investigation. Many times, administrators have accidentally corrupted evidence themselves or, in looking for evidence, were noticed by the hackers, who then deleted log files and their hacker tools before logging off the system.
- Ask the network architects for the network diagrams and descriptions of the affected network.
- Indentify critical business components related to the affected network (for example, financial, contractual, legal).
- Determine if disaster recovery plans exist and can permit certain systems or even the whole portal to be restored in a clean state without interfering with the ability for the investigators to complete forensic analysis of the affected systems.
- Ask the security organization for any recent security audit reports of the affected network, systems, and applications.
- Establish the initial goals of the investigation. Goals are not always the same; however, they would generally include these:

  - Identify and preserve evidence.
  - Determine, as accurately as possible, the method, time frame, and the scope of the compromise.
  - Provide feedback about containment, remediation, and security enhancement.
  - Perform the investigation with as little disruption to the corporation as possible.
  - Identify, immediately, the firewall logs, centralized syslogs, router logs, IDS/IPS logs, sniffer data, application logs, and any other data that could help in the investigation.[7]
  - Implement, immediately, a plan for the preservation of logs so that historical evidence is not deleted.
  - Identify, immediately, the available data storage to handle copies of all the logs. Note that this is often a challenge because corporations do not always have available and accessible storage handy. Sometimes, the easy answer is to ship out large-capacity USB external hard drives.

- Implement proper controls: that is, large corporations are likely to have different teams and organizations related to different areas of potential evidence. Knowledge of cyber incidents in corporations is usually on a "need-to-know" basis. The appropriate controls must be implemented as various teams become involved.
- Decide which preliminary tools would be helpful from a forensics perspective. A sniffer on the subnet can be useful in identifying unusual network traffic between systems or into internal network space. An intrusion detection system (IDS) can help by providing warnings of continued exploitation attempts, although in many cases, further exploitation is through credentials or trusts obtained via the currently exploited system(s).

Investigators need to be careful to not jump to any conclusions or make assumptions. There may be some pressure to take the "just re-image the system" approach to return to a known clean operating state or, perhaps, pressure to limit the time to perform proper analysis. Anything that limits the ability for investigators to properly perform their jobs can leave unidentified compromises in corporate assets and preclude any understanding of what information the hacker(s) may have obtained. If the investigation is thorough, the investigators can usually determine the method and scope of the attack and provide proper input about containment, eradication, and recovery.

To estimate the amount of time needed to resolve a compromise, there are many factors to consider. Time is needed for all the following steps: the work to identify, collect, and analyze logs, to perform forensic analysis of the servers, to analyze malware, to correlate data from different sources, and to manage the various corporate responsibilities such as reporting the status and coordinating meetings. Overall, it can take weeks or months to complete a large enterprise-level case. Naturally, the sooner an attack is recognized, the better. It is common to hear how the first 24 or 48 h are critical in physical law enforcement cases. The same is true for most cyberforensics investigations. Hackers will usually work as quickly as possible to get their rootkits, backdoors, and various tools fully implemented. They usually have scripts that very quickly download tools and install them, which permit them to hop from machine to machine, installing as they go. A speedy cyberforensics response, very early in the hacker's attack phase, will contain and mitigate much of the damage. Corporate forensics also has what could be called the "golden weeks," usually a period of about three weeks. During this time period, the cyberforensics investigation team has the full attention and cooperation of the key people in the various business units. Then, sometime during the third week, this starts to "dry up" because people get pulled back into their daily routines. Also, the investigators naturally start to slow down physically and mentally as a result of the many long hours they have already put into the case. The lead investigator has to contend with these issues by making sure that the critical path of the investigation is followed and that certain critical steps (perhaps different in each case) are completed as soon as possible.

In addition to working hard to maximize their progress during the valuable "golden weeks," the investigators will need to provide information about the case to upper management and the other key people. In this case, similar to most cases in the corporate world, everyone is waiting to find out what was compromised, how the compromise occurred, what needs to be done to contain the problem, how to eradicate the problem, and how to get back to normal business. The investigators, as soon as possible, should collect enough evidence and perform enough analysis to start providing feedback regarding the containment, eradication, and recovery steps. If the case is well managed, then the business application owners, network engineers, firewall administrators, systems administrators, and others can start implementing containment, cleanup, and recovery steps at appropriate times without impeding the additional analysis that the investigators must perform to finalize their assessment of the incident.

An important part of the investigative approach, in any potential hacking intrusion case, is for the investigators to think in a way similar to hackers. The ability to think similar to hackers comes basically from a combination of cyberforensics experience and penetration testing expertise. Hackers often take advantage of the "low-hanging fruit" (the easiest exploitable vulnerabilities). Identifying such "low-hanging fruit" may allow investigators to more quickly identify areas likely to contain potential evidence. Investigators should analyze any recent security audit reports that relate to the environment. Any vulnerability noted in the report(s) may be the avenue used by the hackers. As a parallel effort to the forensics work, a penetration tester could perform a pen-test of a test environment (an internal test or a development environment containing the same applications) to find vulnerabilities. Proper security protocol would also dictate a full penetration test of the affected environment after the investigation was complete and all fixes and patches were put in place. Before any kind of penetration testing is performed, however, it is important to clearly understand the implications. Any testing of the compromised environment could destroy evidence, and all penetration tests must align with legal and corporate policies. The key point to remember is that it is critical for investigators to have a clear and accurate understanding of the environment.

Because of the number of servers and network elements that may be affected in most enterprise incidents, many are classified as large-scale incidents. Such incidents generate so much data to be identified, acquired, and analyzed that investigators need an efficient way to manage it all. One way to do this is to have a team of experienced cyberforensics analysts and others working on various tasks at the same time. Thus, a lot of work is performed in parallel and the approach works well to save time. However, more effort is needed to ensure the quality of the work and to combine the distributed knowledge into a proper understanding of the incident.

As soon as possible, investigators should start analyzing any known or suspected compromised systems and their related logs. Some cases are somewhat benign, such as web defacement or retrieval of non-critical information. Even though an attack may look relatively benign, it may not be. It is important to be thorough, to pursue all leads, and to look further, beyond initial findings, to understand the scope of the compromise. For example, a compromise could be serious if there are signs of escalated privileges, rootkit installation, or remnants of hacker tools. Also, investigators may identify artifacts that can be used to determine if other systems have been compromised.[8] Search engines, such as Google®, and other tools should be used to look for potential comments about the compromised systems on blogs, hacker websites, chat rooms, etc.

If the investigators are lucky, only one or two systems have been compromised. However, the investigators have to consider several possible scenarios.

- The same hackers may have compromised other systems in the portal using the same vulnerability.
- The same hackers may have compromised other systems in the portal using a different vulnerability.
- Different hackers may have compromised other systems in the portal using the same vulnerability.
- Different hackers may have compromised other systems in the portal using a different vulnerability.
- Multiple hackers may have compromised the same systems, each with their own agendas.

Many investigations involve load balanced web farms, or sets of computers that all host the same web server platforms for use by multiple user communities. A key problem in web farms is that the vulnerability that the hackers used on a given system is likely to exist on all the other web servers. Ideally, in a compromised web farm, every single web server would be analyzed and then be completely rebuilt, whether or not it was found to be compromised. This decision, however, is based on an understanding of the compromise, level of risk, time, and cost.

If the known scope and complexity of the compromise grow as the investigation progresses, then naturally the required cleanup and mitigation efforts will expand. In addition, the realized level of risk to the company changes and the investigative approach might have to change as well. In extreme cases, the whole service or web portal might have to be shut down to protect corporate assets and allow containment, eradication, and recovery.

As already mentioned, investigators must determine which tools would be best to use to analyze systems in a given case. The author is a firm believer in the principle supported by the great Japanese sword master, Miyamoto Musashi, who said, "You should not have a favorite weapon. To become over-familiar with one weapon is as much a fault as not knowing it sufficiently well."[9] Having a favorite tool could impair the investigators' performance during forensics analysis because they might ignore other tools and options. Investigators should know how to use a wide range of digital forensics tools appropriately, and know which tools are the most effective in various types of circumstances.

That being said, there are types of cases that benefit from extensive use of "live" analysis tools, which gather and process data such as running processes, lists of open files, and network activity on running computers. Live tools are distinguished from "static" analysis tools, which only work with data stored on disk drives. The typical "static" analysis example is that of analyzing data from a shut down computer. Investigation techniques to retrieve both volatile and static data are more thoroughly described in Chapter 8. The enterprise investigator must thoroughly understand the pros and cons of each type of tool when making choices for the upcoming steps of the investigation.

A web farm is a good example of an environment where forensic analysis would benefit by using live rather than static analysis because:

1. Volatile data such as network activity, running processes, and open files may be critical.
2. Memory dumps could be very useful.
3. The large number of systems could take weeks to image, potentially causing costly downtime.
4. Analysis needs to begin as soon as possible.
5. Remote access (a network connection to the computer) saves travel costs.
6. The investigators need to perform incident response on many systems at the same time.
7. The needs of the business require that the systems remain running and performing as usual.

Many of the live analysis tools require investigators to be on site with physical access to the systems. Enterprise-wide investigations requiring live data analysis require, very conservatively, a team of at least three investigators to stay for a minimum of two to three weeks. This is quite costly. So, using any tools that can perform the required tasks remotely would be of considerable value. The remote forensics analysis tools, such as Guidance Software's (R) Encase® Enterprise Edition, MANDIANT Intelligent Response™, ProDiscover(R) Incident Response, and AccessData® Enterprise use a light footprint and are carefully designed to preserve evidence.[10] Even though they do not rely on any system programs, they will, however, modify memory. Here are some advantages of using remote vendor forensics tools:

- Their usage may be harder to detect by hackers.
- Volatile evidence (processes, network activity, open files) and file system analysis can be performed online in ways that are less likely to tip off hackers.
- They can allow multiple systems to be analyzed and compared at the same time.
- They are generally reliable with the preservation and acquisition of evidence.
- They can capture evidence files and store them in special evidence containers.
- They contain a broad spectrum of features.
- Some support snapshot comparisons of volatile data; this can be very useful in identifying malicious programs and processes if comparisons are made against a known clean snapshot.
- A pre-incident installation of a remote forensics tool applet would offer very quick incident response and forensic access to the systems.
- The courts are often familiar with these tools.

Some of the disadvantages of these vendor tools are these:

- They do not support all OS/hardware configurations and file systems.
- They can take a very long time to parse and display Linux/UNIX directories and files.
- They are quite expensive.
- They tend to work better analyzing Windows environments rather than Linux and UNIX.
- They are sometimes harder to use in certain investigations.
- They need to be well tested in different scenarios to develop appropriate operating guidelines.

Although the major vendor tools just mentioned are popular, they are not the only choice for investigators. Other forensics tools containing scripts for live analysis and acquisition are also effective, especially if known binaries and libraries are used to ensure trusted results and avoid changing the "modify, access, and create" (MAC)[11] times of system programs. Microsoft's older Windows OnLine Forensics (WOLF), and their tools for law enforcement, Computer Online Forensic Evidence Extractor (COFEE) and Windows FE, are examples of useful script-based tools. Other scripts to acquire volatile data can be found in the older free versions of Helix as well as e-fense's Helix3 Pro and Live Response tools. Most of these scripts are designed to run from a CD or USB drive mounted on the target system. Scripts can then be run from the media to acquire memory and other volatile data. Additionally, the CD or USB drive is often bootable to permit a complete reboot of the target system without using data from the hard drive, and thus is ideal for the task of performing hard drive imaging or static analysis. Even though, in general, these scripts are not specifically designed to be run remotely, it might be possible to turn them into remotely run scripts such that an administrative login account or an administrative remote execution capability such as WMI[12] or psexec[13] could be used to run them. Because the major forensics software vendors offer limited support for Linux and UNIX, homegrown scripts are common to support these operating systems. Unfortunately, many Windows and Linux/UNIX scripts, by default, will modify evidence as they peruse through operating system files. It is, therefore, important for the investigator to understand the functionality of script tools and use them appropriately. Some of the advantages of the script utilities are these:

- They often provide a better view of system activity, running processes, and network activity.
- They can provide a more real time monitoring environment compared to the snapshot approach used in the vendor tools.
- They can provide more detail and a wider range of volatile data information.
- They can be tailored for different kinds of investigations.
- They are sometimes the only option for the incident/environment.

Some of the disadvantages of scripts are these:

- They might be more noticeable to hackers.
- Depending on many factors, they are more likely to modify MAC times.
- They might not work as expected due to differences in OSs and hardware.
- They need to be developed and tested on a variety of platforms.
- They may have to be defended in court.

Sometimes a combination of vendor software and script utilities might be needed. Investigators should be prepared for occasions where the expensive vendor tool cannot quite get the job done, as happens in a variety of cases. Probably the most frequent problems occur in the Linux/UNIX environments. Vendor tools can have problems with certain file system types because most of these tools rely only on their own code to read and analyze the file system structure. Because native operating system binaries are not used or trusted to display directories, files, unallocated space, or volatile data in memory, the integrity of the results can be supported. The tools also do not modify file access times when opening directories or files. This is the very best forensics approach, but it limits the tool's functionality to only the files systems that are supported. For example, SAN storage, the Solaris ZFS file system, and Linux LVM[14] can be problematic for some tools. Additionally, applets running in virtualized environments such as Solaris 10 zones may not permit the forensics tool access to the physical devices. Even certain RAID hardware implementations can cause problems for these tools. One possible solution for some of these problems can be found in an interesting tool called F-Response®, which connects to a small applet on the target computer. The tool makes the drive on the target computer read-only and accessible to the investigators' computers. It appears as a local, raw, read-only, physical storage device that can be examined with local forensics or other specialized software.

Sometimes the vendor tool just will not work as the investigators would like. For example, one tool will capture volatile data but cannot display the data unless it is connected to the target system. In this case, after the incident is over, there is no way to view the volatile evidence. Additionally, investigators may find operating or performance issues with any given tool. A tool might take too long to open and parse certain system log files or perhaps it cannot sufficiently identify rootkits or malware. The point is that many tools are usually needed to fully process an incident.

It is important to note that hackers constantly watch for administrative activity and, if they see anything of which they are suspicious, they will run cleanup scripts that greatly hamper forensic analysis. Stealthy investigative techniques should be considered when performing any type of live analysis of systems still connected to a network. By "stealthy" the author means that the investigators should consider exactly which names are used when they deploy their tools and how these tools look and behave when run on the live system. When performing incident response, running a program called "dbindex" will draw less attention from hackers than a program called "forensic-script." The goal is to have hackers think that the incident response script is a normal, everyday process.

Before running the selected tools, the investigators need to carefully consider the order in which to collect evidence. Naturally, the most volatile data should be gathered first, as it will be the first to disappear.[15] Volatility is the first concern, but there are other concerns when performing live forensic analysis through a remote connection. Some tasks take a long time to run and keep the investigators from performing any other work. This can be a real issue when using some of the vendor remote forensics tools to remotely view data on Linux or UNIX data storage drives. In these cases, the investigators should find out the mount points of the drives and the size of all the slices before starting to attach to them for preview. The reason this is important is that, as already mentioned, the investigators will have to wait a long time before they can view the drive data. Therefore, investigators must prioritize which slices to look at. It can be highly frustrating to be waiting on the system to preview a terabyte slice that holds user data, when the much smaller /, /var, /etc, /tmp, and other operating system directories that may be on individual slices could have already been analyzed. System directories are usually the first place to start, because frequently hacking artifacts will be found there. Other tasks, such as imaging a drive/partition or performing a string search, or parsing a registry, or indexing can force investigators to wait many hours for completion. Depending on the tool being used, investigators may just have to wait until it completes. Developing and using recommended guidelines that are tool specific can help alleviate some of these issues. For example, a good procedure would be to immediately forensically extract copies of key system files and obvious artifacts (hacker tools and malware) that other investigators can start analyzing. As an initial starting point, certain key files should be obtained and additional files extracted as the need arises. In the Windows environment, some of these key operating system files include registry files, event logs, web logs, database logs, various configuration files, and files wherein operating systems may store information related to the activity of a given user, such as user index.dat files. In the Linux/UNIX environments, files such as /proc files, hidden files and directories, /etc/passwd, /etc/security/passwd (AIX), /etc/shadow, /etc/group, /etc/hosts, various other config files, plus the logs in /var/log and application logs would be of initial interest. From the user space, root and possibly other user history files should be retrieved. Additionally, at a minimum, a report of running processes, open files, and network status should be obtained using forensically sound methods to gather volatile information. This approach enables parallel work flow, which circumvents the single investigator and forensics tool bottleneck issues.

There are occasions on which a vendor's remote forensics tools and other tools cannot be used for network access reasons. One issue that appears in corporate environments is that some networks and systems can only be reached remotely via a jump server.[16] Such restricted access can limit the ability to extract data from the systems. It is key to remember that the remote forensics vendor tools need to have direct network access to the target applet or vice versa. There is often difficulty in finding tools to use to quickly respond in "jump server" Linux/UNIX environments. Firewall and router ACL rules could be changed to permit other tools to effectively gain access, but this can take a long time. Incident response teams need to quickly determine that a compromise occurred because a great deal of decision making, planning, and organization must take place right away before proceeding with a full forensics investigation. Hence, it is advisable for an enterprise incident response team to become familiar with potential access paths available within the enterprise and work with operations teams on access plans in advance of the occurrence of an incident.

Whenever critical to the case and whenever possible, obtaining images of memory and disks is beneficial. The process of imaging usually demands most of the resources of the system, network, and/or a forensics tool. As a result, sometimes other forensics activities can only be performed on evidence that has already been extracted for analysis. The question of when to start the imaging depends on the case. It is often important to obtain a copy of memory before any other work is performed. Both physical memory and "paged out" (swap) memory should be obtained if possible. Note that the process of acquiring memory actually modifies the memory, so this needs to be taken into account. Imaging the drive(s) could occur later in the investigation, for example, once evidence of intrusion has been validated. Numerous factors are involved in this decision, such as legal requirements, the type of incident, the forensics tools in use, disk storage, network capacity, and access issues.

Once the investigators find key evidence, some of the remote forensics tools can be used to concurrently search all the other systems for the same evidence. After the forensics tool is connected to all the systems, searches can be as simple as sorting by file name across all the systems to see similar names grouped together, using advanced string search capabilities, or by identifying similar hash values. As anyone might assume, finding the evidence is just part of the process. Understanding what the evidence means will fill in the blanks. Hackers use all different kinds of tools in their trade. To understand the scope of the compromise, analysis of these tools, that hackers installed, needs to be performed. Some of the common tools hackers implement are keyloggers, IRC bot software, distributed ssh dictionary attack software, web command shell programs, rootkits, trojans, stored cross-site scripting attacks, sniffers, local and remote exploits, phishing sites, malware distribution websites, and malware command and control code.[17]

To better understand exactly what the hacker tools really do, investigators will need to perform "malware analysis" of any suspicious programs found on the system. Malware can be submitted to various free Internet services, which run the code in a sandbox[18] environment to determine what the program does. This analysis works pretty well for code extracted from the Windows environments but not so well for Linux and UNIX environments. Commercial sandbox analysis software is available for in-house analysis, such as, Truman, Norman Sandbox®, and CWsandbox. Additionally, investigators can imitate the commercial sandboxes by manually performing behavioral analysis of binaries in self-created sandbox environments using debuggers such as Ollydbg or gdb. Disassemblers such as IDA pro can be used to statically analyze the malicious programs as well. Much of this analysis is technically demanding, requiring a good knowledge of assembler language as well as knowledge of specifically how various functions look when compiled by different compilers. In many cases, the malware code is made intentionally difficult to analyze by using packing techniques and run-time tricks to deter reverse engineering. Although the effort to analyze malware can be costly, time consuming, and technically challenging, the intent of the hacker(s) and potential scope of the compromise usually begin to come into focus. Additionally, when the tools themselves are run, they may create artifacts that could contain important information, such as keylogger output files, imported registry files, or activity logs. Understanding how malware and hacker tools work can help investigators determine if and how the tools were used. Malware investigations are more thoroughly described in Chapter 6.

Applications and operating system programs provide all kinds of status in the form of log output. Many levels of error messages, authentication status, activity logging, debugging, and other information are continually reported to log files. The example web portal environment used in this chapter is likely to have significant amounts of historical log data in addition to the logs residing on the servers. The cyberforensics investigation team could easily have terabytes of data from application logs, windows event logs, Linux/UNIX syslogs, firewall logs, and sniffer logs. When appropriate levels of logging are used, logs will usually provide the best resource for determining the time frame, attack vectors, and scope of a compromised system. There can be many challenges involved in preserving these logs, fingerprinting the files with MD5 or SHA1 hashes, collecting and/or disseminating log evidence for analysis, analyzing the logs, understanding time zones of time stamp data, and correlating log activity with system or other activity. There are simply no easy answers as to how to determine the best approach to handling large volumes of log data. Also, no single tool can *easily* incorporate any and all log types. There are tools that can import many common log formats, but it is very likely some logs will require manual intervention. Often, unique skills are required to be able to recognize different attack profiles in logs. Someone familiar with web attacks should be looking at web logs, someone else familiar with Linux/UNIX system attacks should view those logs, and so on. Then, items of interest are extracted, as well as compared and correlated with other data. Depending on the amount of data, key data points from different sources could be loaded into log parsing software or even spreadsheets for sorting and filtering. Some of the freeware log parsing tools, such as the popular Microsoft® LogParser.exe, are great for providing query capabilities and log correlation. Of course, Specialized Log Manager or Security Incident and Event Manager (SIEM) appliances may have already been deployed. If they already contain the logs that the investigators need, they could probably be used to perform most of the log analysis. Either a database or some SIEM/log appliance is the answer for large volumes of data that need indexing and query capabilities. The goal is to gain insight from the data, while preserving evidence. Advanced data analytic techniques are more thoroughly addressed in Chapter 9.

Sometimes, anomalies or suspicious activity in network traffic leads investigators to such things as bot software communications, spamming software, or even live hacking efforts. Therefore, at some point, there might be real value in deploying sniffer technology in the compromised network space on switch spanning ports or taps; this can be done at any time, but early on in the investigation is preferable. Investigators might not know what to look for in the early stages of the investigation. For example, they might not know how to identify malicious traffic from valid traffic. Once they become more familiar with the environment and the nature of the compromise, their ability to target "suspicious" traffic improves. The tools used can be a great help as well. An AT&T-developed tool called GS Tool can handle huge network volumes. Another tool called NetWitness® Investigator presents data in a unique aggregated form that can help find unusual traffic, and a tool called SilentRunner™ is worth noting. Wireshark and tcpdump are free tools and very useful for smaller-volume situations. It also is important to remember the intrusion detection systems (IDS) and intrusion prevention systems (IPS). They sniff network traffic looking for known attack signatures. An often-used IDS/IPS called snort developed by SOURCEfire® is fairly easily deployed. IDS/IPS and sniffers can also assist in monitoring a "cleaned" compromised environment to see if any unusual traffic still exists. There are many choices available in the sniffer and IDS/IPS arenas. The trick is finding what works best for the situation at hand. The utility of network forensics tools is more thoroughly covered in Chapter 7.

There are many ways for hackers to gain access to systems. Some of the most common are through web application vulnerabilities, but also, a variety of vulnerable services can be exploited with remote buffer overflow or format string attacks. Unfortunately, access to systems is often much easier than expected. Hackers are frequently successful at guessing account names and passwords to systems and applications; this is usually done by using tools that attempt multiple logins using lists of common IDs and passwords. Investigators sometimes need to determine if the passwords to known compromised accounts were easily guessed. For example, the investigators may know that the hackers logged in using the "jsmith" account. It might not be possible to find out and verify the password of the jsmith account because jsmith could have forgotten the password, or left the company, or is a customer, or maybe the account was put in by previous hackers. The only choice in this case is to try to crack the password. After cracking the password, if it turned out to be an "easy-to-guess" password, that is, a commonly used password found in password dictionaries, then it is more likely that access to the account was gained through guessing the password.

Usually passwords are stored in some encrypted form called a hash. Commonly used encryption algorithms are LANMAN, NT hash, MD5, SHA1, crypt, and XOR; there are many others as well. Some algorithms can also be "salted,"[19] which adds more complexity.

There are basically three approaches to "cracking" passwords. The first method is to use Rainbow tables, which works well with the "unsalted" LANMAN and NT hashes used in Windows systems. In simple terms, Rainbow tables use a special lookup algorithm that scans through precomputed hashes stored in chains that are optimized lengths of hash sequences. The algorithm can very quickly search through chains to look up lists of reference hashes (hashes retrieved from the compromised system), which then return the clear-text passwords.

The second method is to use a dictionary attack (an extensive list of common passwords) with tools such as John the Ripper. Using the reference hashes, the program takes every word in the dictionary, encrypts it with the same salt (if used) and encryption algorithm used on the reference, then compares the resulting hash to the reference hashes. If the two hashes are the same, then the password is the word in the dictionary that created the matching hash.

The third method is to use a brute force attack, which tries every possible combination of a set of characters. A set of characters is made up by choosing some combination of the following: all lowercase letters, all uppercase letters, numbers, or special characters. The cracking process will take longer if more complex character sets are used and/or longer passwords are used. The investigators should find out if password complexity rules were enforced by the application or operating system that used the reference hashes. For example, user policy could enforce the practice of requiring a minimum 6-character-long password that contains lowercase letters and numbers. This knowledge is valuable in being able to apply the correct character set and password length settings to the password cracking software. Once the appropriate settings are applied, the password cracking software tries every combination of the character set to create a hash and compares it with the original reference hash sample(s). Simple passwords are usually cracked within a day, if not sooner. Complex passwords can take weeks, months, and even years. The investigators have to identify the type of encryption to be able to crack it: this can be simple, hard, or even impossible. In most cases, the hashes are in recognizable formats and salts are usually delimited for easy identification, such as this UNIX /etc/shadow MD5 hash: "1YUf57J75$fS4wB5AW6t188vTu6F.guM." The "$" is the delimiter, so "1" denotes the hash type as MD5, "YUf57J75" is the 8-character salt, and "fS4wB5AW6t188vTu6F.guM" is the actual hash. However, sometimes investigators find themselves working with hashes that are just raw data and information about the hash type or salting is not available. For example, this hex representation of a 28-byte cipher: "09e5e70a554d71fb9d2bd4ab5552ff7850dc1878913b 17091377374d" turned out to be a SHA1 20-byte cipher appended to an 8-byte salt. Once the encryption method is identified, a tool that can be used to crack the password(s) needs to be identified. Sometimes a special tool or patch to an existing program such as John the Ripper needs to be written. In addition, some applications use proprietary hashing algorithms that can make it just about impossible to figure out.

For a long time investigators have been using images of memory to extract "strings" data that could contain passwords, program usage/comment information, and communication session content [for example, Internet Relay Chat (IRC), instant messaging (IM), and other useful information]. In the past, most investigators did not have the skill set and/or time to manually parse through memory structures to extract the breadth of information contained in memory. In a white paper written by Greg Hoglund called *The Value of Physical Memory for Incident Response*,[20] Greg mentions various challenges of Windows physical memory analysis. Below is an abridged summary of some of these challenges.

- To properly understand the memory structure and potential data structure differences, the operating system, the version, and the service pack level need to be determined.
- Undocumented operating system data structures need to be understood to effectively extract useful data.
- Both physical and "swapped" or "paged" memory needs to be properly organized and structured to rebuild a complete memory model.
- Binary EXE or DLL code extracted from memory needs to be modified to add a portable executable (PE) header to make the code an executable file.
- MD5 or SHA1 hashes of files are not useful in identifying those files loaded in memory because the hashes will not match.

Tools are becoming more and more sophisticated in their ability to parse a memory image (live or static) and extract key information about the contents in memory, such as running processes and drivers (even those hidden by rootkits), open files and registry keys, as well as network connections, etc. These tools are predominantly supporting the Windows operating systems, and they are effective enough in this arena that investigators should seriously consider grabbing a memory image as the first step in a live forensics investigation.

There are commercial tools such as HB Gary's Responder, Encase® Enterprise Edition, and Forensic Toolkit® 3.0 that image and analyze memory. Also, there are free tools available such as MANDIANT's Memoryze, Volatile Systems' Volatility Framework, and Andreas Schuster's PTfinder.

In large enterprises that house Personally Identifiable Information (PII) about consumers, protecting data privacy is always a concern. Laws such as the California Database Security Breach Notification Act (SB 1386) have been initiated as has similar legislation in other states. Therefore, if possible, the investigators should consider performing database forensics, especially if they contain credit card or other personal data or there is reason to suspect unlawful database access. This is, however, a new field of investigation for investigators. Few tools exist, and they would most likely have to be database specific. Oracle®, Sybase®, Informix®, MySQL, and Microsoft SQL Server® are just some of the many types of databases that exist. Each one would have specific methods of obtaining database information. Areas that may contain potential evidence are audit trails that would have information about database changes such as updates, inserts, and deletes. These audit records would generally record the date and time of the transactions and information on the user who performed these activities. Unfortunately, many databases are so large and so heavily used that it can often be impractical to perform forensic analysis.

David Litchfield, a renowned database security expert, has explored developing a database forensics tool called the "Forensic Examiners Database Scalpel." Various sources, primarily metadata from transaction logs, web logs, and deleted data are used for analysis. Litchfield says, "It will be able to do comparisons between backup files and the metadata of the database to look at differences between the two and work out who did what when.[21]" Even in cases where database auditing is disabled, it may still be possible to find evidence of SQL queries, and Litchfield provides an example of this in his article, "Oracle Forensics Part 5: Finding Evidence of Data Theft in the Absence of Auditing." He explains that in Oracle10g Release 2 queries are compiled into an execution plan that leaves behind potentially useful evidence in special tables used to optimize database resources.[22] The contents of these tables can be dumped and carefully analyzed to provide information pertaining to database usage.

For the most part, databases are targeted to extract valuable data, but sometimes databases are used to store persistent cross-site scripting (XSS) code used to further exploit anyone viewing that content with a browser.[23] The hacking community will always be creative and innovative in how compromised assets are used. Because databases are often so vital and heavily integrated with corporate products and services, the reasons to perform database forensics will undoubtedly keep growing.

2.3 Case Study

The enterprise environment provides numerous opportunities for a discussion of cyberforensics cases. Standards of professional ethics prevent the author from a detailed description of a specific case. However, there are enough examples of cases wherein a hacker compromises a web portal to be able to use this scenario as a case study without unnecessary disclosure.[24] Web portal investigations provide excellent case studies because these environments can be enormously complex in many dimensions:

- Technically: because they often employ a complex mixture of networking, computing and application technologies
- Functionally: because web services can use complex authentication mechanisms, large databases can be involved, and multiple applications may be designed to interact with each other and other support utilities
- Legally: because the Payment Card Industry Data Security Standard (PCI DSS), the Sarbanes-Oxley Act (SOX) of 2002, the Health Insurance Portability and Accountability Act (HIPAA), and numerous other federal and state government regulations or contractual requirements may entail certain actions
- Economically: because these environments can be a source of invaluable income
- Politically: because various parties such as corporate clients, internal organizations, the press, and other interests may be involved

A breakdown of cyberforensics issues in such an environment permits the author to synthesize known cases into an example of the issues and challenges related to cyber investigations in a corporate IT world. From this discussion, the reader will be able to construe how other types of cases would be investigated.

2.3.1 The Incident

A company can become informed of an incident in many ways. Perhaps someone sees disturbing data in a log file or an IDS issues an alarm. Companies can even be informed about an incident from an outside party. In this case, an administrator notices TCP traffic on a strange port and immediately calls for incident response and forensics support.

2.3.2 The Environment

Web portals are often implemented in load-balanced web farms.[25] It is common to find 20, 40, 60, or more systems supporting the corporation's website content. In today's environments, the web servers are probably virtualized and are likely to be supporting multiple sites on virtualized IP addresses.[26] There could also be a variety of other servers such as back-end database servers, domain controllers, LDAP servers, DNS servers, mail servers, firewalls, management jump servers, and the list goes on. The first task of the investigator is to obtain or create documentation that clearly identifies the infrastructure and application architecture of the supported components, including the focus of the investigation.

2.3.3 Initial Investigation

After initial information gathering, interviews and meetings with various parties such as the application team, network administrators, and the legal department, the investigators realize that incident response and forensics have to be performed on live systems. In this case, remote forensics vendor tools would have to be supplemented with additional tools to evaluate all the systems in the affected environment; this is caused by the very restricted network ACLs and a broad mixture of operating systems including Windows, Linux, and various UNIX systems. For the Linux/UNIX systems, the investigators have to work through a jump server and need to use their own UNIX shell script incident response tool. Although many of these kinds of scripts exist, they need something that is portable across Linux, Solaris, AIX, and HP-UX. Also, all the freely available scripts use netcat to shovel evidence back to the investigators, which does not always work because of firewall/router ACLs. The investigators' script automates collection of volatile data,

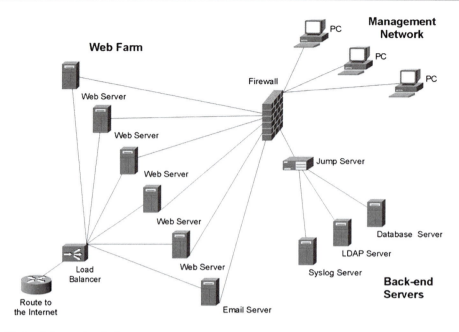

Fig. 2.1 Simplified web farm network diagram

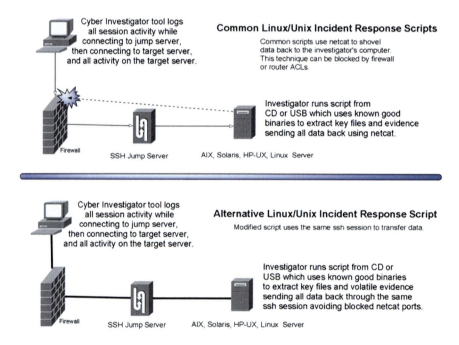

Fig. 2.2 Remote Linux/UNIX incident response in port-restricted environments

common log and configuration files through a terminal connection. The tool uses known safe binaries that are statically compiled when possible. Additionally, this script opens files using Dan Farmer's and Wietse Venema's icat[27] program to preserve MAC times. When icat does not work (for example, with an incompatible file system), MAC times of these files are recorded before copies are hashed, encrypted, encoded, and sent back on the same channel as the ssh or telnet session. Using the same ssh or telnet session to transport the data avoids the problems associated with using netcat in port-restricted environments. On the investigators' workstations, all activity on the systems is recorded for validation and auditing. All received evidence and the activity log data are hashed and stored in a zipped archive. Investigators use workstation-based scripts to copy evidence from the zipped archives, then decode and decrypt them for purposes of analysis.

Memory images are obtained on all systems that support the capability. This is done because:

1. Processes hidden by kernel level or Trojan rootkits are visible.
2. Much of the volatile information is captured in one shot, just by capturing memory.
3. The investigator, as far as possible, goes unnoticed by an intruder that is still logged into the system because dumping memory can be a more stealthy process than running a whole suite of tools to otherwise capture volatile data.

The initial analysis of the collected evidence provides some insight into the method of compromise and enables input to support preliminary containment efforts. Web servers are usually compromised by misconfigurations or code without proper input validation, providing an opening for a hacker. Recent security audit reports were useful in identifying potential vulnerabilities to focus on. In this example, it turns out that a local file inclusion (LFI) vulnerability in a particular page would allow reading some files on the web server. If the hacker can inject code into a known file, perhaps a log file, they can once again use the LFI to read and execute the code. Once this occurs, further exploitation is likely. Ultimately, administrative level access of the compromised systems could be possible. In this web portal scenario, evidence of an LFI attack is found in web logs. Because a user account is required to gain access to the vulnerable web page, it is obvious that either the actual user identified in the logs is the hacker or, more likely, the account is compromised. Analysis of log files shows that code was injected to upload and run an IRC bot with the permissions of the web user. File system analysis also finds IRC bot

executable and configuration files with MAC times that correlate the log file data.

2.3.4 Extended Analysis

After initial investigation of the target web servers, investigators must determine if the hacker managed to elevate privileges and whether hacker activity extends to other systems on the network. Management of all these systems requires various types of login accounts and the administration of them can be very challenging. In an effort to make this as easy as possible, administrative accounts (used by system administrators) and application accounts (used by application administrators) might have the same or similar types of passwords. They are also likely to be used across multiple systems. In a Windows environment, administrators may authenticate locally or through a domain controller that can permit access to a wide range of systems. In a Linux/UNIX environment, it is possible that ssh keys have been set up to permit "password-free" access between systems. Unfortunately, the compromise of a key administrative ID could permit access to many systems. Hackers are not usually content with compromising just one system. They often identify other targets through various techniques while on the first system. If the compromised system ID can access other servers without being challenged to provide a password, or if the passwords are the same, hackers can access other systems easily. A common practice that makes life easier[28] for hackers is that many systems are on the same subnet or broadcast domain.[29] Even when systems are on different subnets, and not visible at the data link layer, they may be listed in configuration files or identified by viewing network activity with the "netstat" command. Basically, it does not take long for hackers to glean knowledge of other potential targets. If they cannot elevate privileges from an application-level ID to an administrative ID or accomplish their goals on the currently compromised system, then jumping to another computer system may provide that opportunity. As hackers are likely to compromise multiple systems, investigators need to look for signs of this activity. System administrators are interviewed and assist in identifying any unusual login log file entries. Systems are searched for unusual artifacts that may be remnants of hacker activity. Systems are evaluated for rootkits. Network activity logs are reviewed for unusual network traffic.

As the investigation progresses, different tools are used as environments and investigative needs change. Many gigabytes of historical web logs and other logs of correlation value that date back to the creation date of the vulnerable web page are collected and analyzed to look for earlier attempts of exploiting the LFI vulnerability. The remote forensics vendor tools extend the search and correlation functions. Key account passwords, in particular, the compromised user account, are cracked to determine password complexity, and the results clearly show that the user account had a simple guessable password, which supports the likelihood that the account was compromised. Without question, hackers can obtain even complex passwords from phishing sites and keyloggers, so this also must be taken into account.

Unallocated space is evaluated for potential deleted evidence. Timelines are created by correlating evidence from a variety of network, system, security and application logs. Evidence-gathering tools report details that are not known to those who reported the incident nor to those who called in the investigators. Information received from both parties conflict with data retrieved from the system itself, and interviews are conducted to sort out misconceptions and misunderstandings. These steps are conducted in an atmosphere of pressure as investigators try to expand knowledge from how the compromise started, to understanding the scope of the compromise, and how best to contain it, all the while fielding constant queries from the legal department, management, application owners, administrative teams, etc.

This web portal scenario has databases associated with the application architecture. Forensic analysis is done with the help of a database administrator who understands the database structure and content. Results from the analysis and interviews are used to narrow the scope of database logs and tables of interest; these are likely to be application-related logs as opposed to error or transaction logs created by the database management system itself. For example, the user account revealed in the web server log is used to focus on queries of the application commands executed by that user. The actual data that the user accesses are inferred from the commands. Queries are carefully chosen in consultation with the database administrator to minimize impact on the production environment while at the same time revealing the maximum amount of information that may be useful to the investigation.

2.3.5 Investigation Conclusions

Investigation and analysis can, in theory, go on forever. A good lead investigator needs to keep the work effort focused and productive with reference to the goals in the case. Because the web portal environment is so large and complex, a good question is, exactly when does the cyberforensics investigation end? No hard-and-fast rule can apply. The investigators' primary goals in this case are to do the following:

1. Identify and preserve evidence.
2. Determine, as accurately as possible, the method, time frame, and scope of the compromise.
3. Provide feedback about containment, remediation, and security enhancement.
4. Perform the investigation with as little impact to the corporation as possible.

Cases can, of course, be closed by corporate management or the legal department. But, normally, the lead investigator determines when to close the case by reviewing the goals and balancing the needs of the business with the overall analysis of case evidence. The investigation of every case arrives at a point when new evidence of probative value starts to dry up and the corporation's financial/business needs prevail. This point sometimes occurs before the goals of the investigation can be reached.

In this web portal example, the owner(s) of any compromised user IDs are informed if the hacker managed to obtain PII database information. Any required legal or regulatory procedures are initiated. Appropriate cleanup measures are performed while continued monitoring of the environment takes place. Network and application security scans are scheduled and are followed by a thorough penetration test. These types of compromises are costly to a company. However, there are benefits. Security awareness is raised and at least one area of the corporate IT infrastructure becomes more secure.

2.4 Issues and Trends

2.4.1 CyberForensics in the Corporate Environment

Based on experiences from many internal and external investigations, some key points may be useful to the reader.

Even the smallest problem on a computer system can lead to identifying a huge compromise. Casually ignoring unusual system behavior or signs of compromise can be devastating. If the unusual behavior was noticed at the beginning of a compromise that no one investigated, the opportunity to nip the attack "in the bud" would be missed and the hackers would have plenty of time to explore, to probe deeper, and to enlist the help of other hackers. On the other hand, if the compromises were already accomplished, no one would be remedying the situation. Here are some examples:

- An administrator notices that files in the /tmp directory are getting deleted. Everyone assumes that it was someone else on their team who is doing it. It turns out that it was poorly written hacker code that is causing the problem, and the investigation identifies that rootkits are now installed on several systems.
- A client's web page is defaced. The investigation determines that the client's ID and password are compromised. The first thought is that the password was easy to guess. However, that is not the problem. The hackers have figured out how to bypass the authentication mechanisms.

Both these cases turn out to be complex investigations.

Any network space that is exposed to the Internet needs to be well secured. Everyone already knows this, but in reality, things do not always go as planned. Unsecured routes to internal network space can exist for a variety of reasons:

- Minor errors in firewall rules
- Errors in router ACLs
- Systems with IP forwarding enabled
- Temporary test systems being casually deployed
- Incorrectly installing or patching systems
- Weak passwords and administrative mistakes

Additionally, often unmonitored corporate entities inadvertently create vulnerabilities and permit access to internal networks: these would include small labs, satellite offices, business partner networks, outsourced computer administration services, consulting services, etc. Cases involving Internet facing systems need to include careful evaluation of all these possibilities.

It is a common practice for development and administration groups to keep documentation on a corporate server: these often include application documents, network diagrams, procedures, and contacts. Additionally, administrative tools (for example, simple database administrative scripts, UNIX shell scripts, Windows batch files) as well as source code can often be found. Unfortunately, this information is sometimes found on production servers. Security scanning tools are not likely to flag these files as potential vulnerabilities, but hackers look for this information. There was a case in which hackers found the source code that detailed how an encryption was deployed to store passwords in a database. This knowledge was later used to circumvent the encryption relating to an application on a completely different network than the one originally compromised.

Hackers will use compromised systems in every way imaginable, including these approaches:

- Setting up phishing sites (for example, a cloned bank website designed to entice users to enter in their ID and passwords)
- Setting up a malware/hacker tool distribution site
- Installing covert communication channels
- Using the system to attack other sites (for example, distributed ssh ID/password guessing attacks)
- Installing sniffers and keyloggers
- Running IRC reflectors and servers
- Setting up a DVD movie distribution site
- Setting up malware infecting sites
- Setting up hacker training sites
- Installing rootkits and backdoors

- Setting up porn distribution sites
- Launching wars on other hacking groups
- Probing into internal networks
- Setting up botnet command and control (software used to communicate and issue commands to many thousands of bot-infected computers)
- Installing spamming software

This chapter uses the theoretical example of a compromised web portal as a discussion platform which, by the nature of the topic, focuses a great deal on hacking. However, cyberforensics in corporations covers many areas. In reality, the majority of cyberforensics cases focus on employees and contractors. The following list contains examples of the kinds of cases frequently investigated:

- Intellectual property
- Corporate espionage
- Corporate violence
- Cyber harassment
- Unauthorized use of the Internet
- Sexual harassment
- Threats
- Pornographic material
- Unauthorized access
- Fraud (for example, medical benefit fraud)
- Off-duty employee conduct
- Bribes
- Burglary
- Using work time inappropriately

Aside from hacking and employee cases, investigators are sometimes asked to analyze systems for potential malware. One such case involved an executive who had spent time in China and wanted to be sure their laptop was not compromised while there. Also, corporations are often involved in legal issues that require the use of e-Discovery.

e-Discovery tools are usually modules of remote forensics tools and, as such, investigators are often involved in these efforts.

2.4.2 Considerations for the Future

The great explosion of smart phone and mobile device usage means corporations now need to provide suitable forensics support. The ever-growing and wide variety of devices forces investigators to purchase and use different hardware connectors and software. The procedures used in handling these devices are quite different than in computer systems. When a need to perform forensics arises and the device is still turned on, it is usually kept on; however, that can cause problems.

Another layer of complexity is applied if there is a long transport time in taking the device back to the lab or if the equipment needs to be shipped out of state for analysis. In these cases, power needs to be maintained on the device. If the device uses a password-protected auto-lock feature, the investigators will need the password or keep the device from entering the protected lock-up mode. Also, communication with the device may have to be prohibited using a Faraday cage.[30] Aside from these complexities, keeping up with the constant change in the cell phone/mobility industry is daunting.

Cloud computing and virtualization have a very bright future for corporations.[31] From a forensics perspective, this is a new territory that comes with its own complexities and issues. There could easily be some real benefits to digital forensics in these environments:

- Nearly instant backups of cloud environments would be possible.
- Storage for backing up log files and other evidence would be available.

- The speed of the cloud in making backups or images would be useful.
- Special forensics systems with a suite of tools could be part of the cloud and called up as needed.

However, there are many questions about data integrity. Cloud Service Delivery Models, such as Infrastructure as a Service (IaaS), Software as a Service (SaaS), and Platform as a Service (PaaS), all have their various controls. In that light, the following questions arise:

- When data is deleted under each of these models, is it really gone? Could there be copies of the data under one of the other service layers?
- Can data cross-contaminate other clouds or trusted boundaries, particularly in multi-tenant operating environments?
- Could data identified through forensic examination be a contaminant or comingled data from other sources?
- How would data encryption methods affect the ability to perform forensics?

Answers to these questions will have to be answered over time and will also vary depending on different cloud architectures and deployment.

It is likely that forensic approaches will need to be modified to support cloud environments. For example, sniffers may need to be installed under a virtual machine to permit the capturing of traffic between virtual systems that are communicating across the hardware backplane. Cloud-provided forensic workstations may need to be used to gain quick access to both static images and live systems. There may be a need to rely more on cloud administrators to perform many of the backing-up and imaging tasks.

Memory forensics is rapidly becoming more mainstream. As this tendency becomes more prevalent, the expectation for investigators to include memory acquisition and analysis as a standard practice will grow. This expectation may cause difficulties when dealing with certain UNIX systems that do not support easy access to memory.

The insidious use of bot malware and the expanding use of client-side attacks[32] drastically change the attack vectors that most threaten corporations. These attack mechanisms place hackers directly inside corporate networks. Ethical and dependable employees can have their systems taken over by hackers and then used to further attack corporate assets. Companies need to focus more and more attention on identifying internal attacks stemming from the use of these methods.

There is a growing need for cyberforensics investigators to rely on various corporate individuals to assist in handling or storing evidence. In most cases these individuals are not properly trained and need to be carefully managed by the investigators. The author expects this trend to continue to grow as the IT world expands in complexity.

Currently, there is a lot of talk in the industry regarding various states in the United States regulating cyberforensics investigations. Many states require that cyberforensics investigators be private investigators. While this is not an issue for investigators performing internal corporate investigations it may affect corporate investigators in other ways. Today discussions exist about requiring standard certifications for all cyberforensics investigators. There are many sides to these issues. It is true that unqualified individuals are working as cyberforensics experts and perhaps some kind of qualifications or controls should be used to separate the qualified from those unqualified. That being said, there are plenty of highly experienced, talented cyberforensics investigators who have no formal training in the field. It will be interesting to see how all this pans out.

In summary, cyberforensics investigations will continue to become much more complex. The knowledge needed to perform investigations is rapidly becoming more diverse, and as a result, there will be a need for investigators with different specializations. Not everyone is cut out for this field. Cyberforensics investigators need to be self-motivated, detailed, critical thinkers with a willingness to keep up with the ever-changing technology. Here are a few other traits that are important:

- Interviewing skills
- Analysis skills
- The ability to focus
- Integrity
- Tenacity
- Report-writing skills

The work pressure can be enormous. However, it is deeply rewarding to solve a complex puzzle and provide a valuable service to the company.

Notes

1. RAID (Redundant Array of Independent Disks) provides a way to store data across different disks; this can improve performance, increase the mean time between failures, and provide fault tolerance. The operating system sees a RAID as a single logical hard disk.

    SAN (Storage Area Network) provides a channel-attached centralized pool of disk storage to servers.

    NAS (Network-Attached Storage) is a server on the network that is dedicated and specialized to handle file reads and writes.
2. LDAP (Lightweight Directory Access Protocol) is a protocol for accessing information directories, often used in authentication mechanisms.
3. Virtual LAN, commonly known as a VLAN, is a group of hosts with a common set of requirements that communicate as if they were attached to the Broadcast domain, regardless of their physical location. See: http://en.wikipedia.org/wiki/Virtual_LAN
4. Electronic discovery (or e-discovery) refers to discovery in civil litigation that deals with information in electronic format, also referred to as electronically stored information (ESI). See: http://en.wikipedia.org/wiki/Electronic_discovery
5. An applet is a generic name for a small program that, in this case, listens on a network port for commands.
6. A "script kiddie" is a hacker culture term used to describe a less-experienced hacker who uses hacking tools without the technical understanding of how the tool works.
7. Intrusion Detection Systems (IDS) and Intrusion Prevention Systems (IPS) are network monitoring devices that identify attack patterns. The prevention system will also terminate a network connection once an attack pattern is identified.
8. An artifact would be files, processes running in memory, database entries, or log data that represent signs of compromise.
9. Musashi, Miyamoto, *Book of Five Rings*, The Overlook Press, 1974, p. 48
10. Footprint, in this case, means that the forensics program running on the compromised system takes little storage space and is minimally invasive to the system.
11. Files usually have associated modify, access, and create time stamps. These times can be critical evidence in a forensics investigation. They help an investigator develop a timeline of activity.
12. Windows Management Instrumentation (WMI) is the primary management technology for Microsoft® Windows® operating systems. It enables consistent and uniform management, control, and monitoring of systems throughout your enterprise. See: http://www.microsoft.com/technet/scriptcenter/guide/sas_wmi_overview.mspx?mfr=true
13. PsExec is a lightweight telnet-replacement that lets you execute processes on other systems, complete with full interactivity for console applications, without having to manually install client software. PsExec's most powerful uses include launching interactive command-prompts on remote systems and remote-enabling tools such as IpConfig that otherwise do not have the ability to show information about remote systems. See: http://technet.microsoft.com/en-us/sysinternals/bb897553.aspx
14. LVM is a logical volume manager for the Linux kernel; it manages disk drives and similar mass-storage devices, in particular large ones. See: http://en.wikipedia.org/wiki/Logical_Volume_Manager_(Linux)
15. The most volatile data, from most to least, are memory, network status and connections, running processes, and data on hard drives or other media.
16. Jump servers are access gateway servers. They are usually used to permit an administrator to securely access network isolated systems by first logging into a jump server using ssh or telnet, then connecting to the target system.
17. An IRC bot is a set of programs that connects to Internet Relay Chat as a client. These connections appear similar to any other IRC user, but the purpose of the bot is to perform automated functions.
18. A sandbox environment is an isolated computer network that can be used to analyze running malware without the risk of infecting anything outside the sandbox.
19. A salt is a set of random characters that are used as part of the encryption key. Both the hash value and the seed are needed to crack a password hash.
20. Hoglund, Greg, *The Value of Physical Memory for Incident Response*, p. 3.

    See: http://www.hbgary.com/wp-content/themes/blackhat/images/the-value-of-physical-memory-for-incident-response.pdf
21. See: http://www.theage.com.au/news/security/owning-database-forensics/2007/05/28/1180205158793.html?page=2 Patrick Gray, May 29, 2007.
22. Litchfield, David, *Oracle Forensics Part 5: Finding Evidence of Data Theft in the Absence of Auditing*, Litchfield, August 2007, p. 2. See: http://www.databasesecurity.com/dbsec/OracleForensicsPt5.pdf
23. Persistent cross-site scripting (XSS) is the storing of malicious scripts that control browser activity. Internet message boards are frequently targeted because user browsers would be affected whenever a XSS stored posting is read.
24. Web portals are networks supporting web servers, usually for a large audience such as the Internet.
25. A web farm is a collection of web servers running the same web application in a manner that distributes the load evenly across the servers.
26. A single computer can run multiple instances of "virtual" operating systems, which saves money on hardware and electricity. Also, a single computer can be referenced by multiple "virtual" IP addresses often used to host different websites on the same computer.
27. Dan Farmer and Wietse Venema developed The Coroner's Toolkit, which included the icat program that opens files based on the inode number without modifying the MAC times. Icat is currently part of the Sleuthkit and Autopsy tools supported by Brian Carrier.

28. Hackers can use sniffer software to capture IDs and passwords or hash credentials. This approach works best when many systems are on the same broadcast domain.
29. A broadcast domain is a logical division of a computer network in which all nodes can reach each other by broadcast at the data link layer. See: http://en.wikipedia.org/wiki/Broadcast_domain
30. A Faraday cage is a metallic enclosure that prevents the entry or escape of an electromagnetic (EM) field. See: http://searchsecurity.techtarget.com/sDefinition/0,sid14_gci942282,00.html
31. Cloud computing is a model for enabling convenient, on-demand network access to a shared pool of configurable computing resources (for example, networks, servers, storage, applications, and services) that can be rapidly provisioned and released with minimal management effort or service provider interaction. See: http://csrc.nist.gov/groups/SNS/cloud-computing/cloud-def-v15.doc

    A virtual machine (VM) is a software implementation of a machine (that is, a computer) that executes programs such as a real machine. See: http://en.wikipedia.org/wiki/Virtual_machine
32. A typical example of a client-side attack is a malicious web page targeting a specific browser vulnerability that, if the attack is successful, would give the malicious server complete control of the client system. See: http://www.honeynet.org/node/157

Chapter 3
Investigating Large-Scale Data Breach Cases

J. Andrew Valentine

J. Andrew Valentine is currently a senior investigator and team lead for the Forensics and Incident Response Team within Verizon Business/Cybertrust Inc. Mr. Valentine has led a number of high-profile investigations involving network breach and data compromise within the United States as well as internationally – many of which have led to successful indictment and prosecution. His work is highly regarded by many United States government agencies, such as the FBI, Secret Service, and the Department of Homeland Security. Mr. Valentine is a highly specialized security professional trained in computer forensics, evidentiary procedures, and investigative techniques. He is well versed in both criminal and civil investigative requirements and regularly interacts with government and state/provincial law enforcement agencies worldwide to transition case evidence and set the stage for prosecution.

Mr. Valentine has more than 9 years of experience as a computer crime and security professional, having spent 4 years in the public sector employed within the Computer Crime Center at the Florida Department of Law Enforcement. Mr. Valentine has been published in Computer Fraud and Security Magazine, SC Magazine, as well as Retail Banking Magazine, and was a contributing author for the American Bar Association's 2008 Cyber Crime Handbook.

3.1 Investigation Characteristics

This chapter discusses the varying challenges surrounding large-scale data breach cases and the forensic investigations that follow them. It focuses directly on specific considerations an investigator should make when conducting such an investigation, not only in terms of technical tools and techniques, but, more importantly, on the primary actions and decisions taken by an investigator that can make or break a case.

Computer forensics involves the complex task of accurately investigating events or activities taking place on computer systems without adversely affecting the integrity of the data retained on those systems. This is a difficult task to perform properly, requiring expert handling and care. At the core of any computer forensic investigation, an investigator is asked to answer fundamental questions surrounding an event: *who did what*, *when did they do it*, and *how was it accomplished*? At the same time, investigators are expected to take precautions that ensure the integrity of the original evidentiary data is maintained.

To that end, investigators follow precise procedures designed to safeguard evidence while still allowing the investigation to move forward. These procedures include maintaining an unbroken chain of custody for all evidentiary material relevant to the case, maintaining the integrity of the data-source media, and creating accurate forensic images of data sources. These procedures are so straightforward that some practitioners have developed widely recognized standards for classifying and investigating types of cybercrimes. For example:[1]

J.A. Valentine (✉)
Senior Investigator and Team Lead,
Forensics and Incident Response Team
Verizon Business/Cybertrust Inc.,
Ashburn, VA, USA

Type 1: Those where the computer is the instrument used to commit a pretechnology crime, such as the distribution of contraband imagery.

Type 2: Those where the computer is incidental to a crime, such as an Excel spreadsheet that contains bookkeeping information related to a criminal activity.

Type 3: Those where the computer is the target of the crime, such as a data breach case where sensitive information is stolen from a computer system.

Arguably, this process has become routine and standardized in both law enforcement and private sector circles relative to Type 1 and Type 2 computer crime cases where the in-scope computer system is either simply a tool used to commit a nontechnical crime (such the hosting and distribution of child pornography; Type 1) or a corollary to some other crime (such as the laptop that is seized during a drug bust; Type 2). Even some Type 3 cases (such as those that involve an individual home user's PC suffering a deliberate intrusion) involve only single systems. In any case, the system will likely retain relevant evidence relative to the case, and a competent investigator will be more than capable of discovering that evidence while maintaining proper chain-of-custody documentation such that it will remain admissible in a courtroom, if necessary.

However, these examples represent cases where the in-scope evidence set is clearly defined, small, and relatively easy to manage. As any investigator will tell you, the larger and more complex a case becomes, the more challenging it becomes for an investigator (or more accurately, multiple investigators) to successfully determine the in-scope systems environment, collect relevant evidence sources, conduct analysis, and accurately report on findings. This factor becomes an especially pressing issue relative to the fleeting nature of digital evidence: the longer it takes for an investigative team to grasp which systems may or may not represent some sort of evidentiary relevance, more and more digital evidence will continue to disappear. In scenarios where a multitude of systems, sometimes comprising an entire corporate environment, are *all* potentially targets of the crime, it is important for investigators to accurately scope their operating environment such that they best serve the investigation and successfully set the stage for prosecution.

And the truth is, accurately scoping the victim environment is only just the first of many challenges an investigator will confront when faced with a large-scale data breach investigation. Recent years have shown us the largest data breach scenarios in history. Case data suggest than in 2008 alone more individual records were compromised during data breach cases than all of the records compromised between 2004 and 2007 *combined* (Fig. 3.1).[2]

In 2008, individual records compromised during data breach cases numbered in the *hundreds* of millions (at least 285,423,000). The bad guys are gaining unauthorized access into larger, more complex environments, and making off with more data, in terms of both volume and cash-transferable value, than during any other period in history. As this trend continues, each year will likely bring newer and larger data breach scenarios involving systems environments that will involve tens, if not hundreds, of systems which potentially retain electronic evidence relevant to the crime.

Almost any computer forensic investigator will tell you that every case brings its own unique challenges. Despite the systematic approach so meticulously described in Chapter 2, there is no such thing as a

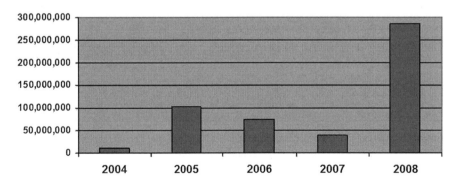

Fig. 3.1 Number of records compromised per year in breaches investigated by Verizon Business

smooth cyberforensics investigation. No environment ever looks like the investigator expects it will, and no forensic tool or utility will function 100% of the time. Worse yet, the investigator may not have the tool they need readily available while on-scene. The best investigators are those who are able to quickly adapt to these challenges, improvising viable workarounds without sacrificing the integrity of the investigation. This is true of any and all cases – those that are high profile, as well as the ones which are conducted under the radar, behind the scenes. For most investigators, there is not a case they work where they do not face *something* unexpected and thus learn something new.

There exists an odd misconception that computer forensics is an instant process. Television programs such as CSI or Law and Order would have viewers believe that computer forensic analysis can be accomplished instantaneously and with a minimum of effort (and conducted against original evidence, no less). Misconceptions about what computer forensics is and how it applies to modern investigations vary in their specific details from person to person, but their overall logic is the same. People tend to think that computer forensics can be performed quickly, directly against the original evidence set, and that rarely are more than one or two systems ever involved. People also often think that digital evidence lasts forever. The idea that an investigation will hinge on the forensic analysis of tens, or perhaps hundreds, of computer systems, is something you'll never see on primetime crime drama. On television, the computer forensic analysis is the easiest, smoothest part of the case. Evidence preservation is never an issue. Digital evidence is never fleeting on television.

In the real world, however, walking into a large-scale data breach investigation will often prove to be chaotic: the victim organization itself is in complete disarray. It is not uncommon for the case investigator to be the last person on-scene to know the basic fundamentals of the case background: as they say within industry parlance, "First to go, last to know." In the aftermath of a large-scale data breach scenario, it is interesting to observe as an organization with a fully documented Computer Incident Response Team (CIRT) procedure sees their predetermined communication channels completely fall apart. It is during these initial moments after the realization that a breach has occurred when organizations often fail to ensure that digital evidence is preserved.

Nevertheless, within large-scale data breach scenarios, where relevant digital evidence is often disappearing with each passing moment, it is the onus of the case investigator to protect evidence in every way possible. The case investigator, depending on the circumstances, might represent law enforcement, be a private sector consultant, or even be employed within the victim organization.

The challenge in protecting relevant (or potentially relevant) evidence is that within large-scale data breach cases, where the in-scope evidence set potentially comprises an entire corporate environment (often spanning multiple locations worldwide), it is a primary task for the investigator to determine which systems *specifically* fall into the scope of the investigation; that is, which systems are most likely to have been involved in the data breach scenario, and/or which systems potentially retain evidence relative to the crime. Determining which of the many systems in a victim environment these are, and where they exist in a victim environment, is by no means an easy task – but this will prove to be one of the investigator's most important steps at the onset of an investigation. Moving through this phase of an investigation is discussed in greater length in the next section of this chapter.

Even so, once an investigator makes an informed and calculated decision around the operating scope of the investigation, there are no guarantees that the operating scope will be small or inherently manageable. Quite to the contrary, larger environments, by their very nature, will likely involve a multitude of systems that are germane to a case. More to the point, a case investigator will need to rely heavily on the knowledge and expertise of personnel internal to the victim organization to gain an understanding of the systems and environment central to the case. Inside larger environments, different personnel will likely own different flavors of systems tied to different functionalities internally. It falls on the investigator not only to accurately scope the victim environment but to identify and interview personnel overseeing those systems. Identifying those individuals can in itself provide a challenge.

A further consideration here is that as the investigator works with personnel from the victim organization, additional variables often work to affect an investigation. Given the often chaotic circumstances surrounding them, large-scale data breach investigations become politically tense. To put it bluntly, it is not uncommon for victim personnel to be fearful for their jobs and livelihood in the aftermath of a data breach. Personnel working inside an organization that has recently suffered a large-scale data compromise event often become very defensive and uncooperative. Information Technology personnel are often hesitant to take ownership of company or network assets that were involved in the data breach. For example, upon the failure of an intrusion detection system (IDS) to accurately predict or notify management during a data breach scenario, persons inside the victim organization will often hesitate to take ownership of the IDS as part of their work responsibility.

Consider this example of an oft-encountered scenario: During the initial interview process, Mr. Gibbs will tell the investigator that Mr. Corey manages and maintains the perimeter IDS.

Following up on that lead, the investigator will interview Mr. Corey. Mr. Corey will then tell the investigator that Mr. Gibbs manages and maintains the perimeter IDS. The investigator is left with no lead on who really manages and maintains the IDS.

This transference of asset ownership is ubiquitous during large scale data breach aftermath scenarios. Even more commonplace are situations where no one maintains ownership over network assets at all. Instead of Mr. Corey and Mr. Gibbs accusing the other of being responsible for the failure, investigators will often find that *no one* maintains responsibility over the affected assets, and that no documentation exists to make any kind of determination either way. This phenomena of non-ownership is supported by the data. To be sure, the use of IDS as an example above is deliberate: in real-world scenarios, it is commonplace for an investigator to be unable to determine who owns the IDS in a victim organization. See Fig. 3.2 below.

Across all data breach scenarios taking place in 2008, only 6% of them were discovered through the use of event monitoring [such as IDS or intrusion prevention system (IPS)] technology. This realization is somewhat counterintuitive, as detecting a security breach is the primary purpose of these technologies. This tends to indicate that ownership issues may have existed before the data breach scenario, but that the breach itself is bringing those issues to light. However, in converse situations, where IDS/IPS functions perfectly and breach situations are prevented and documented, it is likely easier to identify personnel who own and maintain those systems.

Relative to Fig. 3.2, many large-scale data breach scenarios are discovered after fraud patterns emerge relative to the stolen data. Most commonly, this is in the form of credit card identity fraud, where stolen credit card information is bartered in the information black market and then used to make both high-dollar and low-dollar (or lifestyle-type) transactions. Large-scale data breach scenarios involve the compromise of often hundreds of thousands, if not millions, of individual records that potentially go to fraud subsequent to the breach.

However, data suggest that large-scale data breaches present yet another challenge to the investigator – navigating the skill set of the intruder who stole the data. Real-world data indicate that the larger the data breach is, the more skilled the intruder is likely to be. See Figs. 3.3 and 3.4. Although highly skilled attacks only accounted for 17% of the data breach cases in 2008, they also accounted for 95% of all records that were compromised in 2008.

This data is rather intuitive but suggests that the larger the data breach scenarios, the more complex the

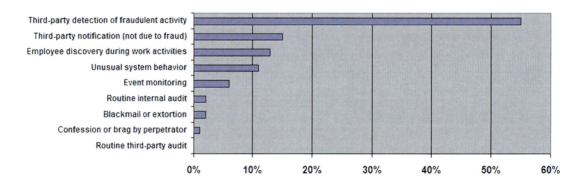

Fig. 3.2 Breach discovery methods by percent of breaches in 2008

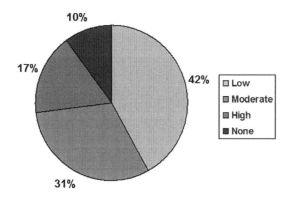

Fig. 3.3 Attack difficulty by percent of breaches in 2008

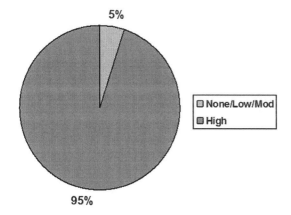

Fig. 3.4 Attack difficulty by percent of records in 2008

Quite simply, the data indicates that large-scale data breaches will be more difficult to investigate because the intruder himself (or herself) was that much better a criminal. In this author's experience, the largest known data breach scenarios taking place so far have resulted in some of the most complex cases, technically speaking, that is, and involved a set of criminals both technically superior and creative enough to use their techniques in new and unforeseen ways.

As a corollary to this improved criminal skill set, large-scale data breach scenarios will also pit investigators against another related challenge – the use of customized malware. Although this point is outside the scope of this chapter, Chapter 6 demonstrates just how complex malware deconstruction and analysis can be. Unfortunately, experience shows that the larger a data breach scenario, the more likely an investigator will encounter previously unseen customized malware, likely operating outside the detection of antivirus tools inside the victim environment. See Fig. 3.5 below.

In 2008 alone, nearly a quarter of all malware discovered during data breach scenarios was fully customized. Given the likelihood that an investigator will discover customized malware tools (built either from existing malware tools, or entirely from scratch) during the course of a large-scale data breach scenario, it is imperative that the investigator have the tools and resources available to conduct accurate malware analysis. A much larger and in-depth discussion of malware analysis is included elsewhere in this volume.

Challenges associated with large data breaches are not limited to those that are strictly technical, however, investigation will become – not only in terms of scope, politics, and asset ownership (as described above), but more specifically in terms of the skill of the intruder.

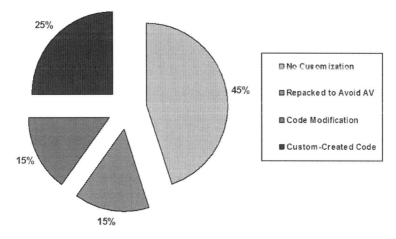

Fig. 3.5 Malware customization by percentage of breaches in 2008. *AV*, anti-virus

as these types of breach and the investigations that follow them often involve political and/or leadership challenges for the case investigator.

Arguably the fastest growing characteristic of large-scale data compromise investigations is the involvement of either internal or external legal counsel, often taking the role of directing the investigation, and in some cases outlining the technical scope of investigative work. Legal counsel will often liaise with law enforcement and/or private sector investigators, acting as a proxy between investigators and the victim organization such that findings are presented to legal counsel instead of the victim organization directly. In these situations, it is critical to work with legal counsel (and either directly or indirectly with the victim organization) to strictly define investigation control points. These investigation control points will define operating parameters of the investigation and remove any ambiguity arising from conflicting ideas of how the investigation will move forward. Examples of investigation control points might include these:

- The flow of information and findings during the case
- The preservation of digital evidence
- The operational scope of the investigation

It is important that any investigator involved with such a case keep in mind that law enforcement, private sector investigators, legal counsel, and the victim organization itself often have differing and conflicting goals. Where private sector and law enforcement investigators may be primarily concerned with solving the crime and apprehending a criminal, legal counsel will be working to reduce liability as much as possible – two often incongruent goals inside an operational investigation. It is not uncommon for the investigator to be asked to step outside the normal analytical role and make political or "influenced" statements inside reporting mechanisms. The best investigators are the ones who do not make political decisions and only present facts of the case that are provable by available digital evidence.

3.2 Investigation Approach

A constant challenge facing computer forensic investigators is the inherently fragile nature of digital evidence. When handled improperly, digital evidence can easily be altered or even eliminated, creating a significant investigative handicap. In the minutes and hours immediately following the discovery of a crime where digital evidence is involved, the actions taken by first responders should ensure that evidence is preserved in a secure and forensically sound manner. This challenge becomes even more pertinent when considering that during large-scale data breach investigations it can become increasingly difficult to accurately identify the in-scope systems that are relevant to the investigation. Essentially, without first being able to identify relevant evidence, it is functionally difficult to protect it.

This difficulty is compounded by the fact that before the onset of a proper forensic investigation, evidence is often tainted by the actions taken by otherwise well-intentioned first responders on scene. Essentially, the first people to discover the crime, if improperly trained or just simply untrained, often "poke around" the system environment attempting to determine what occurred. In so doing, these first responders can potentially alter the digital evidence, rendering it useless to an operational investigation. Consequently, it is important that before the onset of a proper forensic investigation no actions are taken that could compromise valuable evidence sources.

After the discovery of a network breach resulting in a massive scale data compromise (or other computer-related crime for that matter) where digital evidence is involved, it is important to adhere to a set of basic guidelines to ensure a smooth and beneficial forensic investigation. This section of the chapter deliberately avoids an investigation-specific "how to" section, as no two cases are the same. Such a discussion could easily fill a 1000-page tome. Instead, this chapter presents several high-level considerations an investigator should pursue when faced with a large-scale data breach investigation—this is with a firm understanding that many investigations, based on their circumstances and/or restrictions, will not allow for some of the considerations discussed here.

3.2.1 Set Investigation Control Points

An investigation control point is a high-level policy decision that serves to focus the investigator on management goals for the investigation process. Another way to look at investigation control points is that of the bottom-line goals of the investigation, prioritized by the investigator and the victim organization. As noted previously, different parties involved in an investigation will likely have different goals for the end product of that investigation. Setting investigative control points up front will remove any ambiguity around actions taken by anyone involved. For example, a victim organization might decide that they are not concerned with *who* committed the crime, but are rather more concerned with identifying *how* the crime was committed and the remediation of the vulnerabilities that allowed it. Common control points, as already noted, might be the following:

- Identification and preservation of evidence
- Determination of scope of data exposure
- Identification of intruders
- Remediation

That said, each of these investigation control points should represent progressive operational phases of the investigation, set by priority and practicality. Specifically, an investigation control point concerning the identification of potential evidence sources should functionally come before a control point around evidence preservation. Either way, upfront reporting should accurately represent agreed-upon control points of the investigation. Preliminary reporting documentation created at the outset of an investigation should document these control points.

For example, the goals for an investigation could be (1) to determine whether a physical or technical breach of the systems environment occurred, and if so, the extent to which the security breach resulted in a compromise of sensitive data; (2) to identify the extent to which sensitive data had been retained on affected systems and were thus at risk; (3) to find any further details of evidentiary value relative to a possible data compromise with specific regard to information derived from the known fraud pattern analysis; (4) to transition relevant case evidence to law enforcement to set the stage for prosecution; (5) to identify the technical vulnerabilities that facilitated the breach; and (6) to remediate these vulnerabilities.

By assuring that all parties involved in the data breach scenario including (and especially) legal counsel sign off on the control points, the investigator should be left with no lingering questions about what his or her next steps should be. It should be additionally noted that creating investigative control points up front will conveniently create an outline for postinvestigation reporting.

3.2.2 Manage the Unknown Unknowns

In most large-scale data breach investigations, the case investigator will be faced with one or more "unknown unknowns." That is to say, most investigations will lead to the discovery of previously unknown, overlooked, or forgotten assets. These are referred to as unknown unknowns, because not only did the victim organization not know they existed, they did not even know there was a possibility for them to exist. The graph below illustrates "unknown unknowns" from 2004 to 2007 casework (Fig. 3.6).

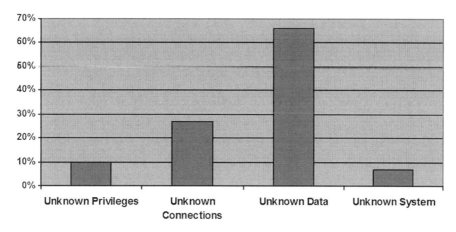

Fig. 3.6 Percent of "unknown unknowns" in 2004–2007 forensic caseload

In conducting interviews with key personnel during the course of an investigation, there is a statistical likelihood that the individual will leave out key information – not because he or she is hiding information, but simply because the person does not know better. That is to say, they may be genuinely convinced of something, but utterly wrong about it. Again, this likelihood often increases with the size of the organization and the data breach itself, as more and more individuals retain ownership of segmented parts of a network. What this means is that investigators will have to be prepared for the scenario where an interviewee is simply incorrect about the nature of a systems environment. As such, an investigator should always validate information gleaned from interviews and existing documentation; this can be accomplished with an Information Flow and Data Discovery Exercise.

3.2.3 Information Flow and Data Discovery Exercise

With the suspicion that a large-scale data breach has taken place within a victim organization, it falls on the case investigator to conduct a more accurate assessment regarding the manner in which the information that was compromised interacts with the victim environment. This assessment includes a review of the at-risk data flow at the organization from the initial entry point into that organization. The investigator should identify any and all systems that the data in question touches, *why* it touches that system, and whether it is *retained* on that system. The objective here is to identify the individual systems and network devices where the sensitive data may have been at risk of compromise. Interviews with key personnel at the victim organization should be compared against a physical examination of the network environment. This examination should give investigators a clear understanding of the information flow and the security measures in place around the data that was compromised.

Additionally, a data discovery exercise may need to be conducted whereby all integral systems and servers that process, store, or transmit sensitive data should be reviewed periodically for old and/or stale content and data structures. During many investigations, investigators are able to discover that plain-text sensitive information was accessed by intruders that the victim organization was unaware even existed. In many similar cases, IT personnel are often unaware that these types of data stores exist in the *volume* that they do.

In conducting data discovery, many investigators heavily rely on the use of the regular expression parsing utility named GREP. GREP is a UNIX-based command line utility that scours datasets for specific patterns and creates reports on their occurrences. GREP's use of "regular expressions" makes it a highly versatile tool, as it can utilize any degree of substitutions and wild cards to provide powerful search-and-replace operations within given datasets. The discovery of these unknown data stores is often the biggest lead an investigator will make in a large-scale data breach case. Unfortunately, the analysis of these types of "unknown unknown" data during a data breach investigation can often be overlooked by case investigators who fail to validate information gleaned from interviews.

3.2.4 Network Discovery

In conjunction with an Information Flow and Data Discovery Exercise, the case investigator should work with the victim to conduct a full-scale network discovery. Any investigator who has worked an intrusion and compromise case will tell you that existing network documentation is rarely accurate, or in some cases it does not exist at all; this is true of small cases, as well as large-scale data breach cases. Relative to "unknown unknowns," the existence of unknown company assets and/or network devices can often be a lead that makes or breaks an investigation. The investigator should consider the use of one or more network discovery tools such as SuperScan, Nmap, or Nessus (or a combination thereof), in conjunction with an active interface-to-interface mapping from known equipment to potential unknowns using tools such as RedSeal and SkyBox, and, in the worst case, a hands-and-knees physical examination and mapping of the network environment. At the culmination of the investigator's mapping exercise, a comparison should be made between the investigator's documented network topography and the one the victim organization has documented.

3.2.5 Accurately Scope Evidence and Acquisition

Given the results of the Information Flow and Data Discovery exercises, the investigator should have a fair idea of the systems within the affected environment that fall in scope for an investigation. Specifically, those systems that store, retain, or transmit the data that were compromised should fall directly into scope for the investigation. Further, any systems that maintain direct access to systems storing the affected data should fall into scope as well. To some extent, the operating scope of the investigation will be discretionary, based on the investigator's instinct, case experience, and information gleaned during on-scene interviews. In any case, the operating scope of the investigation represents quite possibly the most important investigative control point, and as any other investigative control point, should be agreed upon by all parties involved in the investigation.

Note that within the context of a criminal investigation that involves any level of law enforcement the investigator should defer to law enforcement to determine the operational scope of the investigation. That said, the investigator should be ready for law enforcement to deem *all* systems within a given environment into scope for analysis.

3.2.6 Detect and Manage Misinformation

In the midst of a large-scale data breach scenario, many organizations move into informational lockdown. This move can be to limit media exposure of the event, to reduce liability based on the information that was compromised, or simply the result of multiple internal personnel working to remain gainfully employed. Unfortunately, this reluctance to share accurate information or to deliberately share misinformation can often adversely affect investigative efforts. Any decent investigator will memorize and recite the following sentence (or something similar) as appropriate during large-scale data breach investigations:

> "You (and/or your organization) have been the victim of a crime. My job here is to help you. However, I cannot help you unless you tell me the truth."

It could be argued that some investigators are simply better capable of detecting, managing, and mitigating information inside the context of a forensic investigation. That said, every investigator should retain the capability to fact-check and validate information presented during interviews. Perhaps the strongest tool an investigator has to manage and mitigate misinformation is his or her ability to validate claims made by on-site personnel. To consistently negotiate misinformation, an investigator should always work to validate statements made during the interview process, through both physical and technical examination. Last, all known instances of misinformation should be retained in case notes.

3.2.7 Leverage Fraud Data

During large-scale data breach situations where the victim organization became aware of a potential problem by an overwhelming amount of fraud occurring against data tied to their systems, investigators can often leverage that fraud data in conducting the investigation. Specifically, the fraud data, given the time frame that it was known or suspected to have passed through the victim's systems, might provide a basic timeline to give some insight as to when a breach may have taken place. During data compromise scenarios, and specifically large-scale ones, the preponderance of fraud data can often lead investigators to a smoking gun. In this section we have discussed the existence and discovery of unknown data structures that can often lead to data compromise. In most cases, the volume of known fraud represents only a fraction of the information that was initially stolen. That is to say, it is rare to find instances where *all* the data stolen from a victim organization goes fraud.

That said, by parsing known fraud data against data discovered during the information flow mapping and data discovery exercise, an investigator can determine a relative hit ratio of fraud data versus data retained on affected systems. Higher ratios, and ratios that are close to 100%, might signify that the investigator has discovered the exact data that was exfiltrated from victim systems. With this knowledge, the investigator can more efficiently hone the investigation to access points to that specific data. More information around leveraging fraud data can be found in the Case Study section of this chapter.

3.3 Case Study

In this particular case study, a major Asia-based retailer suffered an information security breach, resulting in the compromise of their customers' debit card information. The intruders were able to extract full debit card track data, including personal identification number (PIN) information, from multiple locations across several countries, and create counterfeit debit cards. This case study examines the investigative response and forensics process from the onset of the engagement, including cooperation with law enforcement, through its conclusion.

3.3.1 Company Profile

Acme Corp is a major retailer within the consumer electronics industry that serves customers based in Japan and surrounding countries as well as in the United States. The company distributes both its own brand of many popular products as well as a host of name brand merchandise. It markets and sells products through field salespeople, telemarketing, catalogues, the Internet, and retail stores.

As of December 31, 2006, Acme Corp operated a dozen distribution centers and more than 300 retail stores across Japan, China, Taiwan, Thailand, Singapore, and Indonesia, among other countries. The company was created in 1955, and has changed its name three times over the course of 20 years before settling on Acme Corp in 1975. Acme Corp is headquartered in Tokyo, Japan, and also maintains redundant data centers in Nagasaki, Japan, and Parsippany, New Jersey.

In addition to the retail store operations already mentioned, Acme Corp also maintains an e-commerce presence through their website www.AcmeCorp.com. Through this e-commerce site, customers can purchase anything that is sold within an Acme Corp brick-and-mortar retail store, as well as find other useful tools such as detailed product fact sheets, specifications, and a retail store locator.

3.3.2 Account Data Compromise

On December 15, 2007, Acme Corp was notified by their bank that they were potentially the victim of an account data compromise. Visa Japan had received reports from issuing banks regarding debit cards used legitimately at Acme Corp from November 2005 through July 2007 that subsequently turned up with fraudulent transactions in late 2007. According to preliminary details provided by the issuing banks and Visa's fraud investigation service, all the fraudulent transactions were card-present PIN-based debit transactions. This information indicated that both track data and PIN data had been compromised and counterfeit debit cards were being created. According to fraud reports relayed to case investigators, the majority of the fraudulent use was being reported as ATM (automated teller machine) fraud taking place in eastern Europe.

The method used to identify Acme Corp as the potential victim was a Common Point of Purchase (CPP) analysis. This method takes a group of accounts experiencing fraud and examines their past transactions for any commonalities (mainly that of legitimate purchases). In doing so, the CPP analysis results indicated a high correlation among accounts experiencing ATM fraud and their past legitimate use at one of the seven[3] Acme Corp retail store locations below:

- Tokyo, Japan
- Shanghai, China
- Taipei, Taiwan
- Kyoto, Japan
- Jakarta, Indonesia
- Seoul, Korea
- Los Angeles, California

Considering the fraudulent debit card use and the CPP analysis indicating the data compromise, Acme Corp, in conjunction with Visa Japan and their debit card transaction acquirer, decided to open a full investigation.

3.3.3 Investigation

Visa Japan and Acme Corp, along with their debit transaction acquirer, contacted a United States-based private forensic firm on December 17, 2007, to discuss the situation and request incident response and forensic analysis services of the Acme Corp environment. Shortly thereafter, and in response to the fraud appearing to originate from the Los Angeles store location, Acme Corp's American division contacted the United States Secret Service (USSS), who had also opened up its respective investigation into the situation and was already working closely with the private sector investigative firm involved in the case.

As in any engagement involving multiple teams, cooperation and communication were critical to the success of the investigation. To that end, the private sector investigative firm clearly outlined expectations, lines of communication, and full engagement goals to both Acme Corp and Visa Japan, as well as the USSS.

3.3.4 Investigation Control Points

The primary objectives during this investigation were to (a) move quickly to identify the source of the suspected compromise, (b) ensure that there was no possibility for continued compromise, and (c) salvage as much data as necessary from the environment to clearly identify the full extent of any potential breach. In a situation where data compromise has occurred, it is important to determine a time frame for that victimization. That is to say, in a worst case scenario, it must be determined how long an organization has been the victim of security breach – how long an intruder had access to sensitive consumer information.

3.3.5 Investigative Procedure

Upon initial analysis, the private sector investigative firm identified two possible avenues of attack into the Acme Corp environment, one being the Internet touch point at the Tokyo, Japan data center, and the second being the individual store connections. The initial fraud pattern information provided to the private sector investigative firm pointed to 7 of Acme Corp's more than 300 store locations as possibly experiencing some level of account data compromise of Visa PIN-based debit transactions. Although there is also an e-commerce side of the Acme Corp business, it was determined to be out of scope because of its payment structure and segmentation from that of the rest of the Acme Corp infrastructure and thus is only mentioned here for the purpose of completeness.

3.3.6 Network Analysis

Given the geographic diversity of the reported Acme Corp locations (involving both Asia and United States locations), the private sector investigative firm's initial focus was on that of a possible centralized breach at Acme Corp's Tokyo, Japan data center, the primary location through which all payment card-related activity must pass for authorization and settlement. Shortly thereafter, the private sector investigative firm's on-site investigation began on December 19, 2007, at Acme Corp's Tokyo office. A full analysis was performed of the entire data flow pathway, along with all systems and infrastructure involved. This phase included reviewing firewall and router configurations along with reports from the authorization switch and on-console examinations across the same. Additionally, the private sector investigative firm also analyzed the Acme Corp lab environment for any signs that malicious code could have been introduced through a rollout process or patch deployment. No sign of a security breach or installation of any malicious code was identified. Furthermore, in examining the systems within the Tokyo data center, it was clear that the data being reported as compromised (Visa PIN-based debit transactions) were not retained at that location to the extent necessary to be used in the reported fashion.

With no sign of a security breach identified at the Tokyo data center, the private sector investigative firm refocused the investigation to center around the idea of a decentralized breach and thus examined a number of the locations in question. Although the locations were geographically diverse from one another, the private sector investigative firm had seen situations in which an individual or group of individuals collaborated over large distances to exploit known vulnerabilities within an organization. Furthermore, because the number of locations had not changed significantly during the course of the investigation, it suggested that this situation could fit the profile of such a scenario. In an effort to cover a sample of the locations in question, the private sector investigative firm, joined by a team from Acme Corp, performed on-site forensic analysis at four locations in the following order: (1) Tokyo,

Japan; (2) Taipei, Taiwan; (3) Los Angeles, CA; and (4) Jakarta, Indonesia.

3.3.7 Forensic Work

The forensic analysis had blanketed every Point of Sale (POS) terminal, server, and workstation that is involved with the payment card operations of the four stores. Approximately one dozen forensic digital images were acquired and analyzed for signs of unauthorized activity, malware, and/or virus/Trojan infections. In addition, routers, switches, and wireless access points were also reviewed. While the results of this extensive analysis uncovered vulnerabilities within the environment and the storage of Track and PIN data, there were no identifiable signs of unauthorized access or account data compromise at any of the four locations.

However, an important facet to the forensic portion of any data compromise investigation is scoping the full potential for a breach. Given the preservation of pertinent evidentiary data, the private sector investigative firm was able to fully quantify the potential data loss within an organization through forensic analysis. This scoping exercise helps to define the damage caused by the data compromise both in terms of the total number of individual victims involved as well as the monetary damages involved in canceling and reissuing a high volume of debit cards.

3.3.8 Scoping Exercise

In addition to the handful of vulnerabilities discovered, it was also learned that data retention at the store level was quite different than that of the corporate data center. The POS application used throughout Acme Corp's retail stores created two log files (Debug.log & Transaction.log) on each register. Both log files were found to contain Track 2 data and encrypted PIN blocks for their respective payment card transactions with an indefinite retention period for the Transaction.log file. Additionally, it was found that the Transaction.log file also retained the Data Encryption Standard (DES) session key for debit transactions.

Without a system-defined data retention policy at the Acme Corp store locations, it might be surmised that each of the brick-and-mortar locations had been storing debit card-related track data since they opened.

Upon examining how debit transactions were handled and PIN Entry Devices (PEDs) were configured, it was determined that each device utilized the same DES Master Key. Upon the login of a new POS terminal operator, the PED would regenerate a new Session Key under the non-unique Master Key. It is the Session Key that is used in the PIN translation/encryption process at the terminal. Although the lack of Master Key uniqueness was a significant fault in security, the retention of the Session Key within the debug.log and transaction.log had more serious implications. Obtaining the Session Key can allow an unauthorized individual to be one step closer to decrypting the PIN block information and revealing the originally entered PIN. Such activity would then permit the unauthorized individual to appear as the legitimate debit card holder to any ATM and thus withdraw cash from the actual cardholder's account. Once aware of the potential compromise and risk associated with storing this data, Acme Corp immediately moved forward with modifications beginning in January 2008 to prevent such logging and eventually the full disabling and purging of both log files across all their stores. This step was completed within several months.

Further inspection of the POS application revealed that the underlying SQL database was vulnerable to exploitation as it did not have a SQL Administrator (SA) password assigned. Without an SA password, anyone with console or network access to the system could perform SQL queries or even issue operating system commands without detection. As in many SQL implementations of organizations that have suffered a data compromise, logging of SQL activity and SQL queries was not enabled, and thus no visibility could be gained into past SQL query or operating system commands that may have been executed. SQL logs often contain crucial evidence that reveals what an intruder looked for and retrieved on a victim system, thereby assisting investigators in identifying the data that was likely compromised on a system.

3.3.9 Wireless Vulnerability

Although the stores do not have direct Internet connections that could be used to facilitate such an exploit, each store does maintain Wireless Access Points (WAPs). Acme's WAPs were primarily for inventory management. Each wireless device contains a Media Access Code, commonly referred to as a MAC address, which identifies that particular device on a wireless network. Acme Corp utilized MAC filtering on each access point to deter rogue associations by unauthorized wireless devices. While MAC filtering used to be an effective deterrent, today's technology allows for it to be circumvented with built-in Windows functionality or with the assistance of a freeware MAC spoofing utility. Given that the store network topology was flat, a compromise to the wireless environment could easily result in unauthorized access to Acme Corp network resources and ultimately the stored payment card data.

In addition to MAC address filtering, another security measure for wireless networks involves disabling the WAP's broadcast of the wireless network's identity, referred to as the Service Set Identifier or SSID. Disabling the broadcast of the SSID is a rudimentary security measure in that it hides the network name; however, with simple freely available tools, an unauthorized individual may still "see" the network and may gain access using a variety of other methods. Although Acme Corp did not broadcast their SSID at the stores, their wireless environment was found to be identifiable from outside the physical store boundaries; this was confirmed by the private sector investigative firm's findings of the Acme Corp SSID on a number of wireless "stumbling" sites. Furthermore, store personnel used a label-maker to place the SSID in a visible fashion on each wireless base station. Given the lack of logging capability across Acme's in-place WAPs, there would be virtually no record of wireless activity regardless of whether it was from a legitimate store system or a spoofed intruder's laptop in the parking lot or nearby store.

At each Acme location, authorized wireless devices are assigned specific IP (Internet protocol) addresses within the store network. By doing this, network administrators have another method by which they can monitor and manage devices connected to their networks. However, in each store location examined during the course of the investigation, IP addresses had been assigned to unknown devices on the wireless network, as evidenced by logging at the Point of Sale (POS) controller. That is, at several points leading up to the suspected data compromise, investigators could prove that unauthorized devices were connected to the store networks.

In each instance, examining log data at the SQL server showed multiple accesses from each of the unaccounted IP addresses at the store locations. Essentially, the intruders obtained access to the network, then found the vulnerable SQL database and targeted it. Once they were able to discover the presence of credit and debit card information, compromise was inevitable.

3.3.10 Lessons Learned

As any retailer that suffers a security breach and data compromise, Acme Corp learned three very important lessons the hard way. First, when they were shown hard evidence of the breach, and subsequent data compromise, they realized that no organization is outside the scope of malicious intruders and hackers who will work to steal sensitive information no matter where it lies. Second, this case demonstrated a coordinated, highly organized, and fully mobilized effort on the part of the intruders. As each location needed to be compromised individually, attackers had to coordinate efforts across Japan, China, Indonesia, and the United States concurrently. This point clearly illustrates the time, patience, and resources the attackers had to accomplish this data breach. Third, when they realized that investigators did not need fancy or expensive forensics tools to find evidence of the breach, it became apparent that the company's own complacency indirectly facilitated their own victimization. More often than not, companies that suffer security breach and data compromise never realize they have a problem until someone else tells them, such as their bank, customers, or law enforcement.

Although Acme Corp had made significant strides in mitigating the risk of future compromise to account data, much of the damage had already occurred. The private sector investigative firm involved in the Acme Corp case had close working relationships with federal, state, and local law enforcement agencies in a number of countries and could easily assist in preparing case evidence and documentation for transition purposes. The U.S. Secret Service (USSS) worked closely with the private investigative response team to transfer relevant Acme Corp case evidence to and from law enforcement. As is standard procedure with these sorts of engagements, the private sector investigative firm ensured through diligent knowledge transfer that law enforcement personnel were kept up to date and clearly understood the facts of the case. In the past, the private sector investigative firm has had extensive experience serving as expert witnesses and providing expert testimony, contributing to successful prosecutions in many high-profile cases. This expertise was transferred to Acme Corp management.

This case study illustrates the investigative procedure used by the private sector investigative firm involved in this case. Forensics analysis is not just about searching for or discovering information about a particular incident, it is about the responsible handling of sensitive, irreplaceable data. Although many techniques exist to create exact disk images for forensics investigations, numerous precautions need to be taken to prevent data corruption during the process. It takes trained, qualified forensics experts to know the right steps to follow and which commands to execute or not execute. Many system administrators make the mistake of rushing to take investigation matters into their own hands, only to find that they have inadvertently overwritten the small, important bits of information a forensics investigator may need. Mistakes made during a forensics investigation can result in an irreversible disaster if the necessary precautions have not been taken. Likewise, a break in the chain of custody of evidence can create an insurmountable obstacle for legal authorities. It is essential that the forensics investigator pay the utmost attention to detail throughout all steps of the analysis process.

3.4 Issues and Trends

When examining digital evidence subsequent to a large-scale security breach and data compromise, forensic investigators face specific challenges as they work to draw out a digital footprint of an intruder's actions during the intrusion scenario. In smaller, single-system cases, forensic examiners are able to determine, in the majority of cases, how the intruder(s) accessed internal networks while trying to locate sensitive information. That is to say, after accessing restricted networks, the smaller scope of single-system cases affords the investigator a limited set of spaces where incriminating evidence could possibly be retained. Consequently, the investigative control points discussed in this chapter become intuitive, natural, and decidedly nonchallenging.

As data breach cases increase in size and scope, this smaller scope is absolutely no longer the case. Today's intruder does not wander aimlessly through a victim network hoping to come across valuable data to steal. Instead, today's hackers break into systems, navigate directly to sensitive data stores, and compromise them. Moreover, they are often able to collect sensitive data that does not natively reside within victim systems. Through the use of customized malware tools, the intruders are collecting and exfiltrating sensitive data, often under the noses of the victim organization. The use of customized malware tools will continue to present additional challenges to forensic investigators facing large-scale data breach cases.

And nowhere else is this more true than with the large-scale compromise of data from payment applications and, specifically, POS software implementations. Where an intruder even 10 years ago may have wandered into a payment-related network segment and not stolen anything, today's intruder routinely has the skills, knowledge, support, and intent to access sensitive data specifically, and directly, and then to disappear, system engineers none the wiser.

It is widely understood that the intruders responsible for recent large-scale data breaches are somewhat supported by organized crime groups worldwide. This, however, is a drastic understatement. Rather, modern large-scale data breaches represent the undivided focus of organized crime groups. Data breach represents probably the largest source of revenue for organized crime, even more so than the international drug trade.[4] No other criminal endeavor is as safe, profitable, and anonymous as the silent theft of millions of credit card and consumer records. No other criminal endeavor is as difficult to prosecute. By refocusing efforts into criminal intrusion and data compromise, organized crime groups are able to net millions of dollars without ever leaving the office. For organized crime groups, large-scale data breach is not just the criminal endeavor of the future. It is the criminal endeavor of right now.

In fact, in the majority of these cases, it is not until vast amounts of fraud are reported that an organization begins to realize that something is wrong. In nearly all data compromise scenarios, victim organizations did not even know they were storing sensitive data in the first place. In case after case, malicious intruders break into networks and steal information that victim organizations did not even know they had. Nevertheless, the bad guys are able to access their networks, navigate directly to stored sensitive consumer information, and steal it. When systems engineers and chief information officers do not know what kinds of data they are storing, but the bad guys do, something has gone terribly wrong.

Often, precautions are taken to protect the network perimeter but not specifically the data within it. The idea here is that so long as the perimeter is secure, it does not matter what kinds of information are being stored or retained. Organizations dealing in the transfer, processing, or storage of any sensitive data that could be converted to cash, be it credit card data or otherwise, are in a unique situation where they must refocus efforts to meet the challenges presented by modern intruders. Rather than focusing efforts on "protecting the network," security engineers must proactively work to inventory sensitive data residing within their systems, and then endeavor to protect that information specifically.

No matter what it may be, if an organization is storing valuable information of any kind, there is a bad guy out there engaged in compromising that information. The days of "benign intruder" are over. Now, there is no such thing as an intrusion without any malicious intent.

Today's intruders have the undivided support of organized crime groups, who, more than likely, know more about victim networks and applications than they do. The bad guys will continue to go after data that can be converted to cash.

Given this move to organized crime-supported data breaches, there are several issues that forensic investigators increasingly must face. First, cases will continue to become more and more complex. That is to say, the data suggest that higher-skilled intrusions result in a higher dollar yield for the criminal: examiners will increasingly need to be prepared to respond to, and investigate, large-scale, complex cases that involve numerous systems. Second, victim organization and private sector forensic examiners will need to streamline cooperation and communication to law enforcement, who may work to define investigation control points in cooperation with the victim organization and the private sector forensic examiners.

Notes

1. Douglas, John E., Ann W. Burgess, Allen G. Burgess, Robert K. Ressler, *Crime Classification Manual: A Standard System for Investigating and Classifying Violent Crimes*, Jossey-Bass, New York, 2006, p. 384.
2. Baker, Wade, Alex. Hutton, C. David Hylender, Christopher Novak, Christopher Porter, Bryan Sartin, Peter Tippet, J. Andrew Valentine, *Data Breach Investigations Report, 2009* Verizon Business, Ashburn, Virginia, 2009.

    Baker, Wade, C. David Hylender, J. Andrew Valentine, *Data Breach Investigations Report, 2008*, Verizon Business, Ashburn, Virginia, 2008.
3. Fraud was also detected at other retail locations, but not in the scope and volume of these initial seven locations.
4. Leyden, John, CyberCrime More Lucrative than Drugs, *Channel and Register*, November 29, 2005.

Chapter 4
Insider Threat Investigations

Shane Sims

Mr. Sims is a director at PricewaterhouseCoopers in the Advisory Forensic Services practice with 24 years of experience in the fields of forensic investigations, cybercrime, national security, and crisis management. He served his country for over 10 years at the Federal Bureau of Investigation as a special agent and supervisory special agent. Mr. Sims has responded to numerous crisis incidents and has helped organizations worldwide solve the gamut of cyber-related and insider crimes. He was the inventor of a new and complex suite of sophisticated cyber-based investigative tools, then led global deployment operations of them in support of all FBI investigative priorities and the US Intelligence Community. Mr. Sims frequently provided advice to the intelligence and security services of friendly foreign governments.

At PwC, Mr. Sims focuses on cyber security breach incident response, data theft investigations, online fraud investigations, insider threat investigations, economic espionage investigations, and anti-cybercrime services. His investigation accomplishments at PwC include the global defrauding of online customer investments accounts to exploit ACH money transfer, complex and persistent network penetrations and PCI data theft at global hospitality and leisure industry organizations, and an advanced network penetration and theft of PCI and PII data at a global financial services organization resulting in mass international ATM fraud dubbed by law enforcement as the largest cyber heist ever.

Before the FBI, Mr. Sims was the CEO of a technology consultancy that provided data protection services. He has a B.A. in computer science, an M.A. in leadership, and is a Certified Information Systems Security Professional (CISSP).

4.1 Investigation Characteristics

Online onslaught. Blurred boundaries. Corrupt insiders. Cyber threats are varied, complex, and always evolving. And cyber threat groups are highly motivated to break down even the strongest security walls. Preventive and defensive measures only reduce risk; they do not eliminate the risk of breach, data loss, asset sabotage, and violations of internal computer usage policies. Therefore, all these risks are inevitable realities. The ability to forensically investigate cybercrime is critical to protecting data, the infrastructures that house and move data, and the organizations responsible for those infrastructures and data. Cybercrime investigative techniques can also be creatively leveraged to investigate suspected or actual insider malfeasance.

Data is valuable – not just to the owners of the data but to others as well. Personally identifiable information, payment card information, medical records, student records, intellectual property, trade secrets, classified information, etc., can all be converted by unsavory forces into financial gain or an operational advantage. The information technology (IT) infrastructures that house data and permit its movement are assets that improve organizational efficiency and effectiveness. Intentional denial of service of these infrastructures can have immediate and detrimental

S. Sims (✉)
PricewaterhouseCoopers, 1800 Tysons Bouvelard, McLean, VA 22102-4261

outcomes on revenue and customer confidence. Worse, disruption of the IT infrastructure of organizations deemed as critical infrastructures by the U.S. government can have national security implications. Gaining unauthorized control of these infrastructures can be quite profitable to those with an extortionate mindset.

The insider threat is human centric and multifaceted: a disgruntled employee/contractor, an employee/contractor experiencing financial difficulty, an actual agent of a foreign intelligence service implanted as an employee/contractor. Many outsiders exploit these human-centric issues, increasing the insider threat if not causing actual corrupt insider behavior.

Foreign intelligence services, also termed the state-sponsored threat, are the best funded and most organized outside influencer. This threat group actively targets the private cyber space of U.S. government, military, and commercial organizations. The primary purpose of the foreign government's intelligence service is to conduct espionage and to acquire intelligence.

Terrorist organizations can convert stolen data into financial gain but also need identities to permit the movement of terrorist operatives around the globe. The most feared objective of this outside influencer of the insider threat is the disruption or sabotage of the cyber space of organizations that have been designated as critical infrastructures by the U.S. government. Such activity would have serious national security implications.

Transnational criminal enterprises are becoming more sophisticated at compromising private cyber space in ways that closely resemble state-sponsored actions. The main objective is to steal data that can be converted to profit (such as identifiers that can be used to defraud personal identities and/or counterfeit payment cards to defraud financial institutions) or extort organizations by holding IT assets hostage.

The human-centric insider threat discussion is traditionally associated with an intentional act by a corruptible insider who is influenced to take action by an outside influencer.

Today, however, the insider threat is much more complex and involves any number of unintentional acts on the part of insiders. Poor IT security practices create threats and exploitable opportunities. The interconnectivity of an organization's network to the Internet, vendors, and customers results in the organization assuming the risk of the poor security postures of those external nodes. However, the insider threat with the highest probability of realization is as simple as the touch of the human finger. Enterprise data protection efforts such as laptops with encrypted hard drives and secure remote access to the private network are no match for the human finger. When the human finger clicks on the wrong e-mail attachment or embedded e-mail link, the computer, the network it has access to, and the data within that network could be compromised. Once the computer is exploited and infected with remote-access software, the threat groups have the same access as the authorized user of that computer and have a platform for exploiting other systems on the insider's network and interconnected networks.

Well-funded, highly motivated threat groups develop exploitation techniques that are designed to evade detection by an organization's defensive measures. Therefore, discovering evidence of intrusion, the implantation of malicious software, and the egress of data becomes more art than science. As described in Chapter 6, the artist, a cybercrime investigator, should be skilled and experienced with investigating a variety of externally borne intrusions and internally borne activity by authorized users, and must also be familiar with sophisticated computer exploitation and data exfiltration techniques.

This chapter explores cyberforensics and the insider threat from two perspectives: intentional acts by trusted insiders with authorized access to critical data and unintentional acts by trusted insiders with authorized access to critical data. Critical data is considered any sensitive data being stored, processed, or transmitted in an organization's private cyber space, including but not limited to intellectual property, trade secrets, payment card industry data, personally identifiable information, medical records, and student records.

4.2 Investigative Approach

4.2.1 Due Diligence

Although this book is "cyber" focused, I would be remiss if I did not briefly comment on the important and often undervalued topic of due diligence. Before authorizing access to critical data, including an employee, vendor, or recently acquired business, organizations must perform a deep-dive background investigation. Background investigations must go beyond quick online records searches. Often, red flags will only be discovered through in-person visits to local police stations and the interview of neighbors at current and past residences. A criminal records search via an online source will only return information that was filed in court, and sometimes this information is inaccurate. Furthermore, not all court records are available online. Certain police records can only be reviewed in person. As costly as a true deep dive may be, it is a mandatory element to cyber risk management and arguably the primary factor in reducing the insider threat.

Organizations must treat their critical data as government agencies treat classified information: people and outside organizations should be fully vetted before being permitted to access it. True due diligence cannot be performed by purchasing a records search from an online background investigator. True due diligence is an art, and real artists are expensive. When an organization loses critical data as a consequence of the insider threat – placing its reputation, stock value, revenue, customers, and business partnerships on the line – scrutiny of its risk management program will be severe.

Due diligence is also not a one-time event. Organizations must periodically evaluate insiders with access to critical data for indicators of corruptibility. Elements discussed in this section can be applied in this manner to detect potential cyber-based indicators of corruption.

4.2.2 Forensic Interviews

Observations made over time have revealed that there are instances when, non-law-enforcement cyber-investigators often overlook the importance of properly documenting conversations during the course of a forensic cyber investigation. To accomplish the elements of the investigative approach discussed in this section, a cyber-investigator will likely have strategic conversations that, in turn, permit the investigator to collect important digital evidence. These conversations have to be memorialized appropriately. At a minimum, forensic investigators must capture the statement of witnesses, but they should also capture non-witness conversations that affect any investigative actions. The investigator should simply ask on-topic and open-ended questions that prompt the interviewee to convey the story in his or her own words, and then document that story within a few days of the conversation using the words of the interviewee. The documentation should also include identifying information of the interviewee. A good practice is to begin an interview report with a preamble such as the following:

> On mm/dd/yyyy Shane Sims of PricewaterhouseCoopers interviewed John Doe at his place of employment Company, Inc, 456 Goshen Drive, Richmond, VA. Doe, born 01/01/1964, social security number 111-22-333, of 123 Elm Street, Bayver, VA, home telephone number 703-555-2323, work telephone number 703-555-1212, work email address john.doe@company.com, provided the following information:

Then, add text that reflects the information provided by the interviewee. If the interviewee took data preservation steps at your direction, document the specific procedures performed by the interviewee. Further, the cyber-investigator should place his or her initials, the date, and the time on all evidentuary media provided by the interviewee.

4.2.3 Cyber Surveillance

Cyber surveillance is the proactive, real-time monitoring and collection of cyber-based activity. Cyber surveillance is necessary to continually investigate the insider threat proactively and reactively. The key to cyber surveillance is for organizations to ensure they have openly communicated to all those who have been granted access to their private cyber space: This communication is designed to achieve consent that the use of private cyber space is subject to monitoring and recording.

Cyber surveillance permits the identification of insider threats, and the collection of evidence that can be leveraged should a threat become an action. The elements of cyber surveillance discussed in this section do not include the identification of specific tools and products. I do, however, submit that tools and products used to perform cyber surveillance should be acquired from a recognized and reputable vendor capable of testifying in court on the inner workings of its tool/product or an in-house-developed capability permitting testimony in the same regard.

In addition to the monitoring and collection product or tool being able to withstand judicial scrutiny, the collection activities discussed hereafter must involve preservation and storage of digital evidence that is forensically sound; this is especially true when the collection is focused on actual or suspected corrupt insider behavior. The cyber-investigator must document who, where, when, and how the evidence was collected; generate a chain of custody; and ensure the safe transport and storage of the evidence.

Management due diligence practices with respect to the preservation of cyber evidence are covered in more detail in Chapter 11.

4.2.3.1 Network Surveillance

It is important for a cyber investigator to understand how data flows through an organization's private cyber space and what network monitoring and traffic collecting technology is available in house. To gain this level of understanding, the investigator must conduct many interviews, all of which should be properly documented. With this knowledge at hand, the cyber-investigator can better focus the forensic surveillance and collection of network traffic based on the investigation.

Network surveillance requires the strategic positioning of sensors to monitor and collect network traffic. Network surveillance permits the investigation and preservation of evidence related to system/data access and data movement. This activity can be focused on specific users, systems, network segments, or the entire enterprise. From an overall proactive standpoint, I recommend that organizations use in-house technology to collect network traffic at all ingress and egress points on an ongoing basis and archive this evidence just like any data backup program. Ongoing analysis of network traffic and network utilization can identify indicators of corrupt insider behavior, such as the transmission of data to external hosts or people. Further, the ongoing collection of network traffic will significantly assist a reactive investigative by providing a historical look at the network environment to assist with identifying past corrupt insider behavior. When a specific insider is suspected of corrupt behavior, the collection of forensic evidence then becomes more focused and the cyber-investigator should use his or her own network surveillance technology that is safe, secure, and inaccessible to anyone else.

More detail on network surveillance, data collection, and evidence-gathering techniques is provided in Chapter 7.

4.2.3.2 Computer Surveillance

Computer surveillance involves the monitoring of system-based activity and the collection of system-based data. The following components of computer surveillance can be useful in the cyber investigation of the insider threat.

E-mail Attachment Surveillance: It may seem unlikely that an insider involved in corrupt behavior would actually use the employer's e-mail system to send coveted data to an outsider. However, criminals tend to make mistakes.

Web-based E-mail Account Surveillance: Often, corrupt insiders will use their employer-supplied computer and access to the Internet to log into Web-based e-mail accounts, attach files, and transmit sensitive data to outsiders.

Universal Serial Bus Surveillance: The universal serial bus (USB) interface is the most dangerous vector of the insider threat. Having a capability to proactively monitor the movement of files to external media is imperative to combating the insider threat. After-the-fact attempts to forensically image an insider's work computer and discover copying of data to external media are unreliable at best.

Data Harvesting Surveillance: Corrupt insiders who intentionally move critical data to outsiders often use their authorized access to structured data to extract or export that data to their local machine. Comparing file-creation times on local machines to access logs on structured storage systems can be quite useful to the cyber-investigator.

Print Job Surveillance: Savvy data theft operatives with an awareness of computer forensics simply print out the desired information and walk out of the office with paper in their briefcase or backpack, making this behavior a strong competitor to the USB-based data theft threat. Capturing spool files is an important element of cyber surveillance.

Mobile Phone Picture Surveillance: The most paranoid of insider deviants assume that employers are monitoring computer activity. Therefore, the mere opening of files that contain data of interest can create an interesting risk. Other than taking notes or simply memorizing data being viewed on a computer monitor, corrupt insiders can leverage mobile devices with cameras to capture data on the computer monitor, thus avoiding typical cyber surveillance. The ability to monitor mobile device activity and collect pictures is an important element of managing the insider threat.

Armed with a strong understanding of the elements of cyber surveillance, organizations can reduce the risk of the insider threat becoming a reality and conduct proper investigations of suspected or actual insider malfeasance, whether intentional or unintentional.

4.3 Case Study

4.3.1 Situation

I have seen the following insider threat scenario unfold at many organizations. This situation is truly irrespective or agnostic to industry. I have merged these experiences into a single case description to avoid any possibility of attribution to a given organization.

Situation: A disenchanted insider has authorized access to trade secrets. The victim organization received notice from a business competitor that it had received a communication from an unidentified individual offering certain information from the victim organization on a monthly basis in exchange for an ongoing financial stipend. The victim organization had all the standard protections in place to electronically monitor computer and network usage, including network sensors that collected and analyzed data transmitting throughout the environment, proxy servers to monitor Web activity, and data loss prevention products to monitor for malicious behavior on user computers.

4.3.2 Action

The victim organization hired a cyber-investigator who interviewed appropriate personnel and determined that the trade secrets in question were stored on a database server that was not accessible from the Internet. The investigator documented each interview to capture the information provided by each interviewee. Working with a database administrator, the investigator ensured that database audit logs were tuned to capture user access information and activities such as data extracts. The investigator documented when and how the database administrator changed auditing settings as requested and also obtained a list of all authorized users to the database. A chain of custody was created for the user access list.

The investigator interviewed human resources personnel to determine if anyone with authorized access to the database was known to be unhappy with their job, other employees, a supervisor, or the company. Each interview was documented, and no leads were developed.

Every day, the investigator worked with the database administrator to forensically preserve audit logs onto external media. A chain of custody was created each time. As users were identified from audit log entries as having exported data, the investigator installed computer surveillance software on the insider's work computer. This software permitted the monitoring and collection of keystrokes, screen shots, Web activity, and USB activity. The investigator also deployed computer forensic software on the target systems that permits the remote collection and preservation of the target systems without having physical access to them. The installations were documented. In addition, the investigator installed network monitoring equipment that captured all traffic transmitting from the Internet Protocol (IP) address of the insiders' work computers. The installation of this technology was documented.

The investigator analyzed data collected from the computer surveillance software daily. Approximately 2 weeks later, the investigator observed screen shots from one particular insider's work computer that depicted the use of a Web-based e-mail account and attachment of a spreadsheet file. The investigator analyzed database audit logs for entries on the same day and observed this same insider had accessed the database and exported data. Network surveillance collections confirmed that the spreadsheet being transmitted from the IP address of this insider's work computer to an external host associated with an online e-mail provider matched the screen shots from the computer surveillance collections.

The investigator met with the physical security department at the victim organization to forensically collect building access logs for the day in question. A chain of custody was created. Building access logs showed that the particular insider's building access badge was used to gain entry several hours before the malicious behavior.

The investigator coordinated an after-hours operation to forensically image the insider's work computer. The image was verified, backed up, and a chain of custody was created. Analysis of the image resulted in the discovery of evidence that corroborated the cyber surveillance evidence, including the existence of a spreadsheet file with the same file name as the file attached to the Web-based e-mail message. This spreadsheet contained trade secrets from the database. The creation time of the spreadsheet was nearly identical to the time of the database audit log entry depicting a data extract by this insider. Further, the analysis determined that no unauthorized software resided on the work computer that would have permitted unauthorized remote access to it. Hence, a claim that someone hacked the computer and hijacked login credentials was not possible.

Having the exact date and time that the spreadsheet file was attached to the Web-based e-mail message and sent, the investigator identified other employees with office space near the corrupt insider's work space to interview them about whether they observed the corrupt insider at that work space using the work computer at the date/time in question. Each interview was documented.

4.3.3 Outcome

The cyber investigation identified the source of the complaint and malicious activity by an insider involving the use of cyber space assets to transmit trade secrets to an unauthorized outsider. The victim organization was positioned to confidently pursue numerous courses of action. Termination of the employee could ensue with the assurance that any potential labor dispute civil action filed by the terminated employee could be vigorously argued by forensically sound evidence. Also, should the victim organization choose to present the evidence to law enforcement for potential criminal action, law enforcement would be positioned to leverage forensically sound evidence that would withstand judicial scrutiny.

4.4 Issues and Trends

4.4.1 Anatomy of a Cyber Attack

The following phases outline today's sophisticated cyber attack. I have personally witnessed the evolution of these phases during my own investigative work during the past 2 years. The cyber attack described here is being conducted by highly motivated, loosely organized, transnational hacker groups.

Phase 1a: Reconnaissance of perimeter systems

This phase is executed when there is no collusion with a corrupt insider.

- Targeting of organizations or entire industries with data of interest
- Reconnaissance of external-facing systems

Phase 1b:

This phase is used in combination with Phase 1a or exclusively, and may or may not involve insider collusion.

- Internal users are spammed via e-mail with Trojans in an attempt to persuade one of them to unintentionally click on a malicious link or attachment that will compromise internal user systems, thus providing an entry point
- Targeting of specific insiders who are believed to have access to data of interest, i.e. spear phishing

Phase 2: System exploitation

- If Phase 1a, then a discovered vulnerability on a Web server or router is exploited using a publicly available or custom-developed tool
- If Phase 1b, then a browser vulnerability is exploited using a publicly available or custom-developed tool

Phase 3: Data location and theft

- Enumeration of network nodes to identify additional systems and types of data available
- Installation of custom-developed malware that anti-virus detection software does not detect, such

as sniffers, backdoors, and counter-forensic file deletion software
- Collection of login credentials
- Discovery and collection of critical data
- Egress of data over authorized network protocols not designed for data transport

To put these real-life observations into historical context, consider the evolution of cyber threat groups in the previous two decades:

Twenty years ago: Foreign intelligence services recruited corruptible insiders with authorized access to target data or implanted their own operative. A corruptible insider typically equated to someone who acquired the position predisposed to corruption or became corruptible for reasons of personal financial challenges or employment disenchantment.

Ten years ago: Transnational criminal enterprises recruited juvenile hackers to exploit private networks via the Internet to steal data that could be converted to profit and/or hold IT assets hostage to extort money. Also, these criminal enterprises bribed corrupt insiders to steal data or provide the outsider with access to data. Disgruntled insiders leveraged their authorized access to disrupt cyber services and/or extort the employer. Business competitors conducted cyber sabotage campaigns to disrupt services.

Today: All these methods are still applicable today. However, hackers have formed their own loosely affiliated and global crews that collaborate and communicate online and often team together to leverage each group's technical skills based on the inventory of cyber assets being discovered during an attack. These global hacker crews are specifically targeting organizations that electronically store data which can be stolen and converted to financial gain.

Constant: Insiders are influenced by outsiders to behave corruptly. Insiders behave corruptly on their own in acts of revenge. Insiders unintentionally create cyber risk and access to sensitive data for outsiders.

4.4.2 Emerging and Key Capabilities for CyberForensics

As cyber-based tactics of corrupt insiders evolve and the techniques of outsider attackers advance to exploit the unintentional acts of an insider, so too must the capabilities and tools used to conduct forensic cyber investigations. Today's cyber-investigators must have the capabilities and tools that are discussed in detail in the chapters that follow, specifically these:

- Accounting Forensics (Chapter 5)
- Analyzing Malicious Software (Chapter 6)
- Network Forensics (Chapter 7)
- Operating System Revelations (Chapter 8)
- Applying Interactive Analytics for Data Breach Response and Risk Mitigation (Chapter 9)

Chapter 5
Accounting Forensics

Tracy McBride

Tracy McBride is a Certified Public Accountant with more than 20 years of experience in the financial services industry. Her background includes more than 10 years at Morgan Stanley where she was a Vice President responsible for corporate-level internal and external reporting and analysis and post-merger Asset Management integration. She also directed the accounting, finance, and operations integration for one of Cendant's $3 billion bankrupt acquisitions in 2003 and has held executive positions in the insurance and broker/dealer industries. Her additional expertise includes information systems, process reengineering, change management, mergers and acquisitions, audit, and financial forensics, and as a collaborative leader in mentoring and creating teams. Tracy McBride holds a B.A. in Accounting from William Paterson University and a Master of Business Administration (MBA) from Cornell University. She is a Certified Public Accountant (CPA) and holds a Certification in Financial Forensics (CFF) from the American Institute of Certified Public Accountants (AICPA). Tracy is a member of the AICPA and the New Jersey Society of Certified Public Accountants (NJSCPA).

5.1 Investigation Characteristics

Accounting forensics is defined as a combination of accounting, audit, and investigative techniques that support actual or future litigations. All Certified Public Accountants have been trained in the first two areas with audit of management control requirements becoming increasingly important given years of expanded regulation and documentation, including the Sarbanes-Oxley Act of 2002 (SOX). However, my early training has always consisted of all three key elements: accounting, audit, and investigative techniques. This is, to be prepared in any event to answer any question about where the numbers came from. Since the beginning of my career at a major financial services organization, where I was responsible for the internal and external financial reporting, analysis, and due diligence to support the analyst's quarterly conference calls, my mentor was an incredible forward-thinking leader. His insight to consistently align our department with the best people, consolidation tools, systems, and efficient workflow processes that permitted our team to work quickly, efficiently, and accurately, inorder to obtain detailed financial information at our fingertips, and at the fingertips of our senior leadership, as well as to the Securities and Exchange Commission (SEC). We understood the key drivers, questioned everything, took pride in our internal controls, and functioned as a lean accounting and finance team for a company of its size. It was very early in my career, well before the new SOX world, that I was diligently trained on information technology, systems, and the critical need for integrity of financial information and internal controls. We could not have been such a successful team without it.

Therefore, why have the most recent and largest frauds in history occurred after Congress passed the plethora of accounting oversight legislation? One word – collusion. A second word, or group of words – where is the integrity? Since the earlier frauds, for example, of Dennis Koslowski and Tyco, collusion at the highest levels of the organization occurred

T. McBride (✉)
Certified Public Accountant [CPA/CFF], TMM Advisors LLC, New Jersey, USA

to facilitate Mr. Koslowski's extravagant lifestyle. The attempt then was to hide the fraud by alleging a single Board of Directors "forgave" his loan. However, perhaps the days of toga parties and gold shower curtains are no match to the most recent frauds that have devastated so many innocent people. In this case, the trail inevitably led to tax evasion issues. Forgiveness of a loan? Perhaps Mr. Koslowski had trouble in explaining why this income was not reported on his personal tax return.

The question now remains: why haven't traditional examinations, even by the SEC and other regulators, such as the Financial Industry Regulatory Authority (FINRA), identified these horrific fraudulent schemes? Limited examination hours? Junior staff? Not asking the "right" questions? Perhaps all of these and perhaps a few other items, which would include a need for a complete, in-depth understanding of an organization's internal controls, and risks and how information technology is utilized within an organization. The three "A's" – Accounting, Auditing, and Asking why – and truly understanding and documenting the complete answer, thinking multifaceted and outside the box.

5.2 Investigative Approach

Initial work in the forensic accounting arena is truly "back to basics" for a CPA. This statement is certainly not meant to minimize the significant value that CPAs bring to the table in a major fraud case. However, this approach is critical to understanding the backbone of any organization and to provide the investigation's stakeholders with a granular understanding of the transactional level detail within the books and records of the organization. This approach combines an understanding of the historical information technology infrastructure, how the current transactions were recorded, and future information technology systems/process updates that can impact the integrity of financial reporting.

The first rule of thumb is to obtain a flow chart of the company's information technology business applications and compare it to the balance sheet. The forensic accountant must fully understand the flow of information within an organization. If the complete flow of information is incomplete or does not exist, the investigator will observe business operations processes to see the workflows and to immediately document them before it occurs to anyone in the business under investigation to change the processes that created the existing books and records.

The next step is to trace transactions of interest to the investigation via sample testing. Sample testing is a process by which a statistically significant number of transactions are randomly identified from the population of transactions in a given financial system and tested for accuracy. Sample tests include verifying the source and authority by which the transaction was executed, as well as its associated mathematical calculations and impact on books and records. Accounting professionals must not only know how each transaction is supposed to be processed, but also instil the discipline of audit sample testing for the flow of information from the front end and subsystems within an organization to validate integrity in internal controls. This is necessary because accountants are often called upon to provide written statements, or opinions, about the effectiveness of internal controls. However, accountants who represent corporations with integrity conduct sample audits not just to form their own opinion but to minimize the opportunity for breaches in integrity of information via a variety of factors, including fraud.

It is helpful if the accounting forensic investigator can identify a senior leader in finance who can provide a clear and detailed description of how transactions are processed and also provide evidence of sample testing. Nevertheless, the investigator must independently complete his or her own assessment of integrity of information and controls around the financial acumen of the accounting/finance staff. Key observations made by the investigator will be whether staff training has been mechanical in nature, or whether the team truly understands the substance behind the financial information for which they are responsible. A senior leader in finance should have personally established the competency of the accounting staff and the integrity of the books and records.

In the U.S., Chief Executive Officers (CEOs) and Chief Financial Officers (CFOs) of public companies must sign the certifications to attest to the maintenance of disclosure controls and procedures and internal control over financial reporting under Section 302 of the Sarbanes-Oxley Act of 2002. A diligent financial manager will have taken pains to provide complete confidence in financial statements for the CEO and CFO. Even CEOs of private companies should expect this level of diligence from their finance organizations.

For audits after December 15, 2002, Statement of Auditing Standards No. 99 (SAS 99) was introduced to further define how independent auditors should approach their audit for detection of potential fraud. The fight against fraud begins with strong antifraud programs and controls that management should have in place to prevent and deter fraud. This aspect includes a strong internal controls system consisting of information technology, automated and people processes that are well documented, and a culture that encourages integrity of business. It continues with an independent auditor.[1] An independent auditor's job is to identify how the business accounts for transactions and perform tests independent of the samples performed by management to validate the statements made by management as to the integrity of the books and records.

The books and records of any organization should tell a clear story. If it does not, it should be suspected that individuals are attempting to hide a fraud. In any case where an investigator's questions lead to a lack of cooperation among accounting staff, this can indicate a "smoke-screen" approach to dealing with the investigation. A smoke screen is an individual or set of individuals who continuously provides unclear, incomplete information in an attempt to waste the investigator's time and to stall and derail the investigation. Forensic accountants can circumvent these tactics via interviewing multiple alternate individuals involved in every step of the transaction, or the use of data-mining techniques via the use of technology.

In the course of either the collecting or documenting of internal controls and transaction samplings, another critical aspect of the investigation is the handling of that documentation and/or anything that may in the future be considered case evidence. There are strict guidelines behind proof of the origin of information, demonstration of how it was located and where it was found, how to show the exact time of the creation of data or the fraud occurring, etc. Archiving information on write once read many (WORM) media with proof of date/time, and controls around the forensic review so as to not disrupt the integrity of the information found, need to be done completely and accurately during the investigative approach. This step is in addition to exceptionally detailed documentation of all source data, and a summary of not only how this information was sourced, but also the investigator's assessment of how each set of archived data provides evidence of the facts discovered in an investigation.

5.3 Case Study

This case study describes the case of SEC v. King Chuen Tang, et al., wherein the SEC Charges Former CFO King Chuen Tang and Six Relatives and Friends in California-based Insider Trading Ring.[2]

The complaint stated that the unlawful trades were based on the securities of Tempur-pedic International, Inc. (Tempur) and Acxiom Corporation. Tang was a former CFO of a venture capital fund (VC Fund) that had been in talks with Tempur-pedic concerning mutually beneficial business interests. The case charge was that there were three related but separate instances of securities fraud wherein six of Tang's relatives and friends committed insider trading with potential alleged illicit profit of greater than $8 million.

The unlawful trades were the securities of Tempur-pedic International, Inc. and Acxiom Corporation. The basis of the complaint was that the accused had, in 2008, been confidentially provided information that normally would be known only to company "insiders" and not known to financial analysts that routinely analyze information that Tempur had made public. The information was that Tempur would not meet its next earnings forecast. Tang tipped this information to three friends, and all began establishing short positions in Tempur securities and purchasing put option contracts that would only be profitable if Tempur's stock price declined.

Financial analysts had published reports on Tempur's performance, and it was the general consensus of these analysts that company forecasts were realistic, based on the information they were given. Of course, given that Tang and his counterparts knew that the Company was going to miss analysts' expectations, they had a sure bet that Tempur's stock would decline, and they made illegal profits of approximately $1.2 million.

The second instance of securities fraud was based on a claim that Tang was aware of plans by his firm to make a large, market-moving purchase of Tempur securities in the days following the pre-annoucement of a decline of earnings. This simply translates to a large purchase of stock at a discount set in advance, as all insiders knew that the Tempur stock price would decline immediately following the earnings announcement. Despite instructions from Tang's firm that employees were not permitted to trade during this time, Tang and his friends traded based on this information and made illegal profits.

The third charge claimed that Tang received illegal trading tips in 2007 from his brother-in-law, who was a CFO for a venture capital firm with plans to acquire Acxiom. Tang in turn shared this information with five defendants who purchased approximately $20 million of Acxion stock and $200,000 of call options in their names and Tang's funds. In an effort to cover his tracks, Tang began posting to a Yahoo! Message board to speculate a uptick in the stock since Axioms' chief executive had stopped selling his shares. In May 2007 this acquisition announcement was made, and these individuals liquidated some Axiom holdings for approximately $5 million in profits. Subsequently, in August 2007, due to some changes in the deal and that the merger may not occur, non-public information was improperly communicated and Tang and others engaged in trading of Acxiom securities and realized additional profits of approximately $900,000 for a total of $6 million of profits from the insider trading of Acxiom securities.

Figure 5.1 is a flowchart of the alleged insider trading scheme.[3]

Regulatory authorities utilized a variety of technology and forensic accounting techniques to follow the trail of illegal insider trading activities. Data mining is one technique that allows a significant amount of data to be collected in trading and execution systems. Data on all trades related to a given security is analyzed for patterns of behavior that may lead to determining if a fraud has occurred. The investigative approach was to take the basic transaction data and interpret it to discover and present a story of facts that can be used in litigation. Evidence suspect for fraud and insider trading allegations are supported by transactions that would not make sense to execute if no insider information was available during a given time frame.

Additionally, the firm that Tang worked for had a compliance responsibility not only to deter this type of activity to occur, and to have adequate internal controls within the organization, but to also report any wrongdoings or patterns of behavior up the chain of command and potentially to the regulatory authorities.

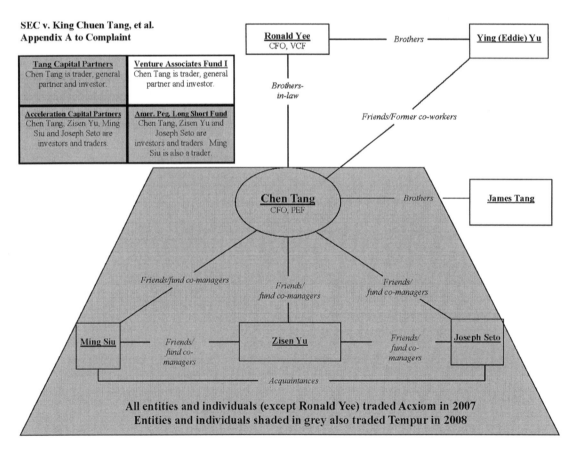

Fig. 5.1 U.S. Securities and Exchange Commission (SEC) publication illustrating relationships among defendants

The firm recognized the unusual trading patterns and reported them to the authorities. This is an example of how technology, integrity of data, internal controls, and investigation are so closely related that all parts need to be 100% accurate, not only to deter fraud but to easily detect fraud and ease of presentation of the facts and evidence.

Although Tang was the CFO at the time of the fraud, and the fraud did not occur within transactions on the books and records of Tang's firm, the firm nevertheless had a responsibility to ensure that its employees followed rules for detecting and preventing insider trading. Tang's firm was a securities firm, so the accounting staff was alert to the potential negative impact of securities fraud violations on the part of its employees. There was plenty of support from the Board of Directors to provide regulatory authorities with evidence that all internal controls were in place to mitigate fraud to keep the Company from wrongdoings and cooperate with authorities on the individual or individuals who perpetuated the illegal schemes.

Once the authorities knew that fraud had occurred, they examined all transactions for the given stock and identified relationships between those who benefited from sales at around the same time as those of the known perpetrators. Because stock transaction flow is well known within the regulatory arena and the data is easily available, transaction tracing was easy to accomplish. A complete list of suspects was generated based on what the investigators knew about the transaction flow and how it affected the balance sheets of potential suspects.

Of course, in many cases, transaction flow is not well understood, and the majority of investigation time is spent documenting it in order to device on what data to search.

Given the current integrity challenges in the financial services industry, there will certainly be increased requirements of internal controls, risk, and the complement of information technology, internal controls, and accounting forensics. Whether or not an organization is potentially under a litigation, the approach by senior leaders of an organization should be to promote a detailed and granular approach by the accounting and finance department to the identification and validation of appropriate transaction level controls. There should be more attempts by management to train staff to fully understand the financials, document the data sources, and proactively monitor and discuss any inconsistencies or anomalies. In other words, companies may be expected to seek ongoing due diligence requiring full appreciation of risk, and at the more senior finance level, estimate the potential for fraud and put processes in place to mitigate and alert if fraud occurs.

Additionally, companies will be held more accountable for their lack of mitigation of fraud that occurs within their organization. This responsibility will then extend to the independent auditors who will be required to expand the review of an organization's internal controls and fraud mitigation. This phase will also be important as financial statements shift from generally accepted accounting principles to international financial reporting standards.[5]

The traditional professional practice of accounting and audit, complemented with financial forensics, will intensify over the next several years. These practices will be further complemented with expanded information technology methods to facilitate, document, and preserve for litigation appropriate evidence to stand up in fraud cases. The entire finance services community should be ready for this next adventure and level of regulatory scrutiny.

5.4 Issues and Trends

The financial industry has just experienced an unprecedented combination of extremely large meltdowns, including the largest Ponzi scheme fraud ever, and the focus is on major insider trading schemes that are uncovered much too regularly.[4] The future should therefore bring a stronger emphasis on information technology and financial integrity, in addition to increased support in the documentation and audit and legal evidence to prove the integrity of an organization.

Notes

1. See http://www.aicpa.org/pubs/cpaltr/nov2002/supps/busind1.htm
2. See http:/www.hflawreport.com/article/588
3. See http:/www.sec.gov/news/press/2009/2009-229.htm
4. References are to Bear Stearns, Lehman, Merrill Lynch, Madoff, and Cerebus, as well as a host of other less publicized cases.
5. IFRS informational website by PriceWaterhouseCoopers: http://www.pwc.com/us/en/issues/ifrs-reporting/publications/ifrs-and-us-gaap-similarities-and-differences-september-2009.jhtml

Chapter 6
Analyzing Malicious Software

Lenny Zeltser

Lenny Zeltser leads the security consulting practice at Savvis and is a member of the Board of Directors at SANS Technology Institute. In addition, he teaches the Reverse-Engineering Malware course at SANS Institute and serves as an incident handler at the SANS Internet Storm Center. Zeltser frequently speaks on technical and business topics related to information security at both public conferences and private events, writes articles, and contributes to books such as this one. Zeltser is one of the few individuals in the world who have earned the highly regarded GIAC Security Expert (GSE) designation. He also holds the CISSP certification and other professional credentials. Mr. Zeltser has an MBA degree from MIT Sloan and a computer science degree from the University of Pennsylvania. To learn about Zeltser's malware course and other projects, visit www.zeltser.com.

laboratory system and network, as well as reverse-engineering the program's code. While the general investigative approach applies to malware running on most computing platform, the chapter focuses on executable files compiled for Microsoft Windows due to the prevalence of such programs in the field.

Malware lies at the heart of many computer intrusions. Attackers may use it to bypass the target's defenses, spread within the internal network, maintain control over the environment, exfiltrate sensitive data, and cover up signs of intrusion. Malware may also play a role in incidents that involve improper employee conduct, policy violations, contract breaches, and numerous illegal or unethical actions that involve computers. To understand the nature of an incident that involves malware, the investigator needs to know how to examine a suspicious program.

6.1 Investigation Characteristics

This chapter explores techniques for analyzing malicious software (malware) discovered as part of a forensic investigation. The chapter assumes that, in the course of an investigation such as those described in chapters 2 and 3, a suspicious program has been identified and isolated. The reader is introduced to key tools and approaches for understanding the capabilities of such a malware specimen.[1] This process involves examining how the specimen interacts with an infected

6.1.1 Malware Analysis as Part of the Forensic Investigation

Malware analysis may need to be conducted as part of both the incident response and forensic analysis processes. The incident response team may need to study a potentially malicious program to confirm that the situation warrants further forensic investigation. When performing forensics, the investigator may need to examine malware to paint a comprehensive picture of the incident. In either case, a malware investigator typically starts after potentially malicious files have been isolated and extracted from the affected system and brought into the laboratory. Knowing what a malware specimen can and cannot do also helps assess

L. Zeltser (✉)
SANS Technology Institute, Bethesda, MD, USA

intentions of the attacker who created, planted, or operated the malicious program.

6.1.2 Common Malware Characteristics

Characteristics of malware vary. They may be affected by fashion of the times, incentives, and opportunities. For instance, as Internet banking grew in popularity, so did the number of malicious programs capable of capturing victims' logon credentials. Propagation techniques change as well. During the days of floppy drives, malware often spread by attaching to the disk's boot record. As ubiquitous networks displaced floppies for data sharing, malware authors increasingly relied on network-based propagation methods. When the popularity of mobile USB drives grew, some malware authors reverted to the "sneaker net" method of moving malware across systems by taking advantage of the drives' auto-run features.

Although malware characteristics evolve with time, they often fall into several categories of traits[2]:

- *Propagation:* How does malware spread across systems? Malicious software may spread over networks and mobile media, and may perform vulnerability exploitation of server or client-side software and social engineering. Malware may also be loaded by an intruder manually. Propagation may be autonomous (as is the case with many worms) and may require user involvement (such as launching an e-mail attachment).
- *Infection:* How does malware embed itself in the system? Malicious software may run once, or may maintain a persistent presence on the system via auto-run features such as the "Run" registry key or by installing itself as a service. Run-once specimens may store themselves solely in RAM. Malware may assemble itself dynamically by downloading additional components. Malware may attach itself to benign programs or may function as a stand-alone process. Specimens also differ in the degree to which they resist disinfection attempts.
- *Self-Defense:* How does malware conceal its presence and resist analysis? Malicious software may attempt to avoid signature-based detection by changing itself. It may time its actions to take place during busy periods or to occur slowly, so that the actions go unnoticed. It may embed itself within existing processes or network streams, modify operation system (OS) functionality, and/or utilize other creative measures to decrease the chances that its presence will be discovered. Malware may be designed to thwart analysis attempts. Such techniques are sometimes referred to as "anti-reversing capabilities," for example, by using a packer that encrypts the original executable, decrypting it at run time.
- *Capabilities:* From the point of view of the malware author, what "business purpose" does malware serve? Malicious software may be designed to collect data by sniffing the network, recording keystrokes and screenshots, and locating sensitive files. Malware may also be programmed to wreck havoc on the system, perhaps by deleting or corrupting data, or to act as a starting point for attacking other systems. It may also provide the attacker with remote access to the system by acting as a backdoor.

Several additional types of malicious traits can be defined as part of the capabilities category. However, these characteristics are sufficiently common that they deserve dedicated subcategories:

- *Exfiltration:* How, if at all, does malware transmit data out of the affected environment? Malicious software may send captured data over the network using clear-text and encrypted channels, and may rely on ICMP, HTTP, SMTP, and many other standard and custom protocols. Malware may also store data locally, waiting for the attacker manually copy it off the infected system.
- *Command and Control:* How, if at all, does malware receive updates and instructions? Malicious software may receive commands from the attacker by listening on a local network port or by making outbound connections to the attacker's system using protocols such as DNS, HTTP, SMTP, or other client-server and peer-to-peer protocols. Malicious executables often have the ability to upgrade themselves according to a predefined schedule or upon the attacker's request.

Malicious software may possess other characteristics that are specific to the program's purpose, and these characteristics often directly reflect unique aspects of the environment(s) for which it was created.

6.1.3 Dual-Phased Analysis Process

To understand the nature of a malware specimen, investigators often examine it from two perspectives:

- *Behavioral analysis* considers the characteristics that malware exhibits as it interacts with its environment. This analysis phase usually involves infecting a laboratory system with the specimen and observing how it accesses the file system, RAM, hardware, and the network.
- *Code analysis* examines the code that comprises the malicious executable, usually with the help of a disassembler and a debugger. The process of locating and understanding "interesting" code sections can be challenging and time consuming. However, code analysis often reveals insights that may be difficult to derive through behavioral analysis.

Incorporating both behavioral and code analysis phases into the investigation allows the researcher to examine the specimen from different perspectives, increasing the likelihood that the findings will be accurate and comprehensive.

Investigators typically start with the phase that comes most naturally to them, based on their background and expertise. Once they exhaust the amount of information they can extract from the specimen using that phase in reasonable time, they move on to the next phase to expand and validate earlier findings. Analysis phases are often intertwined: investigators may begin with behavioral analysis, move on to code analysis, return to behavioral analysis armed with newly discovered details, then jump to code analysis, and so on (Fig. 6.1).

6.2 Investigative Approach

The following section discusses an approach to examining malicious software in a systematic, reliable manner using behavioral and code analysis phases. It offers recommendations for setting up a malware analysis laboratory and describes tools and techniques for examining malware in the context of a forensic investigation. The framework described in this section is reinforced in the *Case Study* section, which shows many of these tools and techniques in action.

6.2.1 Malware Analysis Laboratory

Malware analysis typically requires an isolated laboratory environment, where malicious software will execute under controlled conditions. The laboratory allows the investigator to observe and interact with the specimen during behavioral analysis and to debug and bypass the specimen's anti-reversing capabilities during code analysis.

A malware analysis lab usually takes the form of several computers connected to an isolated network. The computers are designed to mimic the configuration of commonly targeted systems and may run various versions and patch levels of operating systems relevant to the investigator. The investigator infects these systems during the analysis. Among the computers may be one or more systems that run network services which malware may attempt accessing; this setup allows the investigator to simulate the presence of the Internet and other networks that malware may seek.

A flexible and frugal way of setting up the lab involves the use of virtualization software to run multiple "virtual" systems on a smaller number of physical computers. Options for virtualization software are numerous, including both free and commercial products such as the following:

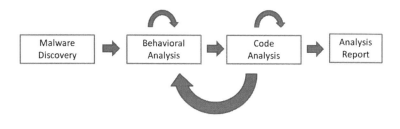

Fig. 6.1 Behavioral and code analysis phases are often intertwined

- VMware Workstation, Server, vSphere, Fusion, and related products
- Microsoft Virtual PC and Virtual Server
- Sun VirtualBox
- Parallels Desktop, Server, and Virtuozzo Containers

Such software allows simultaneously running multiple instances of laboratory systems that operate independently, yet exist on the same physical host. By minimizing the number of physically distinct systems, the investigator usually saves money, while benefiting from the small physical footprint and flexibility offered by virtualization software (Fig. 6.2).

One of the conveniences provided by most virtualization technologies is the simulated network, which allows virtualized systems to communicate as if they are plugged into a regular network without physical network device dependencies. Another major benefit is the ability to take instant snapshots of the lab system's state, with some products supporting multiple snapshots. A snapshot preserves the state of the virtualized system at a given point in time, making it easy to revert to the desired state with a click of a button. An investigator may take a snapshot while the system is still clean and later take several snapshots during different stages of the analysis. Multiple snapshots allow the investigator to repeat behavioral experiments without restarting the analysis from the beginning (Fig. 6.3).

One of the biggest drawbacks of using physical, rather than virtualized, systems in the lab is the loss of the flexible snapshot-taking capabilities. With physical systems, investigators usually can take a single snapshot of the system in its pristine state using file system-cloning tools such as dd. Another possibility is to use system state-restoring software such as Windows SteadyState or Faronics DeepFreeze. Note that such software is not as reliable as virtualization snapshots or partition copies; malware has been known to target state-restoring software, bypassing the boundaries of its snapshots. A more reliable alternative is to use hardware-based "snapshot" products, such as CenturionGuard[3] and Reborn PCI Card.[4]

The biggest advantage of implementing the lab using physical hardware is the stronger isolation of the laboratory environment. Because isolation of virtualized systems is software enforced, there is a chance that a specially crafted specimen will exploit a bug or a configuration weakness to escape to another virtual system in the lab or onto the physical system that hosts the lab. With physically distinct systems, such a possibility is very small because of the true air gap between the lab's components.

6.2.1.1 Isolating the Malware Laboratory

The lab's systems are networked, so they can access each other to support network-related characteristics exhibited by many specimens. The lab network should be disconnected from other network segments to mitigate the risk of malware escaping the laboratory sandbox. Isolating the lab from external factors also helps in reliably determining the cause of the characteristics in the lab.

For situations that require live Internet access, investigators may temporarily connect the laboratory

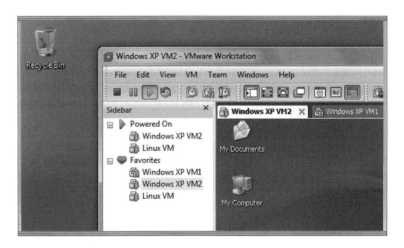

Fig. 6.2 Virtualization software allows implementing multiple laboratory systems on a single physical computer

Fig. 6.3 VMware Workstation Snapshot Manager supports multiple snapshots

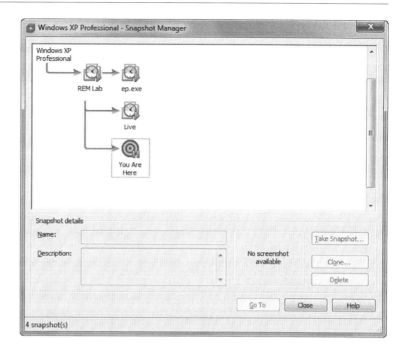

network to the Internet using a dedicated connection that is not publicly associated with their organization, such as a separate DSL line. This connection may be used to observe how a network bot establishes a command and control channel, or to allow a specimen to interact with a malicious website and to observe subsequent infections steps. In these cases, care must be taken to avoid the issue of "downstream liability," wherein the investigator's instance of the malware specimen may attack someone else.

If using virtualization software, investigators mitigate the risk of the specimen escaping from the lab by regularly applying security patches to the virtualization software and by following hardening guidelines from the virtualization software manufacturer. In addition, investigators avoid connecting the physical system hosting the virtualized lab to nonlaboratory networks, except for controlled Internet access as described in the previous paragraph

6.2.2 Behavioral Analysis

Behavioral analysis involves infecting a laboratory system with the malicious executable to observe how it interacts with the network, file system, the registry, and other processes. Multiple tools exist to capture such activities, as discussed next. Many of them need to run directly on the infected system, which may allow malware to attempt interfering with proper operation of the tools. To mitigate this risk, it is advisable to use multiple tools that provide different perspectives on the same set of events.

6.2.2.1 Real-Time Monitoring of the System

Process Monitor is a popular tool for observing activities on the laboratory system in real time using a graphical user interface.[5] This functionality allows the investigator to profile malicious processes after infecting the laboratory system. Once activated, Process Monitor begins capturing details about all locally running processes, recording events related to the following aspects of the environment:

- *File System:* Process Monitor can capture file system-related actions, such as attempts to create, read, modify, and delete local files.
- *Registry:* Process Monitor can capture registry-related actions, such as attempts to create, read, modify, and delete local registry keys (Fig. 6.4).
- *Process:* Process Monitor can capture activities related to local process and thread creation and termination.

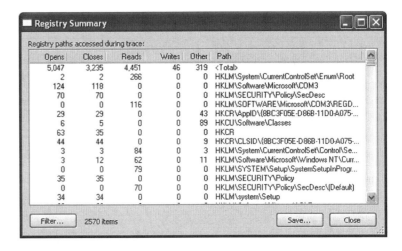

Fig. 6.4 Process Monitor can display the summary of local process activities, such as access to the registry

- *Network:* Process Monitor can capture TCP and UDP network activities that initiate or terminate on the system, including Internet protocol (IP) and port information, but omitting packet payload.

Process Monitor generates an extensive log file, recording one event per line. Each record includes a process name and ID, operation, path and additional details. The log file grows very quickly, due to the high level of activity even on a clean unused system. Therefore, the tool includes filtering capabilities, allowing the user to include or exclude events that match the desired criteria. Regardless of the filtering settings, the tool allows users to export the full log file for archival and further analysis.

Process Monitor can generate summary reports, based on contents of the log file the tool generated. For instance, the Network Summary report lists all network connections that the tool detected, including remote IP addresses and port numbers, as well as the number of transmitted bytes.

Another comprehensive tool for observing the specimen's interactions with its environment is CaptureBAT,[6] which provides another perspective on a set of events similar to those captured by Process Monitor. CaptureBAT is a command-line tool that can record file system, registry, process, and network-level events on the local system. If invoked with the "-c" parameter, CaptureBAT can capture files that malware specimens delete in the background; such files are usually not recoverable using the built-in Windows Recycle Bin (Fig. 6.5).

CaptureBAT comes with several filters, enabled by default, to eliminate much of standard Windows process activities from the log files the tool creates. This filtering helps cut down the noise that is present by default in Process Monitor logs; however, it may also prevent the investigator from seeing important

Fig. 6.5 Capture bat is able to capture local process, network, and registry activities

activities that masquerade as normal Windows actions. Fortunately, the investigator can modify CaptureBAT's filters as needed.

6.2.2.2 Identifying Important Changes to the System

Tools such as Process Monitor and CaptureBAT can capture so much information about local processes that the investigator may miss an important event in a large log file. To address this risk, it is useful to add a change-detection tool to the behavioral analysis toolkit. For instance, freely available Regshot allows the investigator to record the state of the lab system before and after infection and then compare the two snapshots to identify the differences.[7] Regshot can detect changes to both the registry and the file system. It will not flag any changes that occur between snapshots, for example, when malware creates a temporary file that it quickly deletes. Alternatives to Regshot include freely available SpyMe Tools[8] and InstallWatch[9] and various commercial utilities.

Another aspect of malware infections is the manner in which the specimen may configure itself to run automatically even after the victim reboots the system. A popular tool for examining this aspect of the specimen's behavior is Autoruns.[10] Autoruns is aware of the many ways in which a program can run automatically on Microsoft Windows, including the Run and other registry keys, services, device drivers, browser add-ons, schedules tasks, and so on. The tool allows taking and comparing snapshots of the autorun state of the system, helping the investigator detect infection-related changes (Fig. 6.6).

6.2.2.3 Monitoring the Network

An investigator also needs to be able to capture network traffic details beyond the general information recorded by Process Monitor. CaptureBAT, when invoked with the "-n" parameter, records all packets, including payload, that are visible from the laboratory system. CaptureBAT saves the capture file in the common PCAP format, which most network sniffers can parse.

Probably the most popular full-featured network sniffer is the freely available Wireshark.[11] In contrast to CaptureBAT, which can only create PCAP files when monitoring the network, Wireshark includes comprehensive network traffic analysis capabilities, accessible through a graphical user interface. This capability allows the analyst to observe how malware interacts with network resources in the lab by examining both packet headers and payload. A lightweight alternative to Wireshark is SmartSniff,[12] which is among the ranks of numerous network sniffers available for Microsoft Windows. Another option is tcpdump,[13] which can both capture network traffic

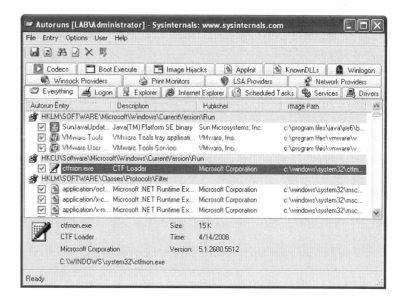

Fig. 6.6 Autoruns identifies the programs configured to run automatically on the system

and parse the data via a command-line interface. More sophisticated examples of network traffic capture are discussed in Chapter 7.

6.2.2.4 Interacting with Malware

Monitoring the laboratory network allows the investigator to discover which network resources the specimen attempts to access. For instance, the sniffer may show an attempt to resolve a hostname by connecting to a DNS server. Because the lab is isolated with minimal services running in it initially, this request will probably fail. However, the investigator can introduce the appropriate service into the lab. In the case of DNS, the investigator may provide the hostname-to-IP mapping by editing the lab system's "hosts" file or by starting a DNS server.

Tools for redirecting DNS-based network connections in the lab include traditional DNS server software, as well as specialized free tools such as the "Mini Fake DNS" Python script[14] and the compiled Windows program fakeDNS.[15] Some malware, such as network worms, use hardcoded IP addresses, rather than hostnames; in this case, honeypot tools such as Honeyd[16] can assist in redirecting the connections to a host in your lab, regardless of the destination IP address.

Allowing the specimen to access the network resource will often lead to the malicious program exhibiting additional characteristics, such as attempting to access a web, IRC, mail, and other services. Malware may rely on these services for the command and control channel (to communicate with the attacker), for exfiltrating data, or for seeking other systems to infect. For instance, after the program can resolve the desired hostname via DNS, it may reveal the service that it will try to access on that IP. A sniffer running in the lab will capture these characteristics. A convenient way to emulate many popular services is to use the freely available INetSim suite of tools.[17]

Interacting with malware is particularly useful when analyzing bots or backdoor-capable malware, which allows the attacker to issue commands to the infected system. By redirecting the specimen to a server in the lab, the investigator can attempt interacting with the specimen as the attacker would; this often helps reveal additional malicious characteristics, as well as to confirm or deny prior theories about the specimen's capabilities.

Consider an example where, after the laboratory system is infected, the sniffer observes attempts to resolve an unfamiliar hostname. With the exception of these DNS queries, which continue as long as the malicious process is running, the sniffer does not show any other network activities. The investigator could respond by allowing DNS resolution to occur, perhaps by using FakeDNS to point the hostname to an IP address that belongs to another system in the lab. Now, by infecting the lab system again, the investigator should see a connection to the laboratory system, and the sniffer should be able to capture the destination port number.

To determine the protocol the specimen is attempting to speak, the investigator would use a tool such as Netcat[18] to listen on the destination port. After repeating the experiment with Netcat running, the investigator would see additional connection details that may reveal the protocol. The investigator would then use this protocol to attempt providing the appropriate response to the specimen's connection in the hope of establishing a "conversation" that would reveal additional malicious characteristics. For instance, if the protocol were IRC, the investigator would launch an IRC server on the uninfected laboratory system, redirect the specimen's connection there, then use an IRC client to connect to the server, and attempt to interact with the specimen.

6.2.2.5 Automated Behavioral Analysis

Several products and services automate some of the behavioral analysis steps just described. Many of these tools are available for free as web-based services; some have commercial counterparts that an investigator can install locally in the lab. Although the free versions of these tools are usually limited in their ability to support interactive analysis of the specimen, they are convenient for jumpstarting the analysis and getting a general sense of the specimen's characteristics.[19]

Before uploading a specimen to these services, the investigator should consider whether such actions are allowed by the organization's policy. By uploading a targeted specimen to these services, the organization may reveal to the attacker that the attack was detected, if the attacker periodically queries such services for information about his executable. In such cases, the organization should consider purchasing commercial versions of such tools that run locally without inadvertently leaking information to outsiders.

Some organizations implemented their own approaches to automating behavioral analysis tasks using free tools and custom scripts. One example of a framework for building such a system is Truman,[20] which implements an isolated "sandbox" for malware to infect and includes scripts to examine malware remnants in a memory dump of the infected system. A similar approach, which builds upon and customizes Truman, was documented by Jim Clausing in an instructional paper titled "Building an Automated Behavioral Analysis Environment."[21]

6.2.3 Code Analysis

The code analysis phase gives the investigator an opportunity to examine the malicious program at the level of assembly language instructions to understand the specimen's inner workings. This section discusses how to perform such analysis of executables compiled to run on x86-compatible CPUs and the Microsoft Windows operating system, because they form the bulk of the specimens encountered during security incidents. Further, the assumption for this discussion is that the specimen's source code is unavailable to the investigator; if it were available, then there would be no need for reverse-engineering the code.

The code analysis phase is often seen as a process distinct from behavioral analysis. However, the two phases are intertwined. The investigator may start with behavioral analysis to identify key characteristics of the specimen. He may then perform some code analysis on "interesting" parts of the program to understand how they work, and then may return to behavioral analysis to test a theory or to investigate the context within which some code sections operate.

The most useful activities for performing code analysis include examining the malicious executable's structure, strings, external function references, and, of course, the actual instructions embedded into it.

6.2.3.1 Structure of the Executable File

Microsoft Windows executables usually follow the Portable Executable (PE) format, which allows the OS to natively load and run the program. The executable's data structure known as the PE Header contains "meta" information about the program, such as the address of the instruction that the OS should execute first (known as the Entry Point), the general layout of the executable's components, and the listing of dynamically linked libraries (DLLs) that the executable uses (known as the Import Table).

Examining the PE header helps the investigator when reversing packed executables, such as those discussed in the Handling Self-Defending Malware section of this chapter. Specialized free tools that can examine and sometimes modify the PE header include xPELister,[22] PEiD,[23] and PE Tools[24] (Fig. 6.7).

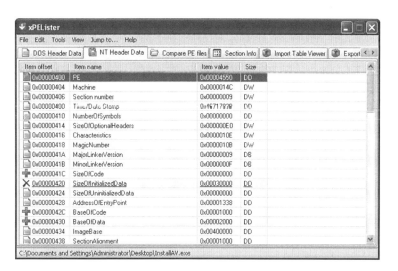

Fig. 6.7 xPELister is among several tools that can examine and modify the executable file's PE header

6.2.3.2 Embedded Strings

When a program refers to static strings, such sequences of ASCII or Unicode characters, they will often be embedded in clear text within the executable file. By looking at the embedded strings, the investigator can sometimes get a sense of the program's capabilities, and can identify potential functionality that may need to be examined further based on the visible function names, section names, potential commands, URLs, IP addresses, and so on.

However, a malicious executable may be written to prevent important strings from being visible in their plain text form. Further, the malware author may embed false strings to throw the investigator off course. Specialized free tools that can extract strings from executables include the numerous variations of the command-line "strings" utility,[25] as well as BinText[26] and TextScan.[27]

6.2.3.3 References to External Functions

An author of a malicious program can compile it to be standalone, including in the executable all the libraries upon which it depends; this is called static linking. A more popular approach is to reference external libraries and the relevant functions within those libraries dynamically, without embedding them directly in the executable. In dynamic linking, the executable loads the versions of libraries located on the infected system when they are needed. This method significantly decreases the size of the executable and improves its portability across various versions of Microsoft Windows. An investigator can learn about the functionality that the specimen possesses by looking at references to external functions, which usually take the form of API calls.

References to external functions can often be seen by examining the executable's Import Table using the tools mentioned earlier for looking at PE Header contents. Packed executables may conceal contents of the original program's Import Table. Therefore, it is also useful to observe the API calls the specimen makes as it runs. This is one of the situations where behavioral and code analysis phases are closely intertwined. Specialized free tools for observing the API calls the specimen's makes as it runs in the lab include Kerberos

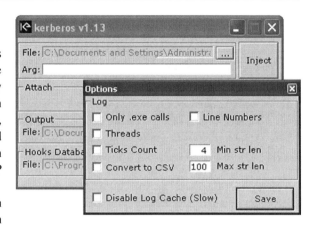

Fig. 6.8 Kerberos is among several tools that can log the specimen's API calls

API Monitor,[28] KaKeeware Application Monitor,[29] and DynLogger[30] (Fig. 6.8).

6.2.3.4 The Executable's Instructions

Perhaps the most important element of the code analysis process is the examination of the actual instructions that comprise the malicious executable. The instructions, which the CPU can understand and execute, are stored in the file as opcodes in a binary form that human beings usually cannot understand without the help of a disassembler. The disassembler can parse the executable and convert opcodes into corresponding assembly instructions that the investigator can examine.

A traditional disassembler allows the investigator to examine the code *statically* by reading the assembly instructions and looking at how they attempt to interact with data. This can be a time-consuming process, especially when the executable is packed or otherwise protected by its author. Therefore, it is useful to include a debugger in the investigator's toolkit. A debugger allows the investigator to examine the specimen's code as it executes, while slowing down the execution of the more "interesting" portions of the code. This process is called *stepping* through the executable, which involves executing an instruction or a function in one step, then pausing, looking around at the changes to the registers, the stack, RAM, and so on, and then continuing the execution. As it is usually impractical to manually step through every instruction, a debugger allows the investigator to define breakpoints, which are the conditions whereby the debugger will pause the normal execution of the specimen, giving the investigator control, so he can step through the relevant code segment. Using the debugger in this manner is called *dynamic analysis*.

Popular disassembler-debugger tools used for reverse-engineering malware are IDA Pro[31] (commercial) and OllyDbg[32] (free), each providing a suite of features useful for analyzing malicious code. Another tool category that is gaining popularity in this field is a decompiler, such as Hex-Rays Decompiler (commercial).[33] While a disassembler translates opcodes into assembly language instructions, a decompiler aims at recreating the source code of the program; this is a challenging task, and does not fully succeed when examining packed or otherwise protected malware.

6.2.4 Creating the Analysis Report

Similar to many other aspects of forensics, malware analysis needs to be performed according to a repeatable process. To accomplish this, the investigator should save logs, take screenshots, and maintain notes during the analysis. This information will allow the investigator to create an analysis report with sufficient detail that will allow a similarly skilled person to arrive at equivalent results.

A typical malware analysis report covers the following areas[34]:

- *Summary of the analysis:* Key takeaways the reader should get from the report regarding the specimen's nature, origin, capabilities, and other relevant characteristics
- *Identification:* The type of the file, its name, size, hashes (such as MD5, SHA1, and ssdeep[35]), malware names (if known), and current anti-virus detection capabilities
- *Characteristics:* The specimen's capabilities for infecting files, self-preservation, spreading, leaking data, interacting with the attacker, and so on
- *Dependencies:* Files and network resources related to the specimen's functionality, such as supported OS versions and required initialization files, custom DLLs, executables, URLs, and scripts
- *Behavioral and code analysis findings:* Overview of the analyst's behavioral, as well as static and dynamic, code analysis observations
- *Supporting figures:* Logs, screenshots, string excerpts, function listings, and other exhibits that support the investigator's analysis
- *Incident recommendations:* Indicators for detecting the specimen on other systems and networks, and possibilities for eradication steps

6.3 Case Study

The following section walks the reader through key steps of analyzing a sample malicious executable. The goal of this case study is to reinforce the discussion in the previous sections and to introduce several additional techniques for analyzing malware. The malware specimen used for this case study is a trojaned version of Windows Live Messenger.[36] This fake instant messaging client, shown in Fig. 6.9, looks like the real Windows Live Messenger. However, users who ran it reported being unable to login to the Live Messenger service using this program.

Fig. 6.9 A trojanized version of Windows Live Messenger looks like the real instant messaging client

6.3.1 Initial Analysis Steps

To start the analysis, the investigator usually performs the following tasks:

1. *Prepare the analysis lab* to include an isolated Microsoft Windows system that would be infected during the examination. Take a snapshot (if using virtualization software) or use another mechanism (if using dedicated physical hardware) to be able to restore the system to a pristine state at the end of the analysis.
2. *Document initial observations* based on any details shared with the investigator about the circumstances of the infection and on victims' or witnesses' perspectives on the incident. In the case of the trojan Messenger, the investigator may have learned that victims downloaded the executable from an unfamiliar website after seeing an ad for an updated version of Windows Live Messenger. The filename of the trojan was "Windows Live Messenger.exe."
3. *Attempt to identify the malware variant* by computing its hashes and searching the web for the mention of the hash, the file name, or other incident characteristics known to date. For instance, this case study's specimen's MD5 hash is A7A75A56B4B960C8532C37D3C705F88F. The investigator can search the VirusTotal website for this hash to see whether this specimen was uploaded to the site earlier and, if so, which anti-virus engines identified it as malicious. This search helps in assessing whether the malware is widespread or is likely to target a single organization. If allowed, the investigator can also upload the executable to automated behavioral analysis services, discussed earlier in the chapter, to get a sense for the specimen's characteristics.
4. *Bring the malicious executable into the lab,* placing it in an easy-to-click location such as the Desktop of the laboratory system the investigator will infect.

6.3.2 Behavioral Analysis Steps

The investigator can use change-detection tools, such as Regshot, to identify key changes the specimen makes to the registry and the file system. The investigator would take the first Regshot snapshot before infecting the laboratory system, take the second snapshot after the system is infected, and compare the two. After launching the malicious program, it is often advisable to try interacting with it to trigger "interesting" behavior. In the case of the trojan Messenger, the investigator might try to login via the program's login screen. Figure 6.10 shows the output of the Regshot comparison report for this specimen's activities: the trojan created two files, "C:\WINDOWS\msnsettings.dat" and "C:\pas.txt".

Real-time monitoring tools, such as Process Monitor, can reveal additional behavioral characteristics and allow the investigator to observe the context within which the changes identified by Regshot were made. As shown in Fig. 6.11, Process Monitor has captured details such as an attempt to locate the "C:\WINDOWS\msnsettings.dat" file (the file was not found), then the creation of this file, and later the creation of the "pas.txt" file.

Figure 6.12 displays contents of the two files that the specimen created on the laboratory system. It

Fig. 6.10 Regshot identifies two files added to the system by the specimen

Fig. 6.11 Process Monitor displays how the specimen queries and creates files

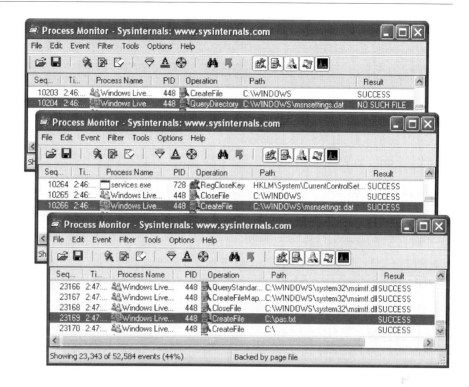

Fig. 6.12 The specimen generated two text files on the infected laboratory system

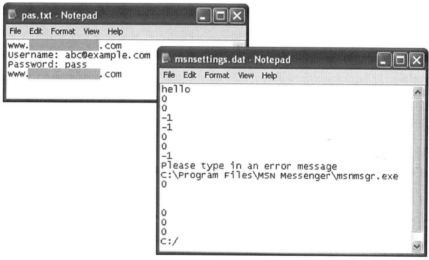

seems that "pas.txt" is storing the logon credentials the investigator used when logging into the specimen. The "msnsettings.dat" file appears to be a configuration file, possible to modify the malicious program's behavior without recompiling the executable.

Looking at these files on the actual infected systems outside the lab would confirm the specimen's password-capturing capabilities. The investigator would also notice the first line in "msnsettings.dat" on the victim's system states "test" while the one in the lab states "hello." Also, the victim's "msnsettings.dat" file includes a reference to an SMTP (mail) server, "gsmtp185.google.com," and an e-mail address, "mastercleanex@gmail.com." This address may be the recipient of the data that the specimen would attempt to send out. The "msnsettings.dat" file generated by the specimen in the lab does not include such e-mail references. The differences may be because the file on

Fig. 6.13 The victim's msnsettings.dat file differed from the one auto-generated in the lab

the victim's system has been customized the attacker whereas the one in the lab was automatically generated by the specimen to include default values (Fig. 6.13).

Having noticed the difference between two versions of "msnsettings.dat," the investigator could continue the analysis after placing the actual victim's file into the lab system's C:\WINDOWS directory to mimic the real-world setup more closely.

To observe how the specimen interacts with the network, the investigator could launch CaptureBAT with the "-n" parameter; this would create a PCAP capture file that could be loaded into most sniffers for the analysis. Alternatively, the investigator could sniff the laboratory network directly with a tool such as Wireshark. As shown in Fig. 6.14, Wireshark captured a packet leaving the infected laboratory system for the IP address that, it believes, is a local DNS server. This is a DNS query; the specimen is attempting to resolve the hostname "gsmtp185.google.com."

The "smtp" suffix suggests that the malware specimen is looking for a mail server and is consistent with the presence of this hostname in the victim's "msnsettings.dat" file.

To identify the port number that malware is attempting to access, the investigator could allow the specimen to resolve the desired hostname, redirecting the hostname and future associated connections to a laboratory system. One way to accomplish this is to use FakeDNS. As shown in Fig. 6.15, after resolving the hostname, the specimen attempts to connect to TCP port 25 on the system it believes to be "gsmtp185.google.com." This port is typically used for sending SMTP messages, which is consistent with an earlier theory. The sniffer shows that the specimen is unable to establish the SMTP connection because the laboratory system to which it is connecting is not listening on port 25.

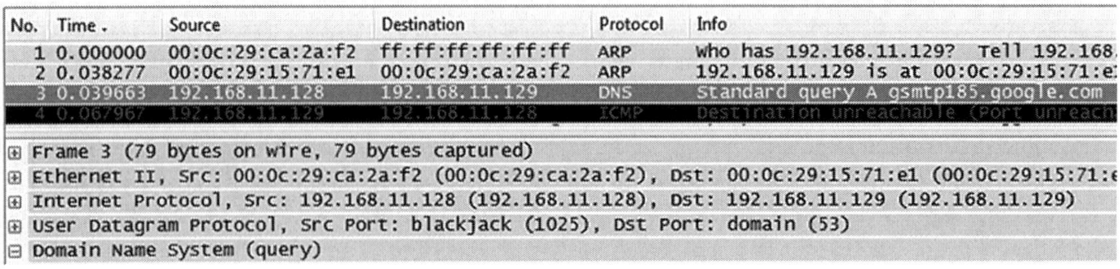

Fig. 6.14 Wireshark captured an attempt to resolve the hostname of an SMTP server

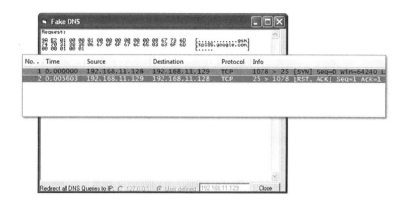

Fig. 6.15 The specimen attempted to connect to TCP port 25 after being able to resolve the desired hostname

The investigator could use Netcat to open a listener on TCP port 25 and repeat the previous experiment to observe what data would be exchanged between the infected system and the laboratory server. Alternatively, the investigator could use a fake mail server called Mailpot[37] for intercepting any e-mail messages that the specimen may attempt to send over TCP port 25. Figure 6.16 shows the e-mail message that Mailpot intercepted in the lab. The message includes the victim's Messenger username and password.

At this point, the investigator has discovered a key characteristic of the malware specimen: its ability to capture Messenger logon credentials and transmit them to the attacker via e-mail, attempting to relay the message through Google's SMTP server to deliver it to the "mastercleanex@gmail.com."

6.3.3 Code Analysis Steps

The code analysis phase can reinforce and expand behavioral findings. The investigator could load the specimen's executable into a disassembler-debugger tool such as IDA Pro and OllyDbg, and look for

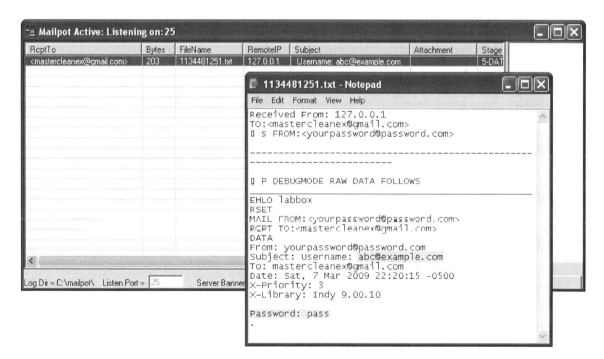

Fig. 6.16 Mailpot intercepted the specimen's e-mail message that attempted to send out captured logon credentials

promising functions, strings, and "interesting" code portions. This case study makes use of OllyDbg and will start code analysis by looking at the strings embedded in the "Windows Live Messenger.exe." The strings can be extracted using tools such as BinText, as shown in Fig. 6.17; however, the investigator can better observe the context within which the strings are used by looking at them in a disassembler.

The investigator can load the malicious executable in OllyDbg on the laboratory system via the "File" > "Open" menu option. To extract embedded strings using OllyDbg, the investigator would right-click on the disassembler window and select "Search for" > "All referenced text strings." OllyDbg would then open a new window, captured in Fig. 6.18, displaying strings that seem to match default contents of the "msnsettings.dat" file.

When the investigator sees an "interesting" string in OllyDbg, he can click on it in the "Text strings referenced…" window and press Enter. OllyDbg would then bring up the segment of the code that makes use of that string, giving the analyst the opportunity to understand its purpose. This is often a convenient way of locating code sections that are worth examining.

For the purpose of this case study, the analyst will make use of another technique to understand the purpose of the "test" string that was in the victim's "msnsettings.dat". This may be worth investigating,

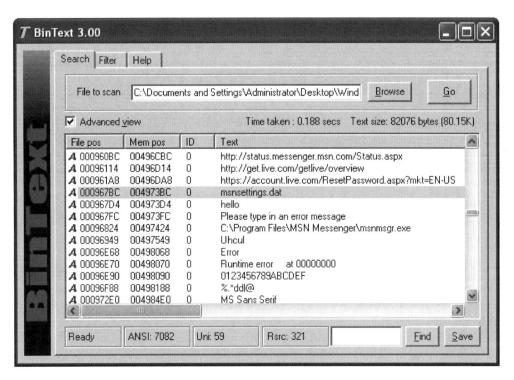

Fig. 6.17 BinText extracted clear-text strings embedded in the malicious executable

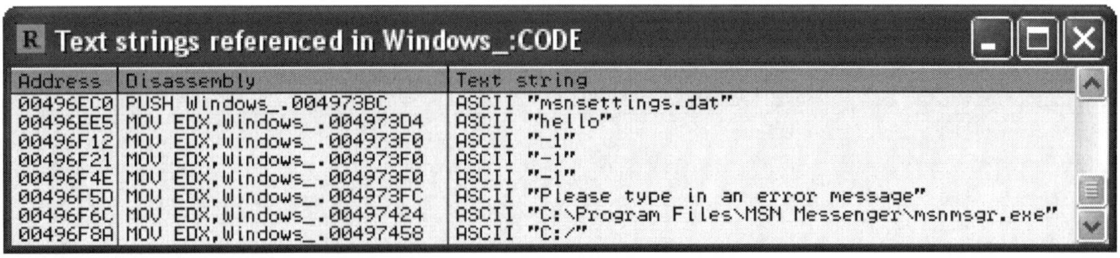

Fig. 6.18 OllyDbg extracted clear-text strings embedded in the malicious executable

because that was one way in which the files on the victim's and the lab's systems differed.

One of the ways to determine how a program makes use of an "interesting" string such as "test" is to run the specimen in OllyDbg, allowing the specimen to load and process all its strings. Then, the investigator could use OllyDbg to locate the desired string in memory of the malicious process and set a breakpoint there. To accomplish this, the investigator would press "Alt+M" in OllyDbg after loading and executing the specimen within OllyDbg. "Alt+M" brings up the Memory Map of the debugged process. To search the executable's memory for a particular string, the investigator would click on top of the memory map window, press "Ctrl+B", and then enter the desired string. In this case, the investigator would enter "test" in the ASCII field of the dialog box, as shown in Fig. 6.19.

A particular string might reside in several locations in memory, some of them not relevant to the analysis. To repeat the previous search, seeking another instance of the string, the investigator would return to the Memory Map window in OllyDbg and press "Ctrl+L", seeing the "correct" instance of the string through trial and error. In this case study, the investigator would need to perform the initial search ("Ctrl+B" once) and a repeat search ("Ctrl+L" once) after returning to the Memory Map window. The investigator would then highlight the desired string ("test"), right-click on it in the disassembler window, and select "Breakpoint" >

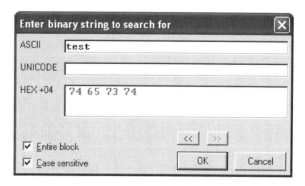

Fig. 6.19 OllyDbg can search memory contents of a running executable

"Memory, on access," as shown in Fig. 6.20. Once the breakpoint is set, whenever OllyDbg detects that the debugged program is attempting to read that portion of memory (e.g., attempts to read the string "test"), it would pause the execution and give the investigator control.

At this point of the analysis, the investigator may be uncertain how to trigger this breakpoint, that is, under what conditions the specimen will make use of the string "test" that it stores in memory. A popular approach in this situation is to interact with the specimen to observe how it reacts. For instance, the investigator could supply various input into the trojan's "E-mail address" and "Password" fields at the login

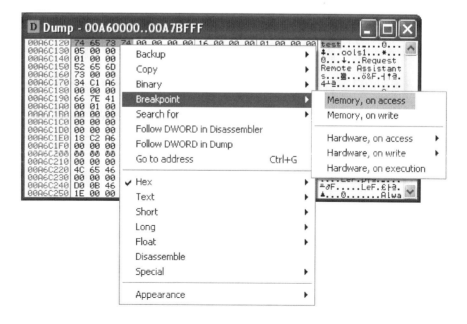

Fig. 6.20 OllyDbg can search memory contents of a running executable

screen. In this specimen, any character entered by the investigator in the "E-mail address" field triggers the breakpoint. Now the investigator can step through the code, look at memory and register values, and attempt to determine the purpose of the string "test." (A register is a specialized location on the CPU that can store data and that is very fast at accessing the data.) One instruction after the breakpoint, this specimen compares the letter that was typed at the login screen to the first letter of the word "test." (Detailed explanation of assembly instructions is outside the scope of this chapter.)

As illustrated on Fig. 6.21, OllyDbg has highlighted the instruction that will be executed next by the program, "CMP CL, BL." This instruction compares the contents of two registers, CL and BL. CL points to the lowest byte of ECX; BL points to the lowest byte of EBX. This is an efficient way of comparing parts of ECX and EBX registers. The ECX register contains hexadecimal value 67, which corresponds to the letter "g"; this is what the investigator happened to have typed into the "E-mail address" in this experiment. EBX contains the string with which the input is being compared, "test" (it is stored backward).

What if the investigator typed "t" as the input? This can be tested in the next experiment, after allowing the specimen to continue running within OllyDbg. In this case, the investigator typed "te" as input into the "E-mail address" field. In this case, the code compares the first typed letter to "t" and the second typed letter to "e," as captured in Fig. 6.22. (The CH register points to the second lowest byte of ECX; the BH register points to the second lowest byte of EBX.)

It seems that the specimen is looking for the string "test" in the "E-mail address" field of its login screen. The investigator can exit OllyDbg, launch the malicious executable by itself, and type "test" to see what happens. In response, the specimen brings up a new, previously unseen window, shown in Fig. 6.23. The screen allows the attacker to overwrite hardcoded options of the trojan, which include the passphrase needed to enter the hidden screen string, the address where the trojan will send captured logon credentials, and so on.

Having performed behavioral and code analysis of the specimen, the investigator confirmed that the trojan is designed to capture the victim's Messenger credentials entered into the trojan version of Windows Live Messenger. As part of the analysis, the investigator identified behavioral characteristics at the system and network levels that could help identify the presence of this malware specimen on other systems. Further, he learned that the specimen saves the captured credentials to a local file, and then sends it to the attacker via

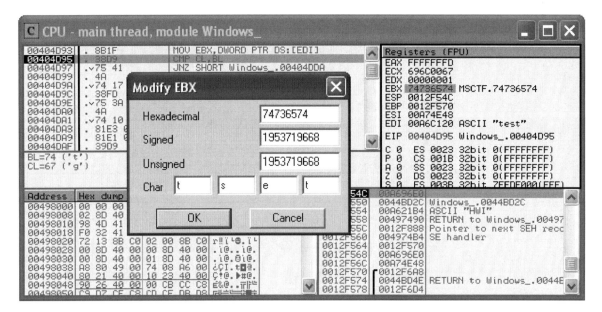

Fig. 6.21 The specimen compares the first letter typed as input to the first letter of the string "test"

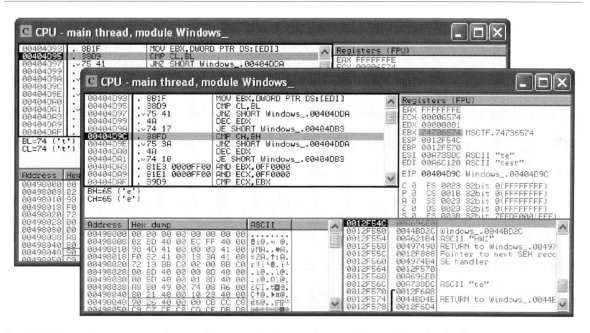

Fig. 6.22 The specimen compares the second letter typed as input to the second letter of the string "test"

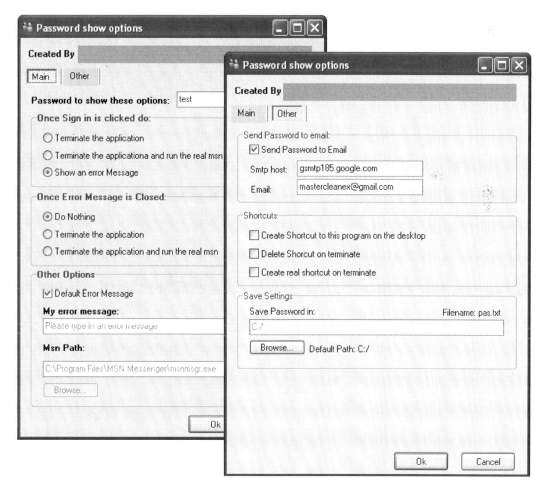

Fig. 6.23 The hidden options screen allows overwriting the specimen's hardcoded characteristics

Gmail. The investigator also identified a file "msnsettings.dat" that the specimen uses to store its configuration; this helped expand the scope of the analysis on the victim's system, allowing the investigator to examine a file that may have gone unnoticed otherwise. The attacker can customize the "msnsettings.dat" file by typing "test" into the "E-mail address" field of the trojan's login screen.

6.4 Issues and Trends

Malware authors frequently construct their creations in attempts to avoid detection and to complicate the reverse-engineering process. This is, perhaps, the biggest challenge that an investigator faces when analyzing malicious software. The following section surveys some of the anti-analysis capabilities the investigator may encounter, as malware authors become increasing sophisticated in the manner of writing, packaging, and distributing their specimens.

6.4.1 Packed Malware

In the context of malicious software, *packing* refers to the process malware authors use to compress, obfuscate, encrypt, or otherwise encode the original executable to produce an executable that is harder to analyze than the original one. Packing an executable also helps attackers bypass signature-based detection for the specimen. Furthermore, a packer can create code of the packed executable in a way that confuses or disables common malware analysis tools. (Packing also has a legitimate use, whereby legitimate software developers are able to protect benign programs from reverse-engineering.)

A packed executable typically stores the originally executable as data. The only part of the packed executable that contains code is the set of unpacking instructions. When the packed executable runs on the victim's system, the unpacking code extracts the original executable into RAM. As a result, the original program is not available as a file to the investigator to analyze (Fig. Fig. 6.24).

One of the signs that a malware specimen has been packed is that the executable no longer reveals many of the embedded strings that were clearly visible in the original file. Therefore, a quick way to check whether the unfamiliar specimen is packed involves looking at its strings, as was described in the *Embedded Strings* section (Fig. Fig. 6.25).

Another sign of many packed executables is the shortened listing of external DLLs that they rely upon, which is stored in the Import Table. The packer often conceals the original Import Table; therefore, if an executable imports very few DLLs and the associated functions, it may be packed. For example, many packers produce an executable that only imports kernel32.dll and its functions LoadLibraryA and GetProcAddress, as shown in Fig. 6.26.

Numerous packers are available to malware authors. Many of these tools are commercial, some are available for free on the web, and some are custom written and kept private. Some of the publicly available packers are these:

- ASPack (commercial)
- FSG (free)
- NsPack (commercial)
- PECompact (commercial)
- Themida (commercial)
- UPX (free)
- Yoda's Crypter (free)

When analyzing a packed executable, the investigator usually starts by attempting to identify the packer used to protect the specimen. Knowing the name of the packer helps research that packer's capabilities and may reveal tips or techniques for bypassing

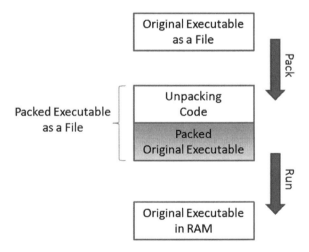

Fig. 6.24 Packing an executable complicates the analysis process

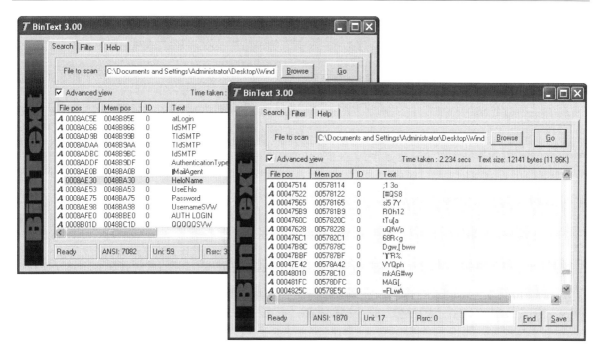

Fig. 6.25 In comparison to the unpacked executable, the packed file has fewer readable strings

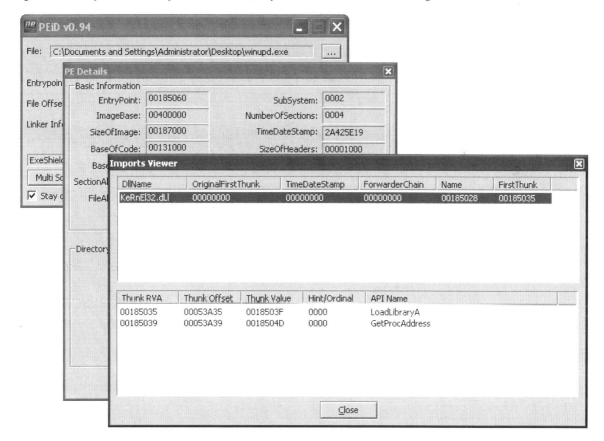

Fig. 6.26 A packed executable often stores very few external DLL references in its Import Table, which can be viewed with tools such as PEiD

its protection. Sometimes, the simplest way of identifying the packer involves noticing packer-specific strings such as "UPX" or "Themida" embedded into the protected executable. Another common way of identifying the packer is to use PEiD, as shown in Fig. 6.27. PEiD includes a database of signatures for many packers.[38] PEiD's signature database can be used for scanning files programmatically using the "pefile" Python module[39] or from the command line using the "packerid.py" script.[40]

A practical approach to bypassing the packer's protection involves allowing the unpacking code to extract the original executable into RAM and catching the program right as the original executable begins running from RAM. At that point, the investigator could use a debugger, such as OllyDbg, to examine the original executable directly in RAM. There are tools that can assist the investigator with this process, such as the OllyDump plug-in[41] for OllyDbg. The process for locating the end of the unpacking code can be challenging, and the complexity of this issue may only be expected to increase.

Alternatively, the investigator could use a tool such as LordPE to "dump" the unpacked executable to a file. The dumped file may not be runnable, because its PE header will often be corrupted; however, a disassembler will usually be able to parse it to make it available for static analysis. Dumping the program with LordPE involves infecting the lab system, right-clicking on the malicious process within LordPE's process listing window, and selecting "dump full." The PE Tools utility, mentioned earlier, offers similar functionality. The investigator can use tools such as Import REConstructor (ImpREC),[42] as well as the functionality built into LordPE and OllyDump, to attempt fixing the dumped program's PE header to make the executable runnable (Fig. 6.28).

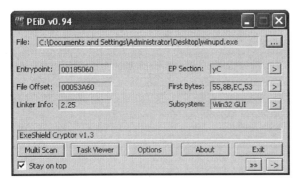

Fig. 6.27 PEiD can identify many common packers based on its signature database

The unpacking code is usually carefully written to be time consuming to analyze. Therefore, it is usually difficult to reverse-engineer the unpacking algorithm.

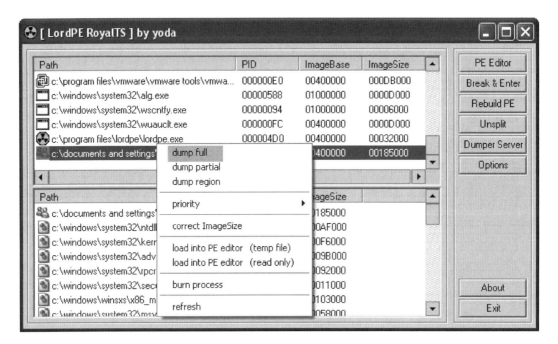

Fig. 6.28 LordPE can "dump" the original executable from RAM to a file

6.4.2 Anti-virtualization Defenses

Many of the defenses built-into malware are incorporated into the malicious executable by the packer. The previous section explained how the packer can significantly complicate the code analysis process. The unpacking code frequently includes other anti-analysis measures designed to slow down the analyst's manual unpacking process and to obstruct behavioral analysis tasks.

A common "feature" of many malware specimens is the ability to detect whether they are running in a virtualized environment, such as VMware. This capability is not uncommon, because malware authors recognize that analysts often use virtualization to implement the lab. If malware detects the virtualized environment, it may refuse to run, or may exhibit characteristics different from those that would occur in a victim's system in the real world.

One approach to handle this defense is to perform code analysis to locate the code that performs the check for the presence of virtualization software. Finding this code can be challenging, but is usually within the realm of practical possibility. Once the investigator identifies the appropriate code section, he can patch the malicious executable to disable or invalidate the check. (Patching refers to the process of modifying the executable's assembly instructions; disassemblers and debuggers such as OllyDbg generally support such functionality.) Many investigators prefer a simpler approach to bypassing the specimen's antivirtualization functionality: they use physical, rather than virtualized, systems when implementing the malware analysis lab.

6.4.3 Other Anti-analysis Trends

Malware may possess other self-defending characteristics that aim at slowing down, misdirecting, or confusing the investigator. For instance, malware may possess rootkit capabilities, whereby it conceals its presence in a way that not only makes detection in the wild difficult, but also makes it challenging to identify which processes on the infected laboratory system need to be analyzed. To hide, rootkits may inject malicious code into legitimate processes, or may override components of the OS kernel to falsify the responses analysis tools receive from the OS when making API calls.

The investigator may be able to disable cloaking capabilities of some rootkits, bringing the processes they are concealing into the foreground for behavioral analysis. Free tools that can accomplish this include RKDetector,[43] GMER,[44] RootkitRevealer,[45] DarkSpy,[46] and IceSword.[47] Another approach to analyzing rootkit malware involves examining RAM contents of the infected laboratory system using tools such as the Volatility Framework.[48] Michael Ligh created several Volatility plugins that can assist in this task, such as malfind.py, usermode_hooks2.py, and kernel_hooks.py.[49] Chapter 8 includes more detail on such approaches.

Malware may also attempt to interfere with the analysis by identifying the investigator's tools by looking for offending process or window names, or by using API calls such as IsDebuggerPresent. To bypass this defense, the investigator can locate and patch the code that performs the check, can use a alternative tool that is not being detected, or to use cloaking utilities, such as the OllyDbg plugins HideOD[50] and Olly Advanced.[51] Specialized utilities for concealing analysis tools also include HideToolz, which provides rootkit-like functionality to use for the investigator's benefit.[52]

Malware may also possess characteristics designed to complicate analysis at the code level. One such technique involves including numerous unneeded instructions in the malicious executable, leading the investigator to spend time disassembling and analyzing useless instructions. Another code-level defensive measure involves implementing an assembly-level jump instruction in unexpected ways; this may involve using the RET instruction, typically meant for returning from a function, to jump to a memory location to execute an unexpected code block. An unexpected jump could also be performed using Windows Structured Exception Handling (SEH) functionality, whereby instead of defining a function to recover from an error condition, the malware author causes the error to occur while the specimen runs, so that Windows invokes the error-handling function to continue executing the malicious program from another code block.

Faced with the ever more sophisticated self-defending capabilities of malicious software, the core aspects of the malware analysis framework will likely remain the same. That is, to understand the nature of the malware specimen requires behavioral and code-level analysis expertise, a laboratory with the ever more sophisticated tools, and plenty of patience and attention to detail.

Notes

1. Another term for "specimen" in the context of malicious software is "sample," which is often used by the anti-virus industry.
2. Adapted from the *Categories of Common Malware Traits* article by Lenny Zeltser (http://isc.sans.org/diary.html?storyid=7186). Used with permission.
3. CenturionGuard is described at http://centuriontech.com/products/hardware
4. Reborn PCI Card is described at http://www.lenten.com/Products.asp
5. rocess Monitor is available at http://technet.microsoft.com/en-us/sysinternals/bb896645.aspx
6. CaptureBAT is available at http://www.nz-honeynet.org/capture-standalone.html
7. Regshot is available at http://sourceforge.net/projects/regshot
8. SpyMe Tools is available at http://www.lcibrossolutions.com
9. InstallWatch is available at http://www.epsilonsquared.com
10. Autoruns is available at http://technet.microsoft.com/en-us/sysinternals/bb963902.aspx
11. Wireshark is available at http://www.wireshark.org
12. SmartSniff is available at http://nirsoft.net/utils/smsniff.html
13. Tcpdump is available as a native package for most Unix distributions, and can also be downloaded from http://www.tcpdump.org. A Windows version of tcpdump, known as windump, is available at http://www.winpcap.org
14. The "Mini Fake DNS" Python script is available at http://code.activestate.com/recipes/491264
15. fakeDNS is available as part of Malcode Analysis Pack at http://labs.idefense.com/software/malcode.php
16. Honeyd is available at http://www.honeyd.org
17. InetSim is available at http://www.inetsim.org
18. Netcat is available for Unix at http://netcat.sourceforge.net and for Windows at http://www.securityfocus.com/tools/139
19. A list of free automated behavioral analysis websites includes the following:

    - Anubis, available at http://anubis.iseclab.org
    - CWSandbox, available at http://www.cwsandbox.org and http://www.sunbeltsecurity.com
    - EUREKA Malware Analysis Internet Service, available at http://eureka.cyber-ta.org
    - Joebox, available at http://www.joebox.org
    - Norman SandBox, available at http://www.norman.com/security_center
    - ThreatExpert, available at http://www.threatexpert.com

20. Truman is available at http://www.secureworks.com/research/tools/truman.html
21. The Building an Automated Behavioral Analysis Environment paper is available at http://www.sans.org/reading_room/whitepapers/tools/rss/building_an_automated_behavioral_malware_analysis_environment_using_open_source_software_33129
22. xPELister is available at http://ap0x.jezgra.net/misc.html
23. PEiD is available at http://peid.has.it
24. PE Tools is available at http://www.uinc.ru/files/neox/PE_Tools.shtml
25. A version of the "strings" utility compiled for Microsoft Windows is available at http://technet.microsoft.com/en-us/sysinternals/bb897439.aspx; another is available at http://www.rnicrosoft.net/tools/nstrings.zip
26. BinText is available at http://www.foundstone.com/us/resources/proddesc/bintext.htm
27. TextScan is available at http://www.analogx.com/contents/download/Programming/textscan/Freeware.htm
28. Kerberos API Monitor is available at http://www.wasm.ru
29. KaKeeware Application Monitor is available at http://www.kakeeware.com/i_kam.php
30. DynLogger is available at http://ntcore.com/dynlogger.php
31. IDA Pro is available at http://www.hex-rays.com/idapro
32. OllyDbg is available at http://www.ollydbg.de
33. Hex-Rays Decompiler is available at http://www.hex-rays.com/decompiler.shtml
34. Adapted from the *What to Include in a Malware Analysis Report* article by Lenny Zeltser (http://zeltser.com/reverse-malware/malware-analysis-report.html). Used with permission.
35. The free ssdeep utility provides "fuzzy" hashing capabilities, useful for identifying similar variants of the same core malware specimen. It is available at http://ssdeep.sourceforge.net
36. The case study is adapted from the presentation by Lenny Zeltser, titled *Introduction to Malware Analysis* (http://zeltser.com/reverse-malware/malware-analysis-webcast.html). Used with permission.
37. Mailpot is available as part of the free Malcode Analysis Pack at http://labs.idefense.com/software/malcode.php#more_malcode+analysis+pack.
38. An expanded database of PEiD-compatible signatures is available as the UserDB.TXT file at http://www.peid.info/BobSoft/Downloads.html
39. The "pefile" Python module is available at http://code.google.com/p/pefile
40. The "packerid.py" script is available at http://handlers.dshield.org/jclausing/packerid.py
41. OllyDump is available at http://www.openrce.org/downloads/details/108/OllyDump
42. ImpREC is available at http://www.woodmann.com/collaborative/tools/index.php/ImpREC
43. RKDetector is available at http://www.rkdetector.com
44. GMER is available at http://www.gmer.net

45. RootkitRevealer is available at http://technet.microsoft.com/en-us/sysinternals/bb897445.aspx
46. DarkSpy is available at http://www.antirootkit.com/software/DarkSpy.htm
47. IceSword is available at http://www.antirootkit.com/software/IceSword.htm
48. The Volatility Framework is available at https://www.volatilesystems.com/default/volatility
49. Michael Ligh's Volatility scripts for malware analysis are available at http://code.google.com/p/mhl-malware-scripts
50. HideOD is available at http://www.pediy.com/tools/Debuggers/ollydbg/plugin.htm
51. OllyAdvanced is available at http://www.woodmann.com/collaborative/tools/index.php/Olly_Advanced
52. HideToolz is available at http://www.woodmann.com/collaborative/tools/index.php/HideToolz

Chapter 7
Network Packet Forensics

Eddie Schwartz

Eddie Schwartz is Chief Security Officer for NetWitness, the world leader in advanced threat intelligence and network forensics. He has 25 years of experience as an information security and privacy expert, specializing in the financial services and federal government sectors. Before joining NetWitness, Eddie was Chief Technology Officer for ManTech Security Technologies Corporation, General Manager for Predictive Systems, where he ran the Global Integrity business unit, and directed numerous Incident Sharing and Analysis Centers (ISAC), SVP of Operations at Guardent, Chief Information Security Officer (CISO) for Nationwide Insurance Enterprise, Technical Director of the Diplomatic Security Service Information Security Laboratory; a Senior Computer Scientist for Computer Sciences Corporation (CSC), and a Foreign Service Officer with the US Department of State. Eddie served on the Boards of Directors of Secured Services, Inc. (OTC: SSVC), and InfoSec (JP), the Executive Committee and Lab Governance Board for the Banking Information Technology Secretariat (BITS) of the Financial Services Roundtable and the Board of Advisors for numerous security start-ups. He has worked as a technical advisor to Boston- and New York-based technology venture capital firms, and the Workgroup for the Computerization of Behavioral Health and Human Services Records. Eddie holds PMP, CISSP, CISA, CISM, CAP, and NSA-IAM certifications, has an M.S. in Information Technology Management, and a B.I.S. in Information Security Management from the George Mason University School of Management.

7.1 Investigation Characteristics

Although many security experts have used network data for forensics purposes for years, historically most network forensics work has been associated with small-scale, post facto analysis in support of internal investigations, or in more infrequent cases, as part of an organized cyber threat intelligence team. During the last few years, however, the arrival of inexpensive memory and hard drives combined with improvements in search algorithms has enabled both technology and the process to advance to where pervasive adoption of real-time network forensics as part of day-to-day security operations across government and commercial organizations is a requirement.

The difference between modern networking forensics and historical usage is that the former has introduced requirements for pervasive versus incident-driven network traffic recording. The difference is best illustrated by analogy with video recording. Imagine that you were trying to use video surveillance to identify criminals who had entered a bank during a robbery. If you waited to activate the video recording device until the robbery was in progress, you might only obtain a visualization of the backs of the criminals' heads as they walked out of the bank, not very useful in terms of downstream investigation. In a scenario where you were recording all the traffic pervasively, the real trick is to both capture and analyze the data properly. As seen in Fig. 7.1, suppose you were looking for the

E. Schwartz (✉)
Chief Security Officer, NetWitness Corporation, 500 Grove Street Herndon, VA 20170, USA

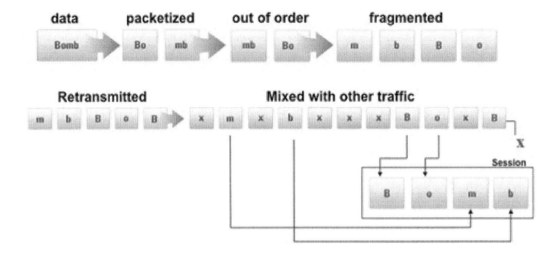

Fig. 7.1 Example of session reconstruction

word "bomb" in a virtual ocean of raw network data: session reconstruction permits the reassembly of these packets so that the word can be recognized easily using automated and interactive processes.

This chapter explores the definition, technology requirements, operational processes, and business value of network forensics as a component of an overall cyberforensics program and as a part of other operational security program elements within your organization.

7.1.1 What Is Network Forensics?

Many vendors and consultants make use of the term network forensics in a variety of ways relative to their products and services. For the purpose of this chapter, network forensics represents:

> Reconstruction of network events to provide definitive insight into the actions and behaviors of users, devices, and applications.

Let's examine this definition more closely to understand the difference between network forensics and other activities discussed elsewhere in this book.

- *Reconstruction of network events* means reassembly of live network sessions based upon each particular network service or application protocol. A simple example would be if the security team needed to review all the Web content of a particular end-user to support an investigation, they would need to reconstruct all the HTTP and HTTPS sessions associated with this individual. To perform this level of reconstruction, we will assume for the purpose of this chapter the security team is performing pervasive full packet capture at a network interface where session-level analysis is desired, such as your Internet point of presence or a business partner link.[1] Keep in mind that session reconstruction is not the same as the simple aggregation or correlation of logs or netflow message statistics. In this case, reconstruction includes the reassembly of all network sessions associated with specific service types or all network traffic.
- *Definitive insight into the actions and behaviors* means deeply inspecting network traffic using recursive parsing and analytic techniques to get to the bottom of what is crossing the wire, and obtaining human-readable views into the full content and context of these network sessions. Achieving this objective requires a port and protocol agnostic approach to session analysis because in today's threat landscape, network characteristics or "metadata," such as port numbers, cannot be trusted as indicators of network or application-layer protocol or traffic types.
- *Users, devices, and applications* includes everything from OSI layer 2 to layer 7 that generates

network traffic or that can have an impact on network traffic. For example, "users" encompass any network object that might represent a user or group of users on the network, such as Microsoft Active Directory usernames, Yahoo e-mail addresses, or AIM or Facebook chat handles. A "device" would include the various nominal descriptors for a workstation, server, or other network device, including Internet protocol (IP) addresses, computer names, MAC addresses, and more. "Applications" include the essential characteristics and components of standard and nonstandard applications operating across the network, legitimately or not. The rubric in Fig. 7.2 includes metadata such as file names, encryption types, error messages, application actions, and passwords. As depicted in the data cube, all these metadata comprise the nouns, verbs, and adjectives in the robust lexicon that describes what is really happening on an organization's network.

It is a failing strategy to rely solely on IP addresses, port numbers, and other numeric addressing as definitive attack identifiers because these numbers are unreliable, and nonstandard network traffic can be tunneled over commonly accepted ports (e.g., SSH over port 443, or non-DNS traffic over port 53). Most serious adversaries operate outside the scope of signature-based defenses and below the radar of "known good" anomaly thresholds, rendering many security technologies blind to advanced threats.

In today's world of advanced threats, complex technology, and savvy insiders, network forensics enables security teams reduce uncertainty and sort through a number of tough problems quickly and efficiently.

There was a time when the use of real-time network forensics techniques were reserved for situations that were highly extreme in nature because of the lengthy time requirements and the technical difficulty level. For example, suppose you were searching for "patient zero" in a designer malware attack on your organization. The attack symptoms eventually may become clear, in terms of data losses and other malicious network traffic characteristics, but in a situation where there are dozens or even hundreds of infected machines, how would you determine the actual point of entry of the malware in an enterprise of 10,000 hosts? If you could ever find it, would your security team know what to do with something that looks like the screenshot shown in Fig. 7.3?

Luckily, the state of the art of network forensics has advanced during the last few years, and the days of "grepping" through millions or billions or sessions in the hope of finding some snippet of obfuscated JavaScript code for secondary analysis in Wireshark have faded into the past.

Today, thanks to advances in both analytic technology and security practice, many organizations are using network forensics every day in a variety of situations, including the following.

1. Improving the Effectiveness of the SOC. Enterprise-wide, real-time, network forensics provides a profound level of network content and context for security operations center (SOC) personnel, augmenting "defense-in-depth" approaches such as firewall and intrusion detection system (IDS) log analysis, statistics-based anomaly detection, and event correlation. The availability of better and deeper information for the SOC staff improves the effectiveness of the SOC by allowing them to make informed decisions faster, thereby reducing the gap exposure for the organization.

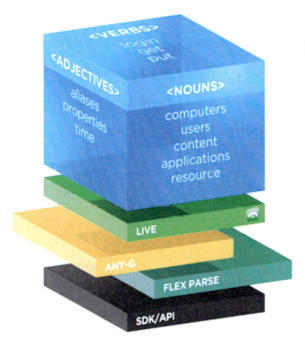

Fig. 7.2 Network forensics metadata

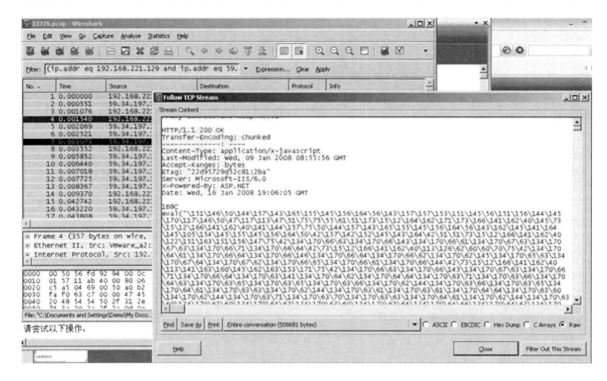

Fig. 7.3 JavaScript obfuscation depicted in Wireshark

2. Situational Awareness. Top security teams constantly are refining proactive views into the threats faced by their respective government and commercial organizations. Advanced threats from organized criminal and state-sponsored groups fall outside the detective capabilities of current security popular platforms and must be viewed from the complete perspective of advanced network intelligence and pervasive network forensics. Network forensics provides security professionals a common lexicon for evaluating, analyzing, and discussing advanced threats and taking proactive defensive steps.
3. Investigatory Support. This broad use category includes a wide range of post facto activities including data breach or information loss impact assessment, Human Resources or Legal Department e-discovery support, antifraud activities, and external investigation support (e.g., law enforcement and others). As discussed in other chapters of this book, many of these investigations historically have taken place at the host level using disk imaging tools such as EnCase, but as you will see in this chapter, there are many situations in which network forensics can play both a support and preemptive role in such investigations.

This chapter examines each of these use cases illustrating the use of network forensics.

7.2 Investigative Approach

Performing network forensics requires a level of understanding within the organization regarding the characteristics of today's threat landscape, the organization's information pathways, and the best ways to visualize the actions and behaviors of users and devices across those information pathways.

Whether your security architecture is organized from the perspective of communities of interest, data classification silos, or regulatory protection enclaves (Fig. 7.4), network forensics can play a critical role in providing your security team timely visibility and intelligence regarding the most advanced threats and

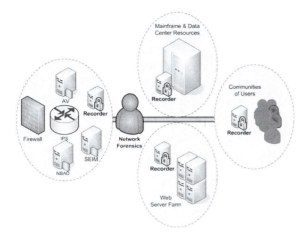

Fig. 7.4 Sample placement of network forensics devices

complex investigative scenarios. Leading organizations have some level of network forensics capture and analysis capability across all mission-critical network interfaces, information assets, and business enclaves.

Every investigation has a starting point: network forensics is no different. With network forensics, the initial approach may originate from one or more of a variety of places, depending upon the maturity of your security infrastructure, the specific use case, and in-house security operations processes.

7.2.1 Input Developed from Existing Security Technology Sources

Most security teams today collect and review firewall logs to some extent or another, and many perform frequent analysis of intrusion detection system logs. In a situation involving any of the three investigation types described earlier, an alert derived from the telemetry from one or more of these legacy security technologies frequently is the starting point for a network forensics investigation.

In this example, the starting point for the network forensics investigation is an alert from the signature-based Sourcefire Defense Center (Fig. 7.5) indicating that an IIS Backslash Evasion was observed between the IP addresses 66.104.20.242 and 207.211.65.16. The SOC team needs to determine quickly whether to escalate this event to an incident or close it out. Without using network forensics techniques, the SOC staff might spend a lot of time gathering and reviewing various sources of information, and after all that time would be limited to the log information contained within the Sourcefire IDS and other devices.

Using network forensics techniques, however, within less than a minute, the SOC team can review the recorded and reconstructed HTTP sessions associated with the alert they received, view the detailed content and context of the alert, and quickly determine that this

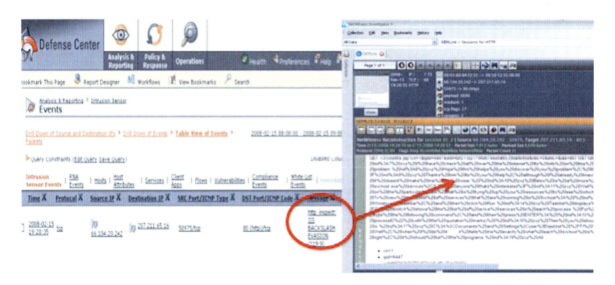

Fig. 7.5 Network forensics content for IDS event

event was indeed a problem. For this type of investigation, network forensics tools and procedures act as a force multiplier for the SOC team, accelerating their work and reducing the uncertainty at the lower tier of the SOC team.[2]

7.2.2 Input Received from Someone in the Organization

The impetus for a network forensics investigation can come from many places outside the SOC team. Regardless of the origin, the same general approach applies: it is essential that the organization captures and analyzes network traffic at critical information pathways to respond to the request. The Internet point of presence is arguably the most important information pathway when dealing with many types of investigations.

For example, suppose someone in the legal department of a public company expresses a concern to the security team that the company's earnings disclosures (confidential "10 K" filings) to the SEC seem to be leaking to the public before general release, thereby affecting stock valuation and potentially creating Sarbanes-Oxley and insider trading issues. A stockholder told the Corporate General Counsel he had seen postings on an "insider tips" group using the e-mail address: jimmy_2_tone@hotmail.com. Assuming that the security team has been capturing all network traffic and focusing on the application layer characteristics in terms of analytics, they can quickly search for any network traffic associated with either the name of the newsgroup or e-mail address in question. Such a search would produce a number a sessions of various types, including Hotmail logins, chat sessions, and other Internet activities. The most interesting sessions, however, show a posting on a Google "corporate.insider.tips" group (Fig. 7.6) by a truncated e-mail address, jimmy_2_...@hotmail.com. The posting appears to contain a 10 K filing.

Assuming the 10 K information only could have leaked from within, it is likely that Mr. "Jimmy 2 Tone" is someone in the company. Using basic network forensics approaches, it is easy to correlate the IP address associated with these outbound sessions to the Google group.

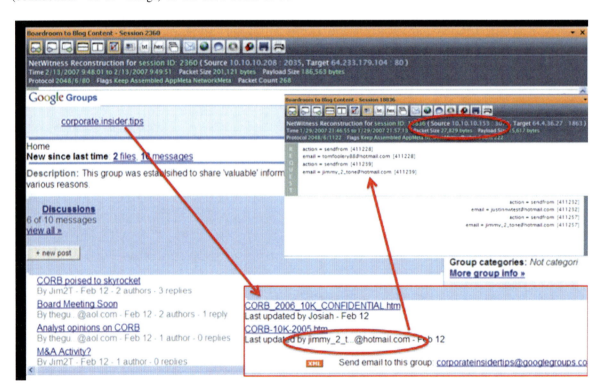

Fig. 7.6 Finding an insider threat

At the time of the posting of the confidential corporate information on Google groups, the person using the e-mail alias Jimmy_2_tone@hotmail.com was working at an internal workstation with IP address 10.10.10.208. Reviewing the network traffic for that device for that day with just a couple of clicks in NetWitness Investigator Freeware, it is easy to observe that a user with Microsoft Active Directory ID "jkenston" (James Kenston) was sitting at the workstation and had printed a confidential document identical the one posted on the Google insider tips group (Fig. 7.7).

With both the evidence that this internal workstation was used to post the confidential 10 K document on Google groups, and that Mr. Kenston's user ID, associated with the identical IP address during the same time period, was used to print the sensitive document in question, additional cyberforensics work such as disk imaging and further log file analysis should be sufficient to close the book on Mr. Kenston and proceed with further disciplinary or legal action.

With that introduction, you now have a sense for the power of network forensics. The next section provides a walkthrough of two different kinds of cases.

7.3 Case Studies

7.3.1 Case Study #1: The "Drive by"

7.3.1.1 Requirements

Imagine the following situation: You work in an environment where the corporate security policy prescribes a zero tolerance for data leakage. The rationale for this policy could be based on a number of business drivers. In this organization, the "data" you are trying to keep from leaking might include some combination of the following, depending upon where you work:

- Customer records including personally identifiable information
- Valuable intellectual property
- Classified national security information
- "Insider" information such as 10 K data or company merger information
- Any other information that has tangible or intangible value to the organization

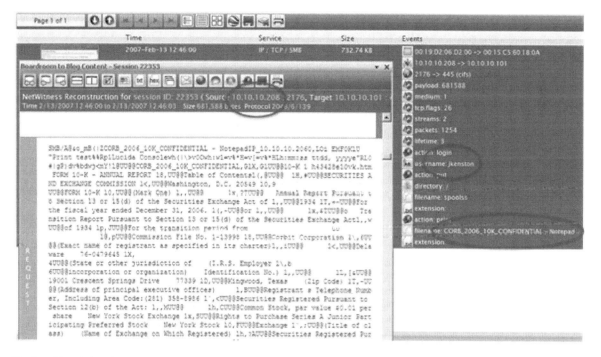

Fig. 7.7 Pinpointing the user

The loss or disclosure of this information may cause harm to the organization and to its people in terms of some combination of dollars, time, lives, or reputation lost. Even if people do not understand the ramifications of the security policy, everyone agrees that these losses would be bad for the organization.

Even though the organization has invested heavily in "data loss prevention" technologies and "defense-in-depth," you have been told by research firms that these point solutions only are 60–80% effective in an ideal world, so your security team is waiting for some unknown "zero-day" bad thing to happen. And, of course, no security policy can completely control the behavior of any organization's end-users. With all this in mind, let's move into the next level:

Assumptions:

1. You have invested in the capability to capture and analyze network traffic 24 × 7 at critical network interfaces in your organization.
2. You have committed your security team to the integration of network forensics into various security processes, including the computer incident response team (CIRT).

Another difference between "old school" network forensics (i.e., packet sniffing and simple capture) and next-generation network forensics is the concept of agility. Once an organization has committed to the use of network intelligence and network forensics in support of security operations, and the deployment of a full packet capture and session analysis infrastructure, the capability can be extended to support many requirements.

Think about the metadata in the cube described in Fig. 7.2. Many of these objects are metadata that can be tracked across the Internet for potential "bad reputations" – either by third-party threat intelligence services, or by your own cyber threat team. For example, domain names of dynamic DNS, file check sums of new malware, or logical combinations of notions such as "if the forensic signature crossing the wire equals a Windows executable, but the file extension doesn't equal a known executable extension (e.g. a GIF file), let me know about it!" Add GeoIP metadata to these "threat feeds" that are mixed with your organization's data at capture time, and the possibilities become fascinating.

The ultimate goal in this "no data leakage" scenario is not to prevent it, because prevention alone is a failing strategy, but to shorten the detection window. Using network forensics and the integration of threat-related metadata, let's review how it would work.

7.3.1.2 Detection and Response

The initial indicator that there is a problem comes from this intersection of the organization's network traffic with the threat feed aggregate. Assuming we have a zero tolerance for communications from devices on the corporate network with a dynamic DNS, if we map the corporate network traffic in real time to all known dynamic DNS domain names and IP addresses, there will be a "hit" any time there is network traffic meeting these criteria.

In this case (Fig. 7.8), there is a sudden spike of 319 network sessions communicating with a dynamic DNS. The CIRT should treat this event as high priority and immediately examine the sessions forensically to determine the context and content of the communications.

Viewing the sessions interactively in NetWitness Investigator Freeware, it is possible to see a broad range of metadata associated with these 319 dynamic DNS sessions. Clearly, training and experience are required to become an expert network forensics investigator, but any experienced CIRT member can use basic network forensics techniques to arrive at important conclusions. In Fig. 7.9, we see that from the metadata alone that the bulk of the 319 network sessions are associated with TCP Destination Port 8090 and a network Service Type with a metadata type labeled "OTHER." Thinking logically and without having to consult other departments, if the sessions associated with port 8090 were part of some normal HTTP proxy, they would render as Service Type HTTP or HTTPS versus OTHER. This conclusion warrants a closer look at the full packet data.

Examining the full packet data (Fig. 7.10) sheds no additional light on the true intent of these communications, except to further confirm that these network sessions are not appropriate. Even someone with no training can see that the sessions on port 8090 clearly are not HTTP/HTTPS and seem to be a series of 366-byte sessions occurring every 15–20 s. The small payload is being sent to an IP address in Shanghai,

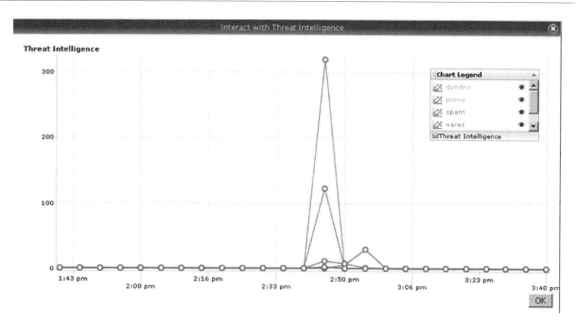

Fig. 7.8 A spike in dynamic DNS activity

China. This network traffic is indicative of the classic behavior of a "Beacon Trojan." The machine is sending a "hello world" message periodically to its controller, letting it know that it is still owned. Of course, this open command and control channel potentially can be used for anything, including additional reconnaissance, software deployment and execution, data transfer, and direct attacks against the organization.

At this point, some questions should come to mind:

- I see the symptoms, but how did this all begin?
- Are there other machines that have similar infestations?
- Is valuable data already leaving the network?

Imagine if you had to sort through log files now to try to answer these questions. Where would you begin if you had 20,000 hosts on your network? Luckily, we are utilizing network forensics, so we can get answers to these questions quickly!

7.3.1.3 Incident Analysis

The previous discovery of the beacon Trojan provided an important clue in this investigation: the IP address of the infected machine. Circled in Fig. 7.10, the IP address is 192.168.221.129. You will recall that this organization performs full packet capture on a 24 × 7 basis at critical network interfaces. Given this advanced network monitoring coverage, the CIRT essentially can go back in time and analyze the historical network traffic associated with this particular workstation in an attempt to determine the moment of compromise. The first step is the isolation of all the network sessions associated with IP 192.168.221.129 for some period.

Viewing the isolated sessions for this IP address in Fig. 7.11, it is immediately clear that the end-user did interact with the workstation and executed a number of HTTP and HTTPS sessions, evident from both the Service Type and TCP Destination meta data types. There also appear to be a relatively high number of JavaScript sessions considering the low number of HTTP sessions, and there are some EXE files that crossed the wire during these sessions. All these issues are worthy of further network forensic analysis.

Examining the reconstructed HTTP sessions in Fig. 7.12, it becomes clear after the first few sessions that the end-user visited a website in China that appeared to be benign but that automatically executed a nefarious obfuscated JavaScript

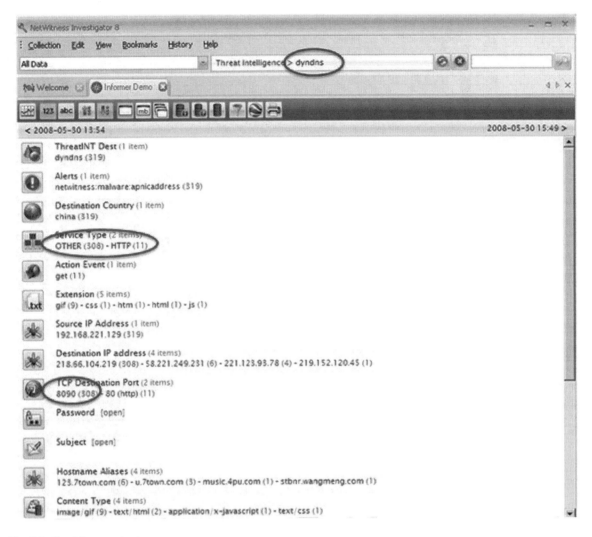

Fig. 7.9 Suspicious service type

sequence in the background, unbeknownst to the user. As indicated in Fig. 7.12, this JavaScript commanded the end-user machine to download and execute a series of executable files under the privilege of the user. One of these executables likely contained the beacon Trojan that triggered this investigation.

7.3.1.4 Resolution

Since this organization is performing full packet capture, the full content of all the executable malware files is available to the CIRT for further testing and analysis. Such testing, which must be performed in a completely isolated environment, generally yields additional information about the nature of the malware and the communications paths it uses. Malware testing should include both network forensics techniques and other techniques described elsewhere in this book such as memory analysis and malware code reverse-engineering. NetWitness Investigator Freeware includes a Google Earth plug-in. In this instance, Google Earth appears to show other geographic network relationships that may require additional investigation by the CIRT.

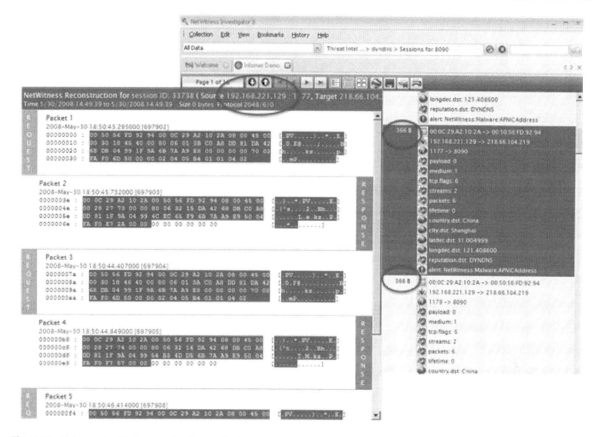

Fig. 7.10 Unknown traffic types and a Beacon Trojan

7.3.2 Case Study #2: Covert Channels, Advanced Data Leakage, and Command Shells

7.3.2.1 Requirements

Network forensics knowledge, processes, and tools are helpful when dealing with covert or unauthorized network communications, complex data leakage scenarios, and command and control exploit situations. In today's cyber war with certain classes of adversaries, the goal of an attack may not be a simple information "grab and run." Many threat agents wish to achieve persistence to perform information operations against your organization that might include ongoing reconnaissance, additional device ownership footholds, continuous data exfiltration, and network traffic analysis. During the past few years, there have been spectacular infiltration and data loss scenarios reported across the government and critical infrastructure sectors attributed to the lack of security team visibility into these advanced persistent threats.

For example, how many organizations closely examine the literal ocean of network traffic flowing over accepted information pathways, that is, network ports that the organization has allowed to do business, such as port 80 or 80xx for HTTP, 443 or 80xx for HTTPS, 53 for DNS, and so on? Today, both legitimate business applications and malware are written to seek an allowed network path if their respective default IP ports are not available. At a high level, this situation creates complexity for the network or security administrator when trying to control traffic simply based on network port-specific approaches. For example, as seen in the forensics analysis in Fig. 7.13, although the firewall administrator may block the standard port for GNUTELLA (6346), deep packet inspection and port

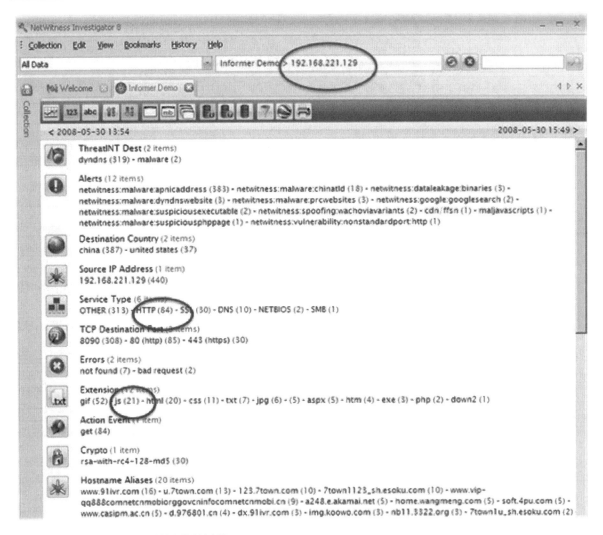

Fig. 7.11 Isolated sessions for 192.168.221.129

agnostic traffic analysis reveals GNUTELLA sessions on other outbound TCP ports. This type of network visibility gap could apply to any peer to peer protocol, whether benign or malicious.

Similarly, in Fig. 7.14, a network forensics-based examination of the traffic flowing across port 443 typically will reveal traffic other than HTTPS, including:

- Chat or instant message services, which may violate security policy
- Skype, SSH, or other disallowed or controlled services and applications seeking allowed pathways
- Tunneling applications such TOR or HTTP anonymizers and proxies
- Unknown or unclassifiable network services ("OTHER") and applications that range from a home-grown application belonging to your organization to a customized communications channel used by malware, a bot, or other intruder

In today's advanced threat environment, it is critical that security teams detect these types of complex problems in as close to real time as possible before additional systems are compromised and information is lost. Once detected, the team should evaluate the appropriateness of the network communications based upon the security policy, desired security controls, and common sense. Network forensics provides the tools and processes for this kind of advanced security operations capability.

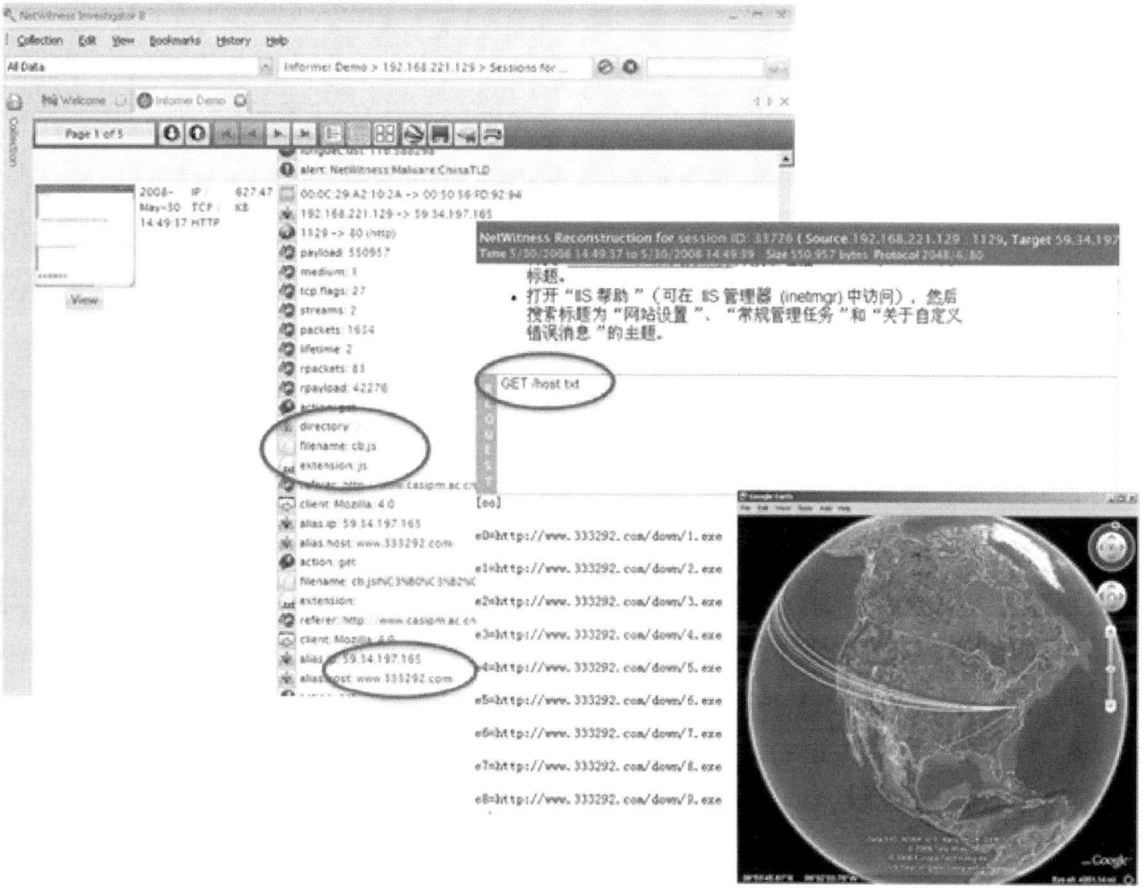

7 Network Packet Forensics

Fig. 7.12 Behavioral analysis reveals malware on the network

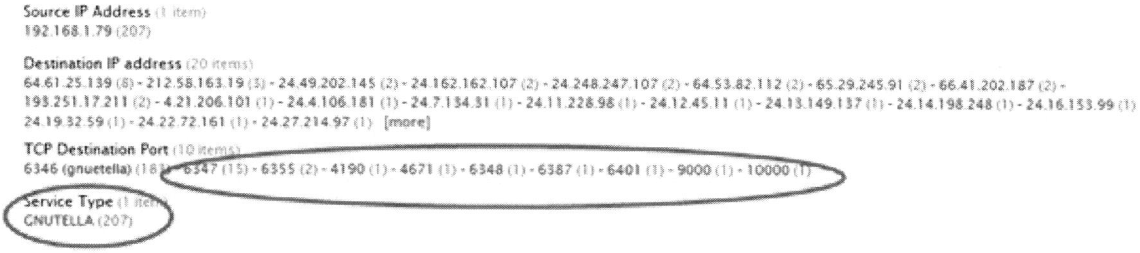

Fig. 7.13 The value of port agnostic traffic inspection

Fig. 7.14 What is running on your common ports?

7.3.2.2 Incident Analysis

Let's assume, once again, that your organization has committed to network forensics and improved network intelligence as a means to improve detection of advanced threats within its information pathways. Prudent security policy and control requirements should specify zero tolerance for nonstandard traffic over accepted ports. As depicted in Fig. 7.15, thanks for pervasive packet capture, the security team is alerted to network activity on TCP port 53 that does not decode as DNS or any other authorized protocol.

As part of its incident response process, the security team should perform additional network forensics steps to determine the content and context of this network traffic. These steps would begin with a review of the sessions involved in this nonstandard network traffic. A quick review at the metadata level in Fig. 7.16 shows unusually large sessions (>500 kb) that are occurring periodically on port 53. These large sessions merit a deeper review by the security team.

Opening the full packet data associated with the large, non-DNS sessions on port 53, and viewing them as TEXT (Fig. 7.17), can often illustrate some unfortunate content. In this example, the attacker appears to running a known command shell across port 53, taking advantage of the open port and the lack of an effective preventive countermeasure.

As with any command and control channel of this type, this backdoor can be utilized by the attacker for a number of nefarious purposes, including: enumeration and shutting down of defensive services (e.g., firewall, anti-virus) on the device, transfer and installation of additional program code, incremental data exfiltration, and additional exploitation attempts or remote control of other assets on the organization's internal network.

7.3.2.3 Resolution

The augmented situational awareness provided by full packet capture, session analytics, and port agnostic session decoding permits the incident response team to easily identify the covert network communications of the command shell. The security team must follow the

Fig. 7.15 Nonstandard network traffic on port 53

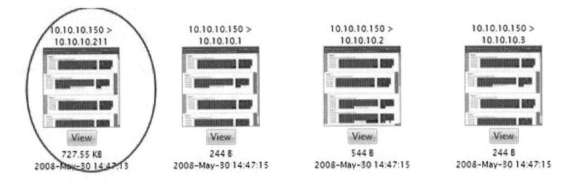

Fig. 7.16 An extra-large "DNS" session

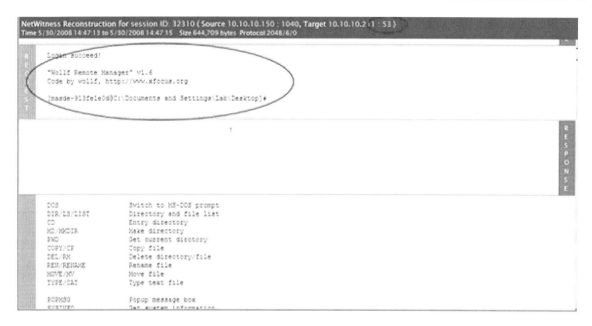

Fig. 7.17 Not DNS, but a backdoor

network forensics investigative track discussed earlier in this chapter and go back in time to find the root cause of the problem. As seen in the prior case study, assuming the organization has been performing pervasive full packet capture, there are numerous clues and actions that can be used to determine whether this command shell entered the system through a network attack or vulnerability, if there are other affected devices, and the impact of this entire incident to the organization.

7.4 Future Trends and the Way Forward

There are two trends worth mentioning to close out this chapter: the emergence of network forensics as a mainstream process within enterprises, and the rise of anti-forensics techniques in the network arena.

7.4.1 Network Forensics Becomes a Mainstream Process

NIST Special Publication 800-86, the "Guide to Integrating Forensic Techniques into Incident Response," discusses the benefits of different types of data sources as part of the incident response process. Chapter 6 specifically recommends the use of network data as part of both the forensic and incident response processes. This table, sorted from lowest to highest information value, summarizes key components of this discussion with the author's comments and opinions.

Within most organizations today, some subset of these technologies exists to support the security incident management process. Leading organizations are putting this information to work as part of a holistic corporate network forensics capability and are retooling internal incident response processes. The goal of sensors and event telemetry always has been to generate what is known in military circles as "situational awareness." For corporate information security teams, situational awareness provides some useful view of the cyber battlefield that helps us understand what the attackers are about to do and to take defensive measures. Network forensics aids this view in two ways:

- Generating unique alerts: as discussed throughout the chapter, unique information is obtained using network forensics techniques and tools regarding advanced threats and complex attacks vectors.
- Enrichment of existing security technologies: legacy security technologies provide indications and warnings (I&W) of potential security problems. Network forensics offers the final truth and confirmation.

Data source	Description
Firewalls	Overwhelming amounts of log data with little context, but can provide useful event data when used within a SEIM and in concert with full packet capture and network forensics reviews
Intrusion detection systems (IDS)	Often the first indicator of a problem for known exploits. Can produce false positives and is constrained by signature libraries
NetFlow monitoring	Network performance management and network behavioral anomaly detection (NBAD) tools. Indicators of changes in traffic flows within a given time period
Security event and information management (SEIM)	Correlates firewall, IDS, and other network and security event data and improves signal-to-noise ratio. Is valuable to the extent that data sources have useful information and are properly integrated
Real-time network forensics	Collects the richest network data. Provides a deeper level of advanced threat identification and analysis and traffic reconstruction. Augments and enriches the value of alerts from all the data sources above

(Rows ordered from Lowest to Highest)

As network forensics becomes a mainstream security operations process within enterprises and integrates with existing incident management and overall risk management activities, organizations will achieve situational awareness of advanced threats and powerful events "continuous augmented awareness" of advanced threats and potential events that could cause harm to the organization and its people.

7.4.2 The Continued Rise of Antiforensics Techniques

The notion of anti-forensics is nothing new in the world of host-based forensics. However, in recent years, there has been a growing trend on the part of sophisticated adversaries to both successfully avoid detection and to obfuscate their tracks pervasively during network attacks. It is certainly in the interest of network-based attackers to avoid detection because the longer they can stay connected to a victim network, the longer the potential period of command and control, network reconnaissance, data exfiltration, or other types of potentially damaging or malicious activities.

For many security experts working in the incident response arena, attack scenarios that include log file tampering, IP spoofing, protocol tunneling, and other obfuscation techniques are nothing new. What is different, however, is the realization on the part of attackers that leading organizations are using real-time network forensics to detect advanced threats and that their attack techniques must appear even more normal to avoid initial detection.

Obvious attempts to defeat detection by pervasive network forensics systems include DDOS attacks or other type of exploits in which the real intent of the attack is hidden within oceans of meaningless or noisy traffic. Fortunately, such blunt techniques usually are easily detected and can be filtered in many cases and parsed in others. There also has been concern relative to the use of tunneling, anonymous routing, and encryption as deterrents to session analysis and detection of inappropriate network activity. Although some of these evasion and obfuscation techniques potentially inhibit some of the visibility gained from network forensics, security teams still benefit greatly from many unique dimensions such as traffic and protocol analysis.

A more crafty approach to avoid both basic and advanced network security monitoring would be to create attacks that most closely resemble normalcy and that introduce additional dimensions of detection complexity. For example:

- Use a common website to obtain command and control instructions (such as pulling a news article and using the text in the article as an algorithm to generate instructions)
- Communicate using 100% RFC protocol compliance
- Randomly communicate with the mother ship, in both time sequence and methodology of communication, mimicking user behavior patterns
- Be a true zero-day and single compromise code base
- The command and control would occur in the geographic area of the target and use a common top-level domain for that area versus some suspect country or region
- Use peer-to-peer communications to avoid a single point of failure

When faced with advanced threats using a combination of these attack vectors, it is only through pervasive, enterprise-wide network forensics that detection and mitigation have a high likelihood of success. In the end, the rise of both advanced threats and anti-network forensics techniques will create an even greater focus on network forensics as both a critical enterprise information assurance technology and a deep technical skill set required within security organizations.

Notes

1. What is full packet capture? At its most basic, full packet capture means "sniffing" the corporate Ethernet or Wi-Fi connection, recording every single packet to one or more hard disk drives at line speed. Sounds simple enough, but there is a lot more than meets the eye. The bandwidth can start at 100 Mbps and reach well over 10 Gbps at a large organization at critical choke points such as core switches and Internet points of presence. Once you have collected 100 terabytes of network traffic, the real challenge has little to do with capturing the traffic and mostly is associated with creating useful analytics that support your organization's security objectives and use cases.
2. This author strongly advocates the use of pervasive full packet capture and session analytics both as a next-generation network security monitoring capability and for organizations wishing to employ network forensics to detect and mitigate advanced threats. A 24 × 7 approach to full packet capture requires an investment in an enterprise network data collection infrastructure.

   If you are new to network forensics, however, and wish to get a sense for the benefits to your organization, there are numerous freely available tools. This table contains some of the best freeware tools, varying across a spectrum of capture and analysis capabilities, as well as in ease of use.

Name	Information and download	Purpose	Notes
NetWitness Investigator	http://www.netwitness.com/	Capture live network sessions and/or import PCAP and TCPDump files. Deep analysis from layer 2 to layer 7	GUI is easy to use and very powerful and provides full session reconstruction, rules-based alerting, and third-party data integration
ngrep	http://ngrep.sourceforge.net/	Provides a grep-like function for analysis of previously captured PCAP and TCPDump files	Command-line interface, difficult to use
sguil	http://sguil.sourceforge.net/	Aggregation of network session information including logs full packet data for data mining	Can integrate data sources including Snort and NW Investigator
tcpdump	http://www.tcpdump.org	Basic writing of packet data from a network interface to a file	
CACE Wireshark	http://www.wireshark.org/	Formerly Ethereal. Capture network traffic, perform packet-level protocol analysis	Useful for packet level analytics, once you find what you are looking for

Chapter 8
RAM and File Systems Investigations

Rita M. Barrios and Yuri Signori

Rita Barrios is an expert in digital forensics, access controls, and secured software development. She has 20 years of Information Technology experience, and is currently an Assistant Professor at University of Detroit Mercy, a National Security Agency Center of Academic Excellence. Following Ms. Barrios' move to the University, she became the program and research manager for the creation and implementation of a DoD-funded knowledge base called the National Software Assurance Repository (NSAR), which houses research from government, industry, and academia on Information Assurance. Ms. Barrios has many years as a senior database administrator, senior application developer, technical project lead, and project manager in the financial and transportation industries. She has participated in all phases of the software development life cycle including requirements gathering, specification, development, testing, and implementation. Her research interests include database intrusion detection and prevention systems, access controls, and the insider threat phenomena. She has published on application data integrity, database security, and on the state of Information Assurance understanding within industry and academia.

Yuri Signori is the President and Lead Analyst for the company that he founded, I-PingU, LLC (i-pingu.com). His company specializes in data forensics, data investigations, data recovery, and human Imaging Services. Yuri Signori started his interest in information technology in 1988, and over the years worked in most major areas of IT until he narrowed his specialty to Information Assurance and Data Forensics. He holds a double master' degree and was a research fellow for University of Detroit Mercy for the Centre of Assurance Studies. Yuri Signori has also taught IT courses for the University of Detroit Mercy.

8.1 Investigation Characteristics

During the investigation process, it is often assumed by those working in the information technology (IT) side of the spectrum that it is only those who possess the technical skills who should be involved. This assumption is false. During the course of an investigation, the IT and legal communities must partner to work together in order to acheive the goals of the investigation.

We operate under the assumption that, unless we are trained as criminal investigators, the IT community does not hold the skills necessary to conduct an effective and legal criminal investigation. The person(s) under suspicion still has to have the standard motive and means regardless of the type of crime. Additionally, the suspect must also be put at the scene of the crime. Only those trained in law-enforcement with specific skills such as investigation techniques, interviewing, and criminal behavior can effectively achieve the desired results without compromising the case. The digital investigation is a team effort where the legal community partners with the technology community in which each performs their specialization.

Working in the "live" investigative environment is a volatile endeavor. To understand this environment, we must define what is meant by the term "live."

R.M. Barrios (✉)
Assistant Professor, University of Detroit Mercy, National Security Agency Center of Academic Excellence, Detroit, MI, USA

The term live, in this context, means that the investigative methodology takes place while the system is still up and running. What this means is that while the investigator is capturing the volatile data as found in RAM (Random Access Memory) as well as temporary system files, these areas of storage may be changing along with the actions of the investigator. Because of the nature of this type of environment, the investigation methodology employed must take care to not destroy the evidence while the capture of information is accomplished. Also, the nature of this environment means that once a machine is shut down, all memory data will be lost. Therefore, the investigator must be sure to take all the volatile data at the point of the live capture. This point is further expanded and clarified in the following paragraphs.

In any investigation, it is important for an investigator to keep a detailed timeline and observations; this is done in part to help the investigators to remember the sequence of events when the need arises during the court presentation, but also to ensure that the investigation proceeded in a methodical and professional manner. Nowhere are the timeline and corresponding documented observations more important than in an investigation on live data. By virtue of working with live data, the investigator is in effect altering the state of the system, so the investigator must prove that the alterations that occur during the investigative process did not contaminate the evidence sought. If contamination does occur, the investigator must also be able to document the contamination as well as to assess the impact of the contamination on the strength of the case. To this end, the detailed timeline and sequence of the actions of the investigator, as well as the systems reactions, must be kept up to date on a minute-by-minute basis. The individual observations of the progressive steps should include detailed descriptions of each action taken by the investigator, including the beginning and ending states of the systems as well as who on the investigative team performed the action.

One cannot say enough about the need for incredibly detailed, precise documentation during the digital forensic investigation. After all the evidence has been captured and analyzed, it will be the documentation that is presented to the judicial body which allows for decision as to the guilt or innocence of the suspects(s).

These documents become the official court record and must be understood not only by the IT specialist but also by the judicial team, which includes the judge, lawyers, defendants, prosecution, and perhaps even a jury made up of a vastly diverse group of individuals. Few in this group of individuals can be assumed to understand information systems. It is because of this reason that the documentation must be clear, concise, and complete, with no gaps presented in the flow of the investigation.

It is also important, in any investigation, to identify who will be responsible for the various tasks of the investigation as well as who will start the timeline of the capture to establish the starting point of this segment of the investigation. Again, nowhere is it more important to document the assignment of accountability than in an investigation into volatile data. Given that we are operating in an environment where the evidence is not physical but virtual and that it holds a high degree of risk in the loss of evidence, we must ensure that each step that is taken during this phase is fully documented with both the beginning and ending dates and times. So, it is imperative to immediately assign accountability for the evidence capture.

When seizing the volatile data of an electronic device, one must remember that it is imperative to capture all the data regardless of whether it has been specifically called for in some management directive or search warrant. The reason for this is that the data, by nature of the temporary state of the device, will be eliminated once the machine is shut down. Therefore, if we were to capture only a portion of the data, then discover at a later time that we needed more, the data being sought after would no longer be available. Therefore, best practices in digital investigations tell us that we must always capture *all* the volatile data at the time of seizure, regardless of its content.

The overall goals of an investigation that encompass the capture of volatile data such as that found in RAM and temporary files may or may not be centered on this investigative approach. It should be noted that the investigation of volatile data capture is only one piece of the digital investigative process and does not assume that the capture of the volatile data will either prove/disprove an investigation but must be taken into consideration with the entirety of the whole case.

8.2 Investigative Approach

8.2.1 General Data Acquisition

The following sections give a view of what can be found in memory as well as a brief overview of the Windows and Unix file systems. It should be noted that this is but an introduction and one should seek out in-depth studies in each of these areas.

8.2.1.1 Volatile Data Versus Nonvolatile Data

The difference between volatile data and nonvolatile data is that volatile data is classified as those data elements that reside in the temporary areas of the digital device whereas nonvolatile data are those data elements that persist on the physical hardware of the device, whether that is on a hard disk or a memory stick.

As noted previously, once the system has been shut down, the volatile data is lost because RAM (main memory) is cleared upon that action. One way to look at this is that RAM is temporary in nature. However, this situation also provides reasons that volatile data may be considered more trustworthy than nonvolatile data. It is an absolutely necessary component of the complete state of a system at the exact time the capture is taken, and it is extremely difficult to "fake" in a consistent manner.

Volatile data can include, but are not limited to, the following items:

- System date and time
- Current network connections
- Open ports
- Logged-on users
- Running services and processes
- Scheduled jobs
- Open files
- Operating system-specific areas as identified next

8.2.1.2 Unix Versus Windows

When investigating a Unix versus a Windows operating system (OS), there is considerable difference in the mapping of the two operating systems and where the various kinds of information can be found. The differences that have a bearing upon this chapter are noted in the following paragraphs.

The Process Hierarchy – When a UNIX process is created, it becomes the child of the creating process whereas a Windows OS does not share the hierarchal relationship without deliberate simulation of the UNIX mode, usually by maintaining the process id and handle of the creator.

Daemon Versus Service – Unix uses daemons, which are processes that are started upon system boot. These typically run as privileged users and provide services to other processes and do not typically interact with users. Windows, on the other hand, uses services that may or may not be started upon bootup and run in the background, with or without special privileges. Simliar to the daemon, the services do not typically interact with the user but are controlled by the Windows Service Control Manager. Windows tends to be more heavily dependent upon threads as opposed to child process generation. A thread is a construct that enables parallel processing within a single process.

Multiple Users – In a Unix system, when a user logs on, a shell process is created to service that user. The Unix operating system keeps track of multiple user-level shells and the associated processes for each. In a Windows system, the GINA (Graphical Identification and Authentication) dynamic link library creates the initial process for the user and is known as the user desktop, to which only that user has access. Generally, other users are not allowed to be logged on to the computer at the same time without the employment of Terminal Services.

Security – Both operating systems authenticate users by ID and password; however, in Unix, the user must be locally identified via a user ID [even though that ID may be supplied via a Network Information System (NIS) or pluggable access module (PAM) domain]. The minimum information by which UNIX will identify the user is the name, password, and group. In the Windows environment, the user may be known locally, via the Windows domain, which is a logical grouping of computers that share common security and user information, or the Microsoft Active Directory service, which provides for an centralized system to automate the management of resources within the distributed environment. The Windows domain contains only the user name, password, and some user groups, whereas the Activity Directory contains the same information as the domain, and optionally may include contact information for the user, organizational data, and the certificates. Additionally, the Unix system utilizes a simple security model in which the operating system applies security by assigning permissions to files because the Unix system uses files to identify devices, memory as well as processes. When a user logs onto Unix, as noted previously a shell is started with the user identifier (UID) and the group identifier (GID) for the user. From this point on, permissions assigned to the UID and the GID control all accesses to the files and other resources. Under Windows, security information is maintained for users in memory, where security context is represented by data generated at each logon session, and objects such as files and folders may have security attributes that are compared with the security context of the logged-in user who attempts to access them.

Consideration of differences in the behavior of operating systems is essential to understanding data captured in a live response. At the heart of an investigation into volatile data is an understanding of the differences in the way the operating system manages the volatile data elements. In-depth operating system knowledge will influence the investigators' actions as they decide where to look for data and how to progress the investigation.

8.2.2 Virtual Memory

In literature on computer systems, we often see the term "virtual memory"; however, it is often misunderstood to only encompass the memory currently being processed by the central processing unit (CPU), or in line to be swapped into the CPU, that is, the "swap" file. Virtual memory is simply a method of extending the main physical memory [a.k.a. Random Access Memory (RAM)] of the system to include both RAM and the swap file. Virtual memory is utilized in both the Windows as well as Unix systems and is not stored by the operating system when the system is powered down.[1] In both operating systems, utilizing a 32-bit architecture, 2 gigabytes (GB) of private virtual address space is assigned to each process in the user/process address space. Similarly, the operating system has an allocation of 2 GB that is referred to as the system address space, or OS memory. With the advent of the 64-bit system, this allocation is raised to 8 terabytes (TB). It should be noted that during a memory dump the paging file may not be included. Care should be taken to ensure that the paging file is acquired along with the RAM allocations to ensure the complete picture of virtual memory.

8.2.2.1 RAM (Random Access Memory)

RAM is also known as "main memory." This is the section of computer memory that maintains the operating system programs, application programs, and data that is in use by the system and is subsequently lost when the system is powered down. The sum total of bytes used in a user session may actually exceed the reserved capacity. When the RAM buffer fills up, older data is replaced with newer data so that, in effect, RAM never fills to capacity. The system may run slower because of the need to refresh RAM with data pulled from the physical hard drive, but typically it does not run out of space.[2]

On the opposite side of the spectrum is ROM (Read Only Memory). This acronym usually refers to data that is always retained on the same physical media, even when the system is powered down. It typically contains a small amount of programming to allow the OS to load the same thing into RAM upon every start-up. ROM is typically found on the microchips that are physically mounted upon the motherboard and is standard on all devices capable of computer-like functions such as PDAs, cell phones, printers, fax machines, and copiers.

As previously noted, during the investigative process, RAM should be captured along with the other data objects of interest using the necessary hardware and/or software to do the information capture. Many items of interest are often stored in RAM in clear text (unencrypted) format, which may include passwords, keys, various types of transactions, account numbers, etc. Additionally, as discussed in Chapter 6, malware can exist in RAM; therefore, if RAM is never captured, that is a lost opportunity for the investigator.

8.2.2.2 SWAP File

As already noted, a swap file is instantiated as a file on the hard drive that is used in conjunction with the RAM allocations to function as a "page" of the machine's virtual memory, which expands the capabilities of RAM. Swap files are used by RAM to "swap" out the data contained within RAM that is not currently being used by the system. When a file is "swapped" in, the computer goes out to the swap file and retrieves that information to be brought into RAM for usage. Other items currently in RAM may be "swapped" out to hard drive space if there is not enough RAM available for both the recalled information as well as what currently resides in RAM. It should be noted that *anything* in RAM may be swapped out, including passwords and logins. Data fragmentation refers to the state that occurs when the swap (paging) file is allowed to temporarily expand beyond its defined boundaries to other areas of the disk. What this means is that there is a possibility that what is captured in the swap file during the acquisition process may not be a full picture of the swap data, because the overflowed temporary expansion allocation is often released back to the availability pool at the next reboot – another reason why we must capture the volatile data before the system is powered down.

8.2.3 File Systems

In the following sections, we cover the basics on the methodology of how data is stored on a hard disk. As is commonly known, when a file is stored, it is stored in blocks of storage called sectors and the size of the sector is usually specified during the installation of the operating system. A typical sector is 512 bytes of data as identified below. As such, when a file that has a length of 536 bytes is stored, it in effect uses 2 sectors, or 1,024 bytes; however, only 536 bytes are actually used. The remaining bytes in the second sector create a form of residual space called slack space (Fig. 8.1).

The interesting information about this area of disk space is that it may actually contain data from files that were marked for deletion which can be captured during the data acquisition process.[3] Slack space can be found at the end of files, sectors, clusters, and disks as well as in RAM. In the case of RAM slack, it is created as a result of RAM data being used to fill the buffer before the hard disk write. As with file slack, if the data being written to RAM does not completely fill the cluster, there may be residual data to be utilized in an investigation.

8.2.3.1 Windows File Systems

The Windows Operating System supports two types of file systems.[3,4] The file systems that are supported and are detailed in the following paragraphs are FAT (File Allocation Table) and NTSF (New Technology File System).

FAT (File Allocation Table) was originally used with DOS (Disk Operating System) and is delivered in three different versions that are identified by the number of bits used to identify a cluster. FAT12 is the earliest version of the FAT file system. This version

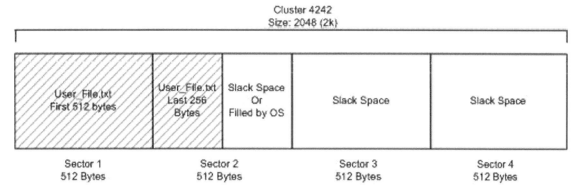

Fig. 8.1 File slack space within a cluster

allows 4,096 clusters per partition with the maximum partition size of 32 MB. Windows 2000 uses FAT12 for floppy disks and for partitions less than 16 MB. In contrast, FAT16 supports volumes of 65,536 clusters with an expanded cluster size to 128 sectors and a maximum volume size of 4 GB. FAT32, which was introduced with Windows 95, uses 32 bits to identify a cluster with the last 4 bits reserved; this allows a volume to contain nearly 270 million clusters. Windows 2000 manages larger volumes, but it limits the size of FAT32 volumes to 32 GB because data processing is inefficient beyond this limit.

NTSF (New Technology File System) is the native file system for Windows NT 4.0, 2000, and XP. As a departure from the FAT-managed system, NTFS is a log-based file system that addresses FAT's reliability and recovery concerns. Partitions are numbered sequentially using a 64-bit logical cluster number and a default cluster size depending on the size of the partition, which is 4 KB for anything more than 2 GB but can be overridden by the administrator. In contrast to the FAT system, an NTFS partition is divided into four sectors: the partition boot sector, Master File Table (MFT), File System data, and finally a backup copy of the MFT.

In the Windows environment, everything is identified as either a file or a directory and is laid out in a hierarchal-type file structure. The file system supports file names of up to 255 characters and can be composed of all characters except for the reserved characters of ?, /,\, ",:, <, >, |, and *.

8.2.3.2 Unix File Systems

The Unix file system is composed of four types: Ordinary Files, Special Files, Directories, and Links.[3,4] Ordinary files contain text, data, or program information. However, ordinary files cannot contain another file or a directory. Directories are the containers that contain pointers to files as well as other directories. In Unix, a directory is implemented as a file that contains a line of data for each file within the directory. This line of data contains the file name, a numerical reference to the file's location, which is known as the i-number and is the reference to the index to a table known as the i-list. It is this i-list that is the complete listing of all the storage space within the file system. Input/output devices are identified by special files. Special files can be character or blocked. If blocked, sizes can be allocated in either 512, 1,024, or 2,048 bytes. Finally, there are links, which are no more than named pointers to another file.

A file is accessed via its own block special file. These files are kept in a special database called the file system table, which is usually located in the /etc/fstab directory. Information included in these entries includes the name of the device, the directory name, and the read/write privileges for the device.

Similar to the Windows OS, Unix implements a hierarchal file structure in which the root directory is the top of the hierarchy. The files can be up 255 characters in length and are case sensitive. Files are located by specifying the file's path from the root.

8.2.4 Data Acquisition

There are two methods of acquisitions available to the investigator: the software acquisition method and the hardware acquisition method. The software acquisition method requires software to be run against the target system such as Guidance Software's Encase or Access Data's FTK as well many other types of utilities and open source solutions. In the hardware-based acquisition view, PCI or PCMICA cards as well as Firewire devices are available that do not require any additional software and are OS independent. It would not be a fair statement to say which methodology is better in the investigative process, as each investigation presents its own unique set of circumstances that have a direct impact on which methodology to use.

8.2.4.1 Steps in the Acquisition Process

As with any type of process in a forensic investigation, the investigator should have a defined, solid set of processes and procedures for the acquisition of volatile memory.[5] This practice ensures that during a potentially chaotic environment the investigator can be assured of an effective, safe investigation where mistakes are less likely to happen, such as changing the data on the targeted system. Before the investigator is called to do an acquisition, care should be taken to test the defined processes, procedures, and controls to ensure that they are in working order. The following is an example of a set of steps that can be used during the acquisition of volatile data. It should be noted that the steps in the acquisition process should be kept to be a few as possible because all actions on the computer under investigation present a degree of risk to the data under scrutiny.

1. Begin the documentation process and be sure to include ALL steps, no matter how small or insignificant the step may seem. As noted previously, this log will become part of the catalogue of evidence that may be presented to a court. In addition, it will give the investigator a historical reference point as to the process that was used in the particular case.
2. Determine if the system is in a locked state. If it is, the investigative process may have to be augmented to include the determination of the password or other authentication mechanism. If authentication cannot be obtained, this is a case in which a hardware acquisition technique would be preferred to a software one. However, unless the hardware acquisition technology is designed for the specific type of device under scrutiny, attempts at live investigation may be compromised.
3. DO NOT change the state of the system by shutting down windows, programs, connections, or anything else. If these processes are shut down, the state of the system (volatile memory) will be changed and potentially vital information will be lost. This change could also compromise the investigational objectives.
4. Acquire the volatile memory areas using the tools (software and/or hardware) necessary for the type of investigation presented. This acquisition is known as creating an image of the volatile memory. If using software tools, the objective is to change the system as little as possible; therefore, smaller memory usage tools are more desirable. Any memory used by the tool may replace memory currently in RAM, which is the target of the capture. It is incredibly important to document this step to its fullest at every action, including identification of the software footprint of the tool being used for the memory acquisition. The term "footprint" of a software component is used to indicate the physical characteristics of a file such as its size and the file names as well as the operating system's resource utilization. These characteristics help to uniquely identify the various software components encountered during the investigative process.

8.2.5 Analysis Approach

To begin the analysis phase, the investigator should make several copies of the newly acquired image of the volatile memory area. The rule of thumb is that one should never perform analysis on the original image unless there is absolutely no other way to perform the investigation. It is acceptable in e-Discovery to present evidence using a copy of the original evidence; this is known as the original copy.

Analysis begins with the identification of the operating system including its version number, the file structure in use running processes, open ports, and current users (including any passwords). Most software acquisition tools will provide this information in the form of a standard acquisition report. Once this information has been obtained, analysis often proceeds via a series of string searches and file carvings (image reassembly) to discover the evidence being sought using established tools and procedures. Only the most sophisticated investigators will attempt to perform image reassembly using methods created on the fly. These methods are beyond the scope of this chapter.

As with any software endeavor, verification and validation of the analyzed data must occur to ensure the evidence being produced is accurate. An effective way to accomplish this is to use more than one tool to do the analysis. The rule of thumb is that if two competing tools produce the same results, it can be said that the evidence is valid and has been verified.

8.2.6 Deliberately Hidden Data

One of the more interesting abilities of the digital forensic investigator is the ability to locate data that has been purposely "hidden" from the general user, or even the administrator, of a computer system. For various reasons to be uncovered by the progression of the case investigation, a suspect may attempt to hide data by placing the data physically on the hard disk or by hiding the data within another file such as an image or sound file. Within the following section, an overview of some of the common methods of data hiding is presented. This section does not cover software hiding in the operating system, as that was covered completely in Chapter 6.

8.2.6.1 Hidden in the Computer

Slack Space

A commonly known method of hiding data is accomplished by physically writing the selected data to the slack space of a formatted hard disk. As previously noted, slack space is that space that is left over at the end of a file, sector, cluster, disk, and RAM that typically contains remnants of deleted files.

The distinct advantage to hiding data in the slack space is that the host file is unaffected by the additional data; therefore, the additional data is easily transparent to the operating system and the file structures. The disadvantage is that this data is often found with simple forensic tools that capture disk images.

Because the slack space at the disk (volume) level is characterized by the space from the end of the file system to the end of the partition where the volume resides as that space which is not allocated to any cluster, the size of the slack space at the disk (volume) level is dependent upon the size of the disk and can be changed by the user at will. File, sector, and cluster slack space, however, is fixed in nature and cannot be altered. To analyze the volume slack one should start by analyzing the file system of the suspect machine utilizing a utility that examines the disk. Should any errors present themselves, further examination for hidden data should be warranted. Checks to the number of sectors allocated to the partition, the file system as well as the boot sector, should also be performed to determine if there are any inconsistencies. If there is more than one sector of slack space present, further analysis is warranted.[3]

File slack is the unused space between the end of the file and the end of a cluster, which can be one of two types, RAM slack or drive slack. RAM slack is found at the end of a file and continues on until the end of a sector (sector 2), while drive slack (sectors 3 and 4) is found from the start of the next sector to the end of the cluster, as shown in Fig. 8.2.[3] Because the analysis of file slack is dependent upon the operating

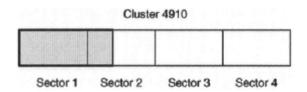

Fig. 8.2 RAM and file slack

system given that the OS decides how to handle slack space, one must take the function of the OS in consideration. For example, the Windows operating system pads RAM slack with 0 s and ignores drive slack when storing a file; therefore, any non-0 bit in RAM slack warrants further examination.

Bad Clusters

A bad cluster is simply a cluster of disk space that is unusable by the operating system and therefore (using current disk technology) is usually remapped to extra sectors so that the operating system is not aware of them. Because bad clusters can be arbitrarily created by a suspect simply by setting the bad cluster flag, the amount of "bad" clusters available to hide data is limited only to the size of the disk. Theoretically, the whole disk could be marked as bad. It is in these "bad" clusters that data can be hidden with little effort and therefore is not visible to the OS because it does not read the bad clusters.

Given that most current technology disk drives handle the remapping of bad clusters, it can be a simple process to determine whether there is hidden data by simply taking note of any marked "bad" clusters. To validate whether a cluster is truly bad, one should run a disk surface scan utility to determine whether the bad cluster is valid. Should the analyst suspect there are arbitrary bad clusters; an effort must be made to analyze the cluster for hidden data using data extraction and carving techniques. It should be noted that if the data is stored randomly in multiple locations or if the file signatures (header and/or footer) are removed, it may become impossible to reassemble the file.

Additional Clusters

With the utilization of common utilities, a suspect may allocate additional clusters to a file to allow for the storage of hidden data. Because the allocation of the file is limited only to the disk space, the suspect can freely allocate as much storage as is needed. The disadvantage of this method is that as the file is modified the hidden data may be lost as the file increases. Using disk analysis utilities may warn the investigator as to the presence of altered file allocations as errors might be generated. Also, systematically comparing the actual file sizes with the allocated file sizes may uncover the possibility of alteration.

8.2.6.2 Hidden Within a File

Steganography is the science of hiding information whose goal is to simply hide as opposed to make unreadable as is done with cryptography. Two of the most common forms of steganography are embedding information into an image or sound file and watermarking. It should be noted that cryptography is often used in conjunction with steganography and should be addressed, if needed, during the investigative process.

Embedding

To begin the discussion on embedded information, one needs to first understand how images are stored. Images are simple binary files where there is a binary representation of color for each pixel of the image. A typical 24-bit color image has a 24-bit color representation per pixel that is represented by 3 bytes of data, 1 each for red, green, and blue (RGB). The size of the image then corresponds to the number of pixels in the image and its associated granularity of color. A typical 1,024 × 768 24-bit image would equate to a file about 2.36 MB (1,024*788*3 bytes). As GIF and BMP files employ a lossless compression scheme, meaning that the software can exactly reconstruct the image, it is more common to see embedding of information in these types of files. If we use the Least Significant Bit approach to embedding, we simply take the binary representation of the information and overlay the least significant bit of each byte within the image. With the 24-bit representation of the image, the change would be minimal and virtually undetectable with simple viewing. Steganography is often accomplished using a variety of tools that are available on both the commercial and open source markets. These tools tend to

be relatively simple to use as well. Conversely, current forensic imaging and analysis tools often can discover and reconstruct the embedded information with relative ease.

Watermarking and Fingerprinting

In the scenario of copyrighted property such as intellectual property or multimedia, steganography techniques known as watermarking and fingerprinting have become commonplace in an attempt to protect the property from pirating as well as to be able to detect when an illegal copy is publicly in use. In this case, using the embedding process as described in the prior section, the copyright or serial number information is purposefully embedded into the protected file. In a situation wherein the investigator is seeking to discovering whether illegal use of copyrighted property has been successful, the investigator would intentionally seek out the proper steganographic information in these files as evidence to the case.

8.3 Case Study

The following case study was contributed to this chapter by Yuri Signori, founder and CEO of I-PingU Investigations (www.i-pingu.com).

8.3.1 Background

An IT and data hosting company had under its employ an IT Manager who had became very unhappy with his job. The company, which we shall call XYZ Corp., had hosted a number of sites to house client organizational applications that encompassed a variety of business purposes.

XYZ Corp. had legal contracts and service-level agreements with each of its clients that focused on the security of their data, uptime, availability, and all metrics associated with providing business data in an accurate and reliable manor. The IT Manager, whom we shall name Fred, was given free reign and access to all the equipment hosting this data, as it was his responsibility to see that the everyday operation was in accordance with all service-level agreements (SLAs) and contracts.

As days passed, animosity grew between Fred and XYZ Corp. because of Fred's performance. It would later be discovered that Fred had a history of unusual and bizarre incidents between himself and his previous employers that involved lawsuits, theft, and blackmail.

One particular day, Fred did not show up for work. The assumption was that Fred was taking yet another day off for an alleged sickness or personal excuse. Business ran as usual that day until just about the end of the business day when a call came to Barney, XYZ's president.

Fred informed Barney, with no hesitation, that earlier in the week, he had taken all onsite and remote backups of all the data for XYZ Corp. and their customers and unless Barney agreed to pay him the exact amount of $10,000, he would destroy all the backups. Moreover, Fred had also removed the data from the servers of XYZ Corp. during that week to ensure that they would have no means to recover the stolen data.

Being that Barney was a man of principle and felt strongly that a greater cause was at stake than the $10,000 or the data, he immediately called the police and the company attorney. The police obtained a warrant and confiscated all computer equipment from Fred's apartment. As criminal charges were being brought against Fred, the prosecuting attorney needed enough evidence to show that not only did Fred steal all copies of XYZ's data, but hopefully to show that he had criminal activity evidence on his personal home equipment.

8.3.2 The Investigation Process

The police had been provided access to all Fred's equipment to substantiate the presence of XYZ's data on his personal equipment. The police investigative team performed the initial image of the machine's volatile data areas before shutting down the machine using sound investigative practices. This initial image included currently running processes, applications, open ports, and users currently logged onto the system. Given that the law enforcement agency obtained the initial image of the volatile data, XYZ was advised by their attorney to obtain a third party data forensics specialist to acquire and examine the hard drive data as well as to investigate the volatile data image; this was advised so that an objective third party would report any findings as evidence to ensure that no slant could be drawn on the findings. If XYZ had conducted the investigation themselves by using the images previously created, the defending attorney could indicate that the data had been tainted because of personal dislike toward Fred.

The company contracted with an external law firm to hire an external forensic specialist. The specialist's approach to gathering evidence followed this process:

1. Obtain written permission by the police and XYZ Corporation to investigate the equipment.
2. Use court-validated toolsets during the investigation. The tools used in this investigation included:

    (a) Digital camera
    (b) DriveMate – USB 2.0 hard drive cable
    (c) External USB 260 GB disk drive
    (d) Software:
    - PowerISO Professional
    - AccessData – Forensic Toolkit
    - X-Ways – WinHex Professional
    - Paraben – Email Examiner
    - Paraben – P2 Explorer
    - FastLynx
    - Several DOS 6.22-based hard disk utilities
    - Several RedHat Linux-based hard disk utilities
    - Boxer Text Editor
    - WinDiff
    - WinGREP
    - SnagIT Pro

3. Follow practices for any forensics investigation:

    a. Make sure that the site is not tampered with.
    b. Photograph all equipment being investigated.
    c. Record serial numbers of all external and internal devices.
    d. Create a case file electronic and hard copy.
    e. Record all tools being used, and in cases of software tools, the version.
    f. Show that the data was processed in an environment that was free from virus contamination.
    g. Extract an image of all hard drives and then make copies of the images, leaving the original drives and original image untouched for future examination.

h. Analyze the data.
i. Present all findings.

The key, as emphasized in the approach section, is to leave the original site untainted while gathering as much raw data as possible. As this information was going to be used in a court of law, the prosecuting attorney would draw his own conclusions and formulate questions for cross-examination during the trial. The end result in presenting any uncovered data had to prove two things to show that the investigation was done in a sound manner:

1. The data being presented had not been tampered or changed in any way during the investigation.
2. That the defendant was not being discriminated against. It is imperative that the investigator only presents the facts of the case with no opinion interjected as this may lead to the presentation of a biased case.

The data analysis in Step 3 h was an in-depth search using court-approved toolsets to uncover hidden files, undelete e-mail and deleted files, and uncover possible hidden data and text. This case was unusual as all the case data found was readily available, had no password protection or encryption of any kind, and could be read using applications that come preloaded with Windows XP.

The results of the data analysis are displayed in Table 8.1. The first column in Table 8.1 lists the data that the forensic analysis team found noteworthy even though they were given no specific direction as to the types of information they might expect to find. The second column in the table indicates whether the investigators expected to find data of the type identified in the first column.

Note that the external forensics recovery team never provided any opinion as to the content of the information they found. Such judgments are the job of the investigator. The data forensics analyst is only to report what is found with as much detail as possible.

This example makes clear that the focus of the data forensics investigator differs from that of a private investigator as a private investigator has a license to allow him or her to draw conclusions that show wrongdoing even before a conviction, in many cases, specifically for the purposes of getting a conviction.

It should be noted that neither the outcome of the court case, nor the identities of Fred, Barney, and XYZ Corporation, were disclosed to the investigative organization and its associates. From the point of view of a data forensics examiner, it is enough success to know that after case evidence is submitted, that further communication is made, as historically this is an indication that the case evidence is complete, is unarguable, and that it served its purpose.

The suspect had been identified, his personal computer confiscated for data forensics study, but what was not specified was the data being sought. The direction was to look for missing data that had been taken from XYZ Corp. The nature of data is that copies are frequently made for backup purposes. Just to find data that had been deleted from XYZ Corp.'s servers could simply mean that as the IT Manager, Fred was making extra backups. Keeping in mind that the only criminal action could be imposed on Fred was a phone call in which he had verbally made the threat of blackmail by specifying that he would destroy the missing backup media from XYZ Corp if his demands were not met. The phone call could have easily turned into a he said/she said scenario, and the recovery of the backup media could have been explained by a claim that he was taking the media off site for any number of reasons that would seem reasonable for an IT Manager with his responsibilities. The prosecution felt strongly that finding the backup media, a copy of the data on the suspect's home computer with the fact that all data had been erased on XYZ's server, and the record of the phone call, would provide sufficient evidence for a case. Additionally, a civil litigation action could be initiated against the defendant for malpractice if XYZ Corp. decided to pursue further actions.

The rest of this investigation was no different than any standard criminal investigations. Data forensics is, after all, one type of criminal forensics methods. If a warrant is issued by the police to find evidence for a murder, for example, and during the process they find illegal weapons, narcotics, or any other evidence of foul play, then that could lead to an entirely new case and prosecution. In this case, once all the equipment being seized was examined, it was the job of the data forensics analysts to simply report all data that was found on the computers. The investigating body in this case had permission to search all data and use all the methods needed to ensure that anything hidden could

Table 8.1 Result of data analysis in case study

Data discovered	Anticipated discovery (did we anticipate finding the data based on the case background?)	Where the data was discovered (volatile versus nonvolatile)
XYZ Corp.'s business and customer data	Yes	Nonvolatile
Images of XYZ Corp. blank checks	No	Nonvolatile
Home pornography	No	Nonvolatile
Letters of criminal intent	No	Nonvolatile
e-mails of criminal intent	No	Nonvolatile
Random Internet blog information regarding check printing	No	Nonvolatile
Bookmarks: - Web pages regarding hacking - Web pages regarding check fraud - Web pages regarding case studies for lawsuits - Web pages regarding wrongful dismissal cases - Statistical web sites for a number of topics	No	Nonvolatile
XYZ Corp.'s HR data	No	Nonvolatile
Several of XYZ Corp.'s software titles pirated and installed on Fred's computer	No	Volatile and nonvolatile
Documents based on Internet queries containing information on various XYZ employees. Information found was indicative of searches based on employee names returning any random information available	No	Nonvolatile
Pictures of Fred with slightly bruised eye. Text on the pictures read comments such as "1 day after Barney hit me, 2 days after Barney hit me, etc..."	No	Nonvolatile
Scanned images of the signature of Barney, the President of XYZ Corp.	No	Nonvolatile

Data Discovered During the XYZ Corp. Investigation.

be revealed regardless of the method. The important point is that the forensic specialist could never express opinion to as to what the data was or why the suspect would hide it; only that there was an opinion that there was hidden data in technical terms in a data forensics context. The forensic specialist team was advised that if the law enforcement agencies had specifically made a request, the team could use a previous case as a comparison if one were available to identify similar circumstances that lead to the determination of the findings.

8.3.3 Conclusion

The investigative team's conclusions with respect to Fred based on common sense and observation of the data artifacts suggested the following:

1. Never anticipated that the police were going to seize his personal computer equipment.
2. Was an individual looking for fast cash.
3. Was likely to be:

   a. Entertaining the idea of participating in misdemeanor and felonious activities.
   b. Engaged in misdemeanor and felonious activities.
   c. Planning the execution of misdemeanor and felonious activities.

4. Had a demonstrated history of filing preconceived law actions based on premeditated and arranged circumstances.
5. Was an inexperienced criminal, with very little "professional" or "experienced" criminal execution.
6. Anticipated that Barney and XYZ Corp. would have paid the $10,000 dollars given that XYZ Corp.'s customer data was stake.
7. Calculated success based on odds rather than a plan or contingency for different outcomes.

8. Premeditated ulterior motives when he was hired by XYZ Corp. and that perhaps he had been attempting actions such as these for years.

8.4 Issues and Trends

8.4.1 Issues

8.4.1.1 Usage of Standards

One of the most heated debates within the field of digital investigations is the lack of standardized methodologies and competencies. Until recently, there really were no set standards of qualifications that the well-qualified digital investigator must possess. Typically, the test of qualification is whether the person possesses the standard batch of the popular certifications, which tend to be focused on the use of the popular acquisition and analysis software suites. It is because of this lack of standards that many states are imposing private investigator licensure requirements before digital evidence can be "officially" presented in the judicial setting.

As of 2009, the industry's recognized groups, The Sans Institute, High Tech Crime Consortium (HTCC) and The International Society of Forensic Computer Examiners (ISCFE), formed a council of digital forensics specialists whose goal is develop industry standards in this regard. This direction was taken as a direct response to various states agencies requiring that digital investigators be licensed as a private investigator to present digital evidence.[6] As noted by these groups, the physical investigation methodologies and skill sets as found in a typical private investigator's capabilities are not necessarily the same as those required for digital evidence investigators. Additionally, in 2008, NIST (National Institute of Standards and Technology) set out to work on three projects that focused on categorizing software, forensic tool testing, and providing reference data for the forensic investigator.[7]

Currently there are many open-source investigative tools on the market, which makes digital forensics a more cost-effective activity for the small/medium business endeavor. As noted by Brian Carrier in 2003, the reliability of an open-source tool must be tested by applying the Daubert guidelines, which focus on testability, error rate, publication for peer review, and acceptance by the community.[8] In a response to the need for testing digital forensic tools for reliability, NIST began a project in 2008 (CFTT, Computer Forensic Tool Testing) to establish a methodology for testing computer forensic software tools via the development of tool specifications, procedures, criteria, test sets, and test hardware. Although this may not negate the need for Daubert, as the test will still have to be presented as evidence to the courts, using the NIST CFTT standard will enable a more stabilized methodology and provide sustainable proof via the documented processes for the creation of tools that will meet Daubert's objectives.

8.4.2 Trends

8.4.2.1 E-Discovery

Discovery is the phase in the legal process in which both parties are required to submit to each other the information and records pertaining to discovered evidence related to the case.[9] This step ensures that both sides in the litigation have a fair representation of the evidence to either prove or disprove the claims made in the court documents. In 2006, an amendment to the U.S. Federal Rules of Civil Procedure codified the requirements to provide electronic information and records, which is known as Electronically Stored Information (ESI). This amendment coined the term *Electronic Discovery* or, more commonly, *e-Discovery*. In the e-Discovery realm, documents include, but are not limited to, word processing documents, electronic spreadsheets, e-mail, audio, and video.

In this type of digital investigation, the investigator is working directly with the legal community to determine what items of interest must be included in the capture/analysis phase. As noted earlier, it is common practice to capture all the information in both the volatile and nonvolatile areas of the system even if it is not clear what evidence is to be obtained, which is done to keep access to the original evidence at an absolute minimum. It should be noted, however, even though all the information will be available to the investigator, only those data components as outlined in the search warrant are permitted to be included in the final analysis of the evidence. If the investigator is unsure of the scope of the information he or she is to collect, he or she should consult with the legal and law enforcement teams for guidance.

8.4.2.2 Anti-forensics

The concepts of anti-forensics presented itself shortly after the onset of digital forensics came onto the investigative scene. To put it simply, anti-forensics are countermeasures to successful usage of the current kit of digital forensic tools that threaten to render the investigation legally unsound. It is believed that for every forensic tool there is a counter tool that will impede its utilization during an investigation. Anti-forensics are tools and techniques that focus on limiting the identification, collection, collation, and validation of electronic data. The goals of these tools, when talking about the investigative process, are to enable the suspect to avoid detection, disrupt the data collection process, and cast doubt on the evidence report.

Because of the increased usage of such tools recently, all digital evidence tends to be questionable as to its validity. What this means is that there will be direct impact on the e-discovery phase of the investigation. Also, anti-forensic tools make it very difficult to find the suspect's footprints in the system and make it almost impossible to prove that the investigator actually did find the suspect.

Some popular anti-forensic tools include the following:

- Timestomp, which can alter a time stamp
- Transmogrify, which allows changes to the header record of files as well as the extension, making it almost impossible to determine whether the file actually is what is purports to be; Slacker is a tool that breaks up a file and stores its pieces in the slack space of files
- Sam Juicer retrieves encrypted passwords but leaves no footprint of its execution; KY inserts data into null directory entries
- Data Mule attacks the reserved space on hard drives
- Ramdomizers generate random file names to avoid signature-based inspections

As can be seen, the usage of these tools makes the investigation incredibly more difficult by the mere fact that one will not know what is valid and what is not, which, as noted previously, leads to the questioning of all digital evidence obtained.

As suspects become more sophisticated, the usage of anti-forensic tools will continue to rise. The investigator must not only be aware of how to do a successful standard investigation but also how to look for and understand the usage of anti-forensics tools and techniques.

Notes

1. Like any bit pattern on digital media, fragments of bit patterns are occasionally recoverable with sophisticated forensics on chips or hardware itself, but such discussion is beyond the scope of this type of investigation.
2. Of course, if the program being loaded is too large to fit in the reserved area, it could, but this topic is outside the scope of this chapter.
3. Carrier, Brian, *File Systems for Forensic Analysis,* Pearson Education, Inc., 2005.
4. Microsoft TechNet, *Interoperability and Migration Guide*, 2009. Retrieved from http://technet.microsoft.com/en-us/library/bb496474.aspx
5. Jones, Keith J., Richard Bejtlich, Curtis W. Rose, *Real Digital Forensics: Computer Security and Incident Response*, Pearson Education, Inc., 2006.
6. http://blogs.sans.org/computer-forensics/2009/04/06/digital-forensics-professionals-might-be-required-to-become-private-investigators-via-new-licensing-amendments-in-north-carolina/
7. See www.nist.gov – *Digital Forensics at the National Institute of Standards and Technology*, 2008. Retrieved on October 31, 2009.
8. Carrier, Brian, *B Open Source Digital Forensic Tools: The Legal Argument*. Retrieved from http://www.digital-evidence.org/papers/opensrc_legal.pdf
9. Mack, Mary, *A Process of Illumination: The Practical Guide to Electronic Discovery*, 2008. Retrieved from http://www.fiosinc.com/livefiles/1/586/Fios-eBook-A-Process-of-Illumination.pdf

Chapter 9
One Picture is Worth a Million Bytes

Don Fergus and Anthony Agresta

Don Fergus has spent more than 30 years in senior roles at national and international telecommunications, financial services, consulting, and public sector organizations. A pioneer in IT risk mitigation and digital forensics, his experience includes international audit, IT governance, product development, international risk management, and global banking sector and data exchange and security standards.

Currently, Fergus is the Vice President of IT Risk Management and Chief Security Officer at Intekras, Inc., where he manages a Cyber Forensics Lab replete with the most progressive data storage, analysis, and monitoring systems available and a team of cyber security specialists supporting a range of government and commercial clients.

Fergus has held the positions of Vice President at Lowers & Associates, an international risk mitigation firm, of Managing Partner of TriVision Partners, a management consulting and training firm, of Enhanced Services Project Director, Business Development & Technology Planning Chief of Staff, and Senior Product Counsel at MCI, and of Vice President, International Communications at Citicorp/Citibank. Fergus is an expert in international communications and data exchange. He served in Geneva at the UN/Economic Commission for Europe, in Brussels as the President of the International Data Exchange Association, and in Paris at the International Chamber of Commerce.

Anthony Agresta has more than 25 years of experience in senior roles with organizations focused on analytics software technology used in a variety of applications including cyber analysis, fraud and intelligence analysis, predictive analytics, business intelligence, and customer relationship management. Agresta is a Vice President at Centrifuge Systems, a provider of next generation interactive analytics technology. He has held the position of Chief Operating Office at DataX, LTD, Consolidata, and Mobile Sciences Knowledge Group, three Selling Source companies that focus on real-time identity verification services, internet list management compilation, and mobile communications, respectively. Agresta was vice president of worldwide product marketing and sales engineering at SPSS, a worldwide leader in analytics technology. Before SPSS, Agresta was a Senior Director at Siebel Systems where he worked on Siebel's marketing automation and analytics product lines.

Earlier in his career, Agresta served as vice president of product marketing and product management at Paragren Technologies where he worked closely with product development, sales, and technical services to enhance Paragren's marketing automation and analytics suite. Agresta launched his career creating estimates and projections for small-area Census and Postal Geography. He has a Master of Arts in Demography from Georgetown University and a Bachelor of Science in Foreign Services from Georgetown University.

9.1 Investigation Characteristics

Every year, the U.S. Department of Homeland Security celebrates *National Cyber-Security Month*. This effort highlights steps being taken by government agencies

D. Fergus (✉)
Vice President of IT Risk Management and Chief Security Officer Intekras, Inc., Sterling, VA, USA

to educate citizens on guarding against cyber-threats at home, work, and school. To kick off a month of cyber-security awareness, the Department of Homeland Security (DHS) Secretary announced the Department's hiring of 1,000 cyber-security experts and professionals. The cyber-security roles will include cyber-risk and strategic analysis, cyber-incident response, vulnerability detection and assessment, intelligence and investigation, and network and systems engineering.

"This new authority will enable DHS to recruit the best cyber-analysts, developers and engineers in the world to serve their country by leading the nation's defenses against cyber-threats," said the secretary. "Effective cyber security requires all partners – individuals, communities, government entities and the private sector – to work together to protect our networks and strengthen our cyber resiliency."[1]

This effort highlights some important characteristics that are needed in digital forensic investigations: analysis, detection, intelligence, and collaboration. Data breach investigations typically involve massive amounts of data. Virtually every device connected to the Internet generates a sea of log data, intrusion detection alarms, firewall alerts, anti-virus warnings, and/or network traffic. The situation is worsened at the enterprise level, where terabytes of security data and millions of alerts may be produced daily. Sifting through very large data sources requires technology to transform the raw data into information and then turn that information into knowledge. Communicating with the ecosystem that Secretary Napolitano references is essential.

Data access, analytical tools, and experience in cyberforensics represent important characteristics of any digital investigative approach. Collaboration is another attribute that warrants considerable attention. A recent cyber-security recommendation to a U.S. Senate Committee notes that four common themes emerged from the research completed. The report lists the first theme as follows:

"A coordinated and collaborative approach is needed. Cyber security research and development efforts in the US must be better coordinated; only through information sharing and collaboration can effective solutions emerge."[2]

This theme holds true for the collaborative side of information sharing. If digital forensic analysts can share results quickly, they can force-multiply their efforts, and this applies to both inter- and intra-organizational collaboration. Through cooperative efforts, this approach can extend across international boundaries to solves cases faster.

While there are a myriad of straightforward processes, techniques, and tools for detecting a data breach (alarms, notifications, and performance degradation), post-incident assessment of a successful cyber-attack can be very complex. The assessment of an attack's impact and its extent is important in determining what was affected and from where the attack originated. Equally important is the understanding of how the attacker was able to penetrate the system(s) and, by applying that information to plans for protection measures, preventing similar attacks from occurring.

Anomalous communication patterns are, of course, useful indicators of system/network intrusions. However, a major problem investigators face is being able to correlate data across various host/network boundaries to see how network connections and running processes on a host are interrelated. To handle today's security and threat landscape, we need new analysis methods.

Criminal activity is moving up the network stack, with an increasing amount of attacks being executed at the application layer. In addition to analyzing network-related data, incident responders must make sure they are taking an in-depth look at application data. However, because of the vast amount of data requiring analysis, more advanced methods are needed. Information visualization of multiple data sets can help address these complex data analysis problems.

If an attack affects only one host and is executed locally on the machine, visualization does not really add much to the investigator's ability to conceptualize what occurred. However, as is more likely, today's attacks are executed across the network and involve multiple machines and databases. In this case, visualization can help shed light on the attack details, can assist in determining where attackers are located, can demonstrate how an attacker was able to penetrate the network perimeter, and can display the set of systems with which the attacker came into contact. These are just some of the capabilities that an investigator can use to perform analytics.

Interactive analytics (IA), a form of information visualization, is one approach that has proven to be helpful in understanding and communicating attack details. It places digital forensic analysts at the center of data breach investigations and empowers them to explore data. IA combines three techniques that can be used in forensic analysis: Interactive Data Visualization, Unified Data Views, and Collaborative Analysis. The more sources of data IA is used to analyze, the more readily can investigators identify those responsible for cybercrime.

Data gathering begins the process of any digital investigation. At the outset of a data breach investigation, pertinent log files (gathered from intrusion detection systems, firewalls, systems, and routers/switches, etc.) are collected. The forensic investigator's primary goals are to (a) isolate the attack and (b) determine the attack's source and methods. After identifying potential attackers, all the activity performed by these "entities of interest" is analyzed. However, given the urgency by which an investigation must be performed, quickly correlating data becomes a challenge for the investigator. This is the defining characteristic of an investigation that requires interactive analytics.

Success is tied to a fundamental premise: when knowledgeable cyber analysts trained in detection and investigation are given the freedom to quickly explore relevant data, faster and more accurate identification of evidence results.

So, what has been missing from current approaches? To date, these analysts have not been able to quickly integrate disparate data sources and create a more complete picture of the breach. Collaborative analysis allowing law enforcement and others to share analytical results has been elusive.

The imperative is straightforward: arm forensic analysts and network security professionals with technology and data to expose the totality of evidence behind cyber-breaches. This chapter describes how digital forensic analysts, network security professionals, and investigators can explore data at the speed of the human mind. It discusses how the application of interactive analytics can be applied to cyber-security problems, focuses on the three principal components of IA, and demonstrates how IA can be used to analyze disparate data sources in a unified way. The net effect is increased accuracy associated with a positive identification of cybercriminals and their methods.

9.2 Investigative Approach

Interactive analytics is well aligned with these initiatives. It includes three main components perfectly suited to detect and identify a cybercrime. The characteristics of IA are these:

1. Interactive data visualization
2. Unified data views
3. Collaborative analysis.

9.2.1 Interactive Data Visualization

Interactive data visualizations means that analysts can interact with rich visual displays of data. As they analyze these pictures, they identify insights that lead them to explore the data in different forms. They may decide to filter the data, create and incorporate new measures in the analysis, and "spin off" (create subsets of data) for a more focused approach.

Interactive data visualization allows forensic analysts to "shift their lens" from one visualization to another. For example, sorting all the data in a table view by payload for e-mail attachments can tell you the source and destination Internet protocol (IP) addresses that are experiencing the largest payload sizes. Maps showing the geographic locations of the source traffic can be generated, as can timelines showing the timing and intervals between network traffic. Charts can be used to uncover the magnitude of the problem by summarizing the number of times destination IPs or servers have received unusually large payloads. Finally, link analysis can be used to visualize linkages between computers from which e-mails have been forwarded. "Shifting your lens" is a powerful component in cyber-security analysis. It is important to note that any single visualization cannot be used to fully explain a cyber-breach, but, when analysts can quickly navigate from one visualization to another, the insights can be remarkable.

9.2.2 Unified Data Views

The volume and velocity of data coming from multiple sources can be overwhelming. Some of this data is automatically stored in the enterprise's data warehouses. Much is not. Third-party sources, both public and private, can provide valuable insights but can further complicate the data landscape. The scope of a single investigation can include any type of data imaginable, from deep packet inspection to spreadsheets residing on desktops. There is no limit to the number of sources of information that may need to be analyzed.

If the forensic analyst has access to all relevant information, she or he can use it to expand the visual canvas. Painting a complete picture (a "360-degree view" of cyber-activity) can dramatically improve the chances of identifying criminal activity. This is where the power of unified data views comes into play. Why is this so important? As the analyst uncovers important insights through interactive data visualization, new questions come to the forefront of the investigation. For example, if an investigator is analyzing suspicious network traffic using IP address, communication type, and payload and port activity, she may want to shift to determine the state or country from which this traffic is originating. Reaching into a second data source that links IP address to states and countries would allow the analyst to perform this level of analysis on demand.

Connecting to the new source from within the analytical software application ensures that the investigator does not lose sight of key findings. By ensuring that the "train of thought" is not broken, cybercrime investigations can be solved much faster.

As a cybercrime investigator, imagine if you could quickly reach into large repositories of name, address, and contact data that also happen to have source IP addresses assigned. Imagine if you were able to successfully match this data to your suspicious network activity. Even with a fairly low percentage of matches, you may identify an important suspect.

Unified data views go beyond data integration to include accessing real-time services such as identify verification services, Internet searches, access to document repositories, URLs, e-mails, social networking sites, and more. As a result, unified data views is an essential component in the investigative approach.

9.2.3 Collaborative Analysis

The idea of collaborative analysis is not new. Essentially, a collaborative system supports location-independent shared analysis of data and extends the physical workplace of participants in a virtual environment, while preserving traditional textual and verbal communication and cooperation. Collaboration's basic aim is to improve productivity and quality.

Collaboration in digital forensics is crucial to the success of an investigation. Evidence must be shared and consistently understood by any number of administrators, technology managers, lawyers, third-party forensic specialists, private investigators, law enforcement officers, and prosecutors. By maintaining a constant, uninterrupted level of analysis, cases can be solved in a much shorter timeframe. Additionally, through controlled collaboration, specialized analysis of forensically preserved data can be achieved while preserving the chain of custody.

Applying this concept to IA, the instant sharing of case data can reveal investigative insights that can be further analyzed across a forensic team. In addition to viewing an artifact or graph, collaborators gain visibility into the entire analytical process, which can lead to swifter conclusions. The result is an investigative effort that can leverage the collective domain knowledge of internal and external forensic specialists to improve efficiency and accurately identify attack activity.

9.3 Case Study

9.3.1 Case Background

In this case study, an international social networking site focused on building communities, sharing knowledge, and e-commerce has experienced a dangerous cyber-breach. Customer service received a series of complaints from customers indicating their accounts have been compromised. They reported that usernames and passwords may have been illegally obtained through a phishing scam. In the scam, customers clicked on an e-mail that appeared to come from the social networking site. The link appeared to bring them to the social networking site, but instead redirected their network traffic to a page that malicious perpetrators had designed to capture the users' confidential password information. Apparently, the unsuspecting members were asked to re-key their usernames and passwords but did not recognize that the data was being keyed into a fictitious website. They had been misled to re-enter the information in forms that looked identical to approved login pages.

More alarming is the fact that accounts of these customers had actually been accessed by someone who had stolen their passwords. Membership communications has taken place illegally, and unsuspecting members were engaging in on-line conversations with individuals whom they believed they could trust. Clearly, time was of the essence. Warnings were immediately posted on the site, and data breach response analysts had immediately been tasked with identifying the cybercriminals. To do this, they needed to quickly and accurately analyze network traffic, private and public data, and expose the "hidden truth" behind this cyber-attack.

With interactive analytics as their chosen method of investigation, the analysts needed to identify the scope, or *dimension,* of the breach and collaborate with law enforcement to stop a malicious ring of cyber-thieves from attacking a larger section of the membership community. Without a swift response, the problem could escalate and the entire site was at risk of being taken down. Negative media exposure loomed in the background if this problem was not solved quickly.

9.3.2 Connecting to Data and Profiling Network Traffic

The site kept all records of all user login activity in a database. The forensic investigator reviewed the most recent login activity by accessing this login data set. Figure 9.1 shows that a connection has been made to a data source. This login data was used as the starting point for the investigation.

As illustrated in Fig. 9.2, using the data set, the investigator can quickly see the usernames for the accounts that have been accessed. Notice that she also has access to source IP address, source organization, payload, communication type, and other data attributes. All this information is presented in a highly interactive format. The investigator can filter the data, sort the table, rearrange columns to simplify analysis, and search for specific accounts based on the country of origin or state of the source IP address.

The interactive analytic tool was also used to display relationship graphs to uncover important linkages between any of the data, which then can expose other risks that require further investigation. In Fig. 9.3, a relationship graph is used to visualize the links between source and destination IP addresses as well as source and destination organizations. Notice that a

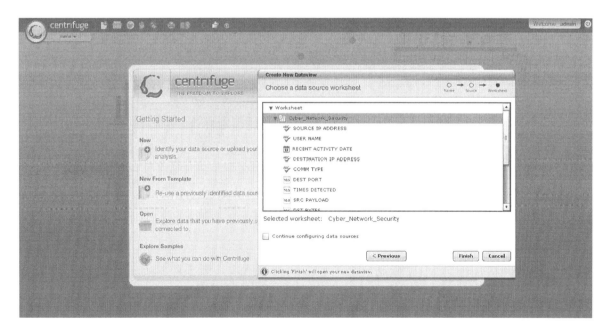

Fig. 9.1 Connecting to important data sources

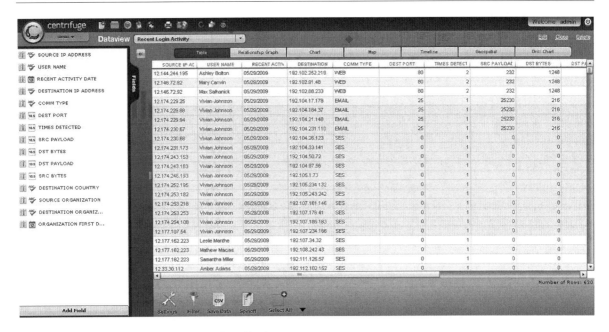

Fig. 9.2 Profiling login activity using interactive table views

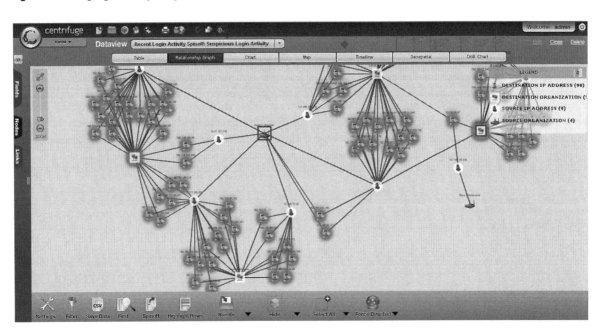

Fig. 9.3 Relationship graph shows linkages between user account IP addresses and source IP addresses. Organization information is also shown as part of the graph

series of destination IP addresses (highlighted in highlighted) along with several destination organization are experiencing a high level of network traffic activity. This traffic could have been legal activity but it did prompt additional investigation.

The investigator then summarized the number of times individual accounts had been accessed from a single IP address, and some hot spots emerged. In Fig. 9.4, the numbers on the right summarized the number of times that single accounts have been

9 One Picture is Worth a Million Bytes

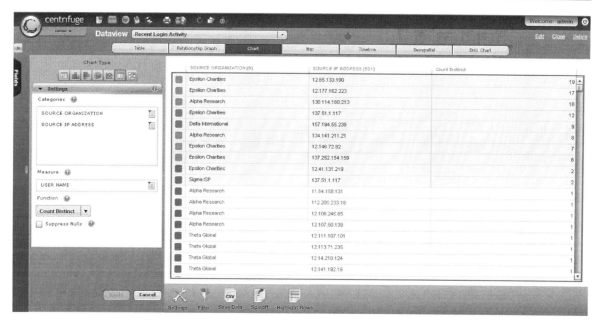

Fig. 9.4 A matrix chart summarizing user account access (cell) from specific source IP addresses. As this is very recent activity, the investigator is surprised at some of the high numbers

accessed from the same IP addresses. Also listed are source IP addresses, the source organization, and the type of communication. Based on the domain expertise of the investigator, this account access appeared to be unusual.

A timeline view (not shown) was also used to indicate that the suspicious source IP addresses were accessing the same accounts within very short time intervals. The timeline view also showed that the session time for each session was quite short, which was unusual for the user community.

9.3.3 Connecting the Dots to Identify Cybercrime Suspects

At this point, the investigator brought additional data into the analysis in an attempt to match source IP addresses to individuals. She used a private data source, which is a national database of 240 million unique consumers along with IP address, name and address, phone, e-mail and other contact information. This database was compiled and is constantly updated by a commercial partner. The original source of this data is individuals applying for products and services online; they complete forms and supply contact information in return for free products. A match on this database does not mean that the people identified in the database were the attackers, but it may mean that the people may have been using the same computer, or perhaps are physically close to the ones involved in the attack. Although strong privacy policies are a part of this third-party data source, users grant the right to use this information in an investigation under specific conditions. Investigation of cybercrime is a situation that meets these conditions. Interactive analytics allows forensic analysts to quickly incorporate this data into the visualization process.

Figure 9.5 shows the investigator adding in the new data to the site's login data sets. Interactive analytics automatically determined how the two sources should be mapped together and presented this to the analyst. After this data source had been added, it became instantly available for use in the investigation. Figure 9.6 shows the data in the actual analysis. Notice the gray shaded new fields on the left. Since "state" is part of this new data source, the investigator now has the ability to map source IP address locations. The darker areas are the states where most of the activity is originating.

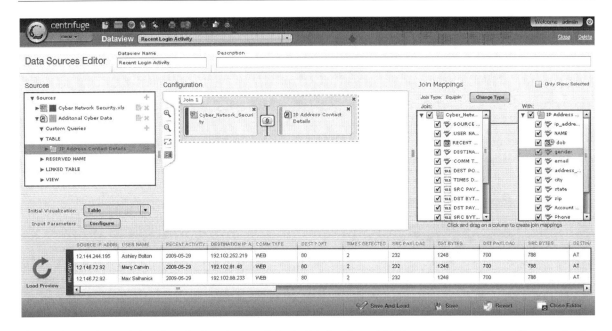

Fig. 9.5 Interactive analytics allows the investigator to bring in data "on demand." This approach saves time while expanding her visual canvas and broadens the investigation

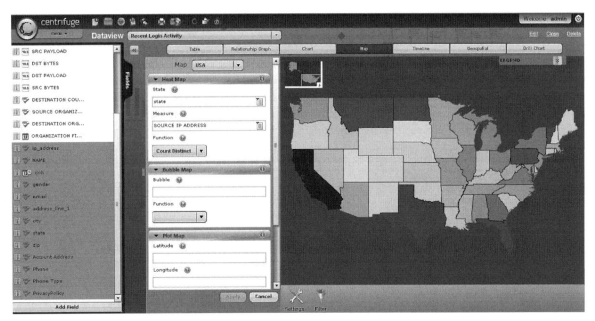

Fig. 9.6 New data available for profiling is in gray on the left. The investigator visualizes the source IP addresses totals by state. There is a concentration of activity in California, Texas, Florida, and Virginia. Also available for analysis are name, e-mail, geographic address, and phone. The investigation is coming into focus

Armed with this new information, the investigator expanded the relationship graph (shown in Fig. 9.7). The NAME of the individual attached to the source IP address in the private source database was brought into the graph. This was linked to the USER NAME field in the login data (that is, the name of the member

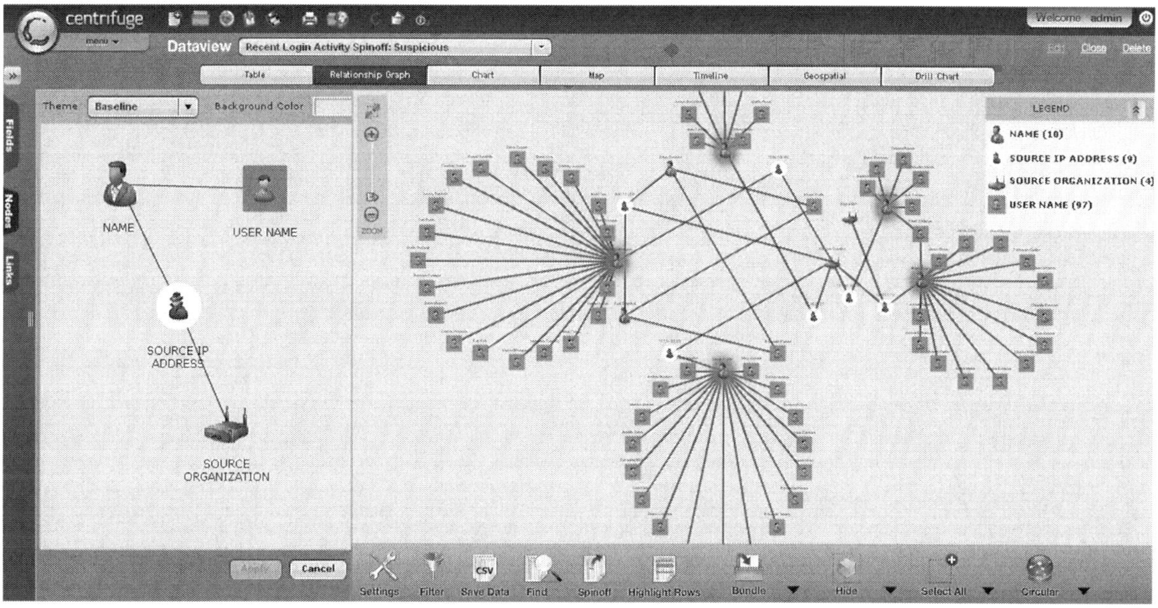

Fig. 9.7 The investigator has identified individuals who have accessed many user accounts. While this is possible, it is very unusual

for the social networking site). Notice that, in Fig. 9.7, a handful of names (highlighted) are linked to many USER ACCOUNTS.

The investigator zoomed in on some names that appeared suspicious. For example, the left side of the graph in Fig. 9.8 exposes one individual who has accessed 19 different user accounts. This individual has accessed more user accounts than anyone else in the analysis.

9.3.4 Integrating Other Sources of Data to Build a Stronger Case

Not content to simply identify a name, investigators continued to reach into internal and external data sources to expand the analysis. Figure 9.9 shows how the investigator linked to a government watch list to see if any of the suspect names are currently on the list. She found that five of the suspect names were on the watch list. In addition, the investigator verified address and phone number corresponding to these names from two other separate data sources, one private and one public. The choices available to the analyst for real-time indentity verification included personal property data, internet searches and both government and commercial databases. It is important to note that this is all done from within the interactive analytics application. As a result, the investigator does not lose her "train of thought." Results are quickly reviewed.

Types of data visualization also include geospatial, which allowed the investigator to locate the suspects while also mapping, roads, high-risk buildings, and other landmarks. Again, this was all done from within the interactive analysis application. Figure 9.10 below shows the location of the individuals on the watch list. These people were originally flagged as suspects through analysis of the suspicious cyber-traffic and methodically correlated with physical locations.

At each point in the process, the investigator saved results for future reference. This is done often to maintain a history of how the analysis evolved in support of litigation that may occur. These "analytical assets" were stored both as live assets that others could use later as well as in PDF form. The PDFs were digitally signed and dated. Figure 9.11 shows a series of analyses on the left with thumbnail descriptions. Each of the assets is tagged enabling key word searches. Note that the files can only be opened by those to whom the investigator has granted privileges to do so.

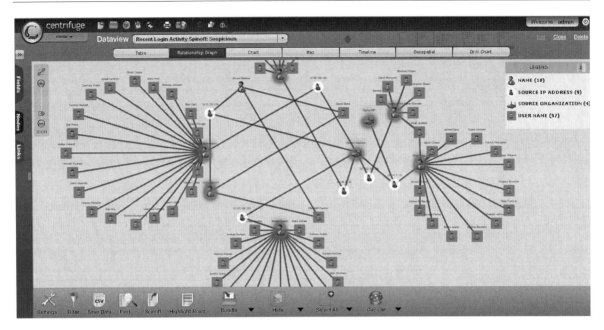

Fig. 9.8 One individual has accessed 19 different user accounts. The investigator has additional contact information for this suspect

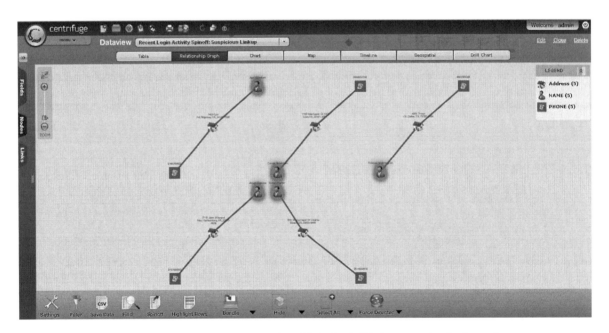

Fig. 9.9 Linking to a government watch list identifies matches; this further builds the case to involve law enforcement

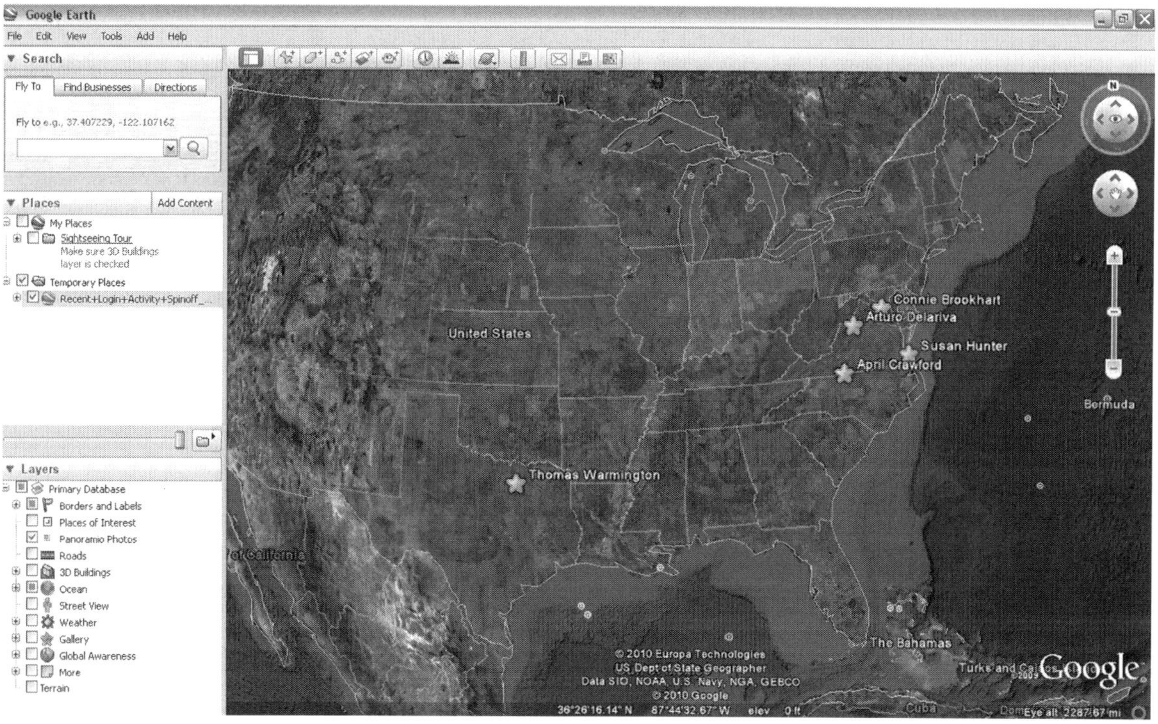

9 One Picture is Worth a Million Bytes

Fig. 9.10 Geospatial map using Google Earth of the suspected cybercriminals. They are located in three different areas of Virginia and northwest Texas

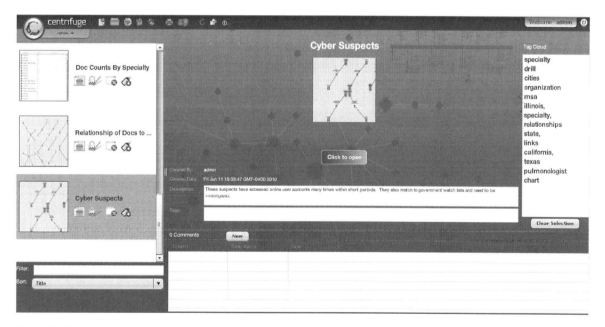

Fig. 9.11 The analytics repository stores any analytical assets that have been saved for future use. The entire breach investigation could have been documented, step by step, in this repository

Throughout this process, the investigator was free to explore data in any visual form and, in so doing, identify hidden relationships useful in solving this case.

9.4 Issues and Trends

Interactive analytics and the application of relationship graphs in cyber-security investigations are growing in popularity with larger private sector companies. Some smaller and mid-market sectors have applied this technology as well. IA has been used widely by federal agencies for years, and adoption rates are increasing as more organizations understand how federal agencies have successfully applied this technology in support of counterterrorism, cyber-security, financial crimes analysis, and homeland security.

Interactive Analytics is also being recognized as a next-generation business intelligence technology, allowing analysts of all levels to quickly connect to data, explore the data interactively, and share insights with others. While there are many reasons why this approach is gaining in popularity, analysts are finding that when easy access to data is combined with the freedom to explore data visually, the results are remarkable within shorter and shorter periods of time. As a result, this approach is being recognized as an effective method in data discovery. It goes far beyond static dashboard analysis, which normally does not allow the analyst to apply her judgment and training to uncover hidden meaning across disparate data sources.

Working with other cyber-breach investigators through collaborative analysis is also becoming more and more common. Whether this involves notifying another cyber-investigator that analytical results are available for them to work with, or publishing a PDF to executives, this form of knowledge sharing will continue to identify breaches more quickly and minimize the risk organizations face.

Increasingly, interactive analytics is being integrated into larger risk intelligence platforms that also include case management, rules management, event monitoring, predictive analysis, and entity resolution technology. Indeed, interactive analytics complements other techniques and technology involved in data breach response and risk mitigation. Both predictive analytics and rules management solutions play an important role in intelligence analysis, data breach, and fraud analysis. IA can be used to explore data and identify important attributes that can be used in more automated forms of predictive modeling. It can also be used to analyze the results of models designed to predict when and where cyber-attacks could take place. Findings from interactive analytics can be used to build or refine data breach rules that are constantly running and used to detect the breach.

Collaboration and knowledge sharing have been identified as key methods to address data breaches because trusted individuals can quickly force-multiply their efforts. Many law firms, cyberforensics labs, and investigative analytics organizations understand the power of supporting evidence in the form of analytic results that prove relationships do exist. Retaining this level of detail has proven instrumental in litigation support activity.

Interactive analytics has proven to work across many federal agencies in support of cyber security, homeland defense, counterterrorism, and financial crimes analysis. Through the combination of interactive data visualization, unified data views, and collaborative analysis, cyber-breach investigators and colleagues inside and outside their organization are armed with technology that can be used to help secure cyber space and minimize the risks that all of us face.

Notes

1. Help Wanted: Homeland Security Sees Cyber Security Pros, *Information Week*, October 1, 2009. http://www.informationweek.com/news/government/security/showArticle.jhtml?articleID=220300746
2. National Cyber Security Research and Development Challenges, *An Industry, Academic and Government Perspective Related to Economics, Physical Infrastructure and Human Behavior*, Institute for Information Infrastructure Protection (www.i3p.org), 2009, p. 5.

Chapter 10
Cybercrime and Law Enforcement Cooperation

Art Ehuan

Art Ehuan is a director with Forward Discovery, an information security company that provides extensive cyber training and services to law enforcement agencies in the United States and internationally. Ehuan currently provides training to international law enforcement organizations through the United States Department of State, Bureau of Diplomatic Security, Office of Antiterrorism Assistance. Ehuan has previously served as a Special Agent with both the Federal Bureau of Investigation (FBI) and Air Force Office of Special Investigations (AFOSI) and was responsible for managing large-scale cyber investigations. Ehuan has also spent considerable time in corporate information security departments and has worked with law enforcement to address cybercrime impacting organizations and companies.

10.1 Investigation Characteristics

Cybercrime is a fact of life for all corporations that have an Internet presence, be they small, medium, or large. Cybercrime will impact these companies in one way or another. No corporation should ever consider themselves immune to this type of crime because they do not think they have anything of value for cybercriminals. All organizations have information, and this data has a value to someone who is willing to pay for the content.

The dynamics of cybercrime has changed tremendously from the days of youthful hackers who were breaking into systems for the thrill or the challenge. Historically, this crime resulted in little monetary loss to the organization other than reputational damage from web defacement/compromise. Now, cybercrime is about financial gain for criminals. There is a tremendous amount of money that can be made from stealing information and selling or trading it for items of value on the Internet.

This realization has created a tremendous interest from organized crime (OC), which has greatly expanded their capability in this emerging area of crime. OC has both the interest and the resources to target corporations across the globe to steal information for the purpose of making grandiose amounts of money.[1]

This chapter describes how a corporation can engage and work with law enforcement to ensure, as much as is practical, that the goals of both organizations are met in addressing the cybercrime threat. Cooperation is not a zero-sum game where one side wins and the other side losses. With mutual understanding, the company and law enforcement goals can be met and the cybercriminals identified and prosecuted. Law enforcement alone cannot hope to defeat cybercrime; it will require extensive teamwork with corporations. Only through mutual working engagement can law enforcement hope to make a dent against this scourge.

10.1.1 Organizational Characteristics

The organizational characteristics of conducting a cyber investigation that will involve law enforcement activity can be quite challenging. A corporate

A. Ehuan (✉)
Forward Discovery, Alexandria, VA, USA

cyber-investigator's primary concern is to eliminate the threat to the organization, and then to ensure that it does not occur again. The corporate cyber-investigator may not be concerned with prosecution, because the decision to contact law enforcement authorities is typically determined by the organization's management. Corporations are many times wary or hesitant to notify law enforcement for reasons of concern about bad publicity that may arise from an incident being reported. This concern normally leads to numerous meetings and discussions taking place between corporate management, attorneys, and corporate investigators to discuss how to proceed and to explore the ramifications to the organization of law enforcement notification.

The mission of the law enforcement cyber-investigator is to investigate and identify the perpetrator to be arrested and prosecuted for unlawful activity. The law enforcement officer may not necessarily be concerned with the reputation of the organization if the media becomes aware of a police investigation. These two very divergent goals can sometime cause conflict between the corporation and law enforcement. If and when a decision is made to notify law enforcement cyber-investigators about an incident, it is best for the corporation to have a plan and be prepared for the events that will be occurring and may get out of control for the company. Planning and preparedness is key to the success of a corporation being able to manage the cyber incident with minimal impact to the corporation.

Corporate management will many times make assumptions of what will take place once law enforcement authorities are contacted and there is a response by authorities. Assumptions such as "They will disrupt operations," "They will notify the press," "They will shut down the company," or a myriad of other fear-driven reasons have little to no basis in fact.

A critical factor for a corporation to succeed when law enforcement notification is required is to establish a partnership with these authorities before an incident occurs. A mutual and trust-based partnership will lead to an understanding and cooperation between both parties. Identifying and coordinating with an appropriate law enforcement agency that has jurisdiction in which the corporation is based is advisable at the earliest possible opportunity.

In the United States, both the Federal Bureau of Investigation (FBI) and the United States Secret Service (USSS) have statutory authority to investigate cybercrime that impacts interstate commerce under *Title 18 United States Code 1030 Fraud and Related Activity in Connection with Computers.*[2] Specifically, the Federal statute spells out the following[3]:

Whoever
(1) having knowingly accessed a computer without authorization or exceeding authorized access, and by means of such conduct having obtained information that has been determined by the United States Government pursuant to an Executive order or statute to require protection against unauthorized disclosure for reasons of national defense or foreign relations, or any restricted data, as defined in paragraph y. of section 11 of the Atomic Energy Act of 1954, with reason to believe that such information so obtained could be used to the injury of the United States, or to the advantage of any foreign nation willfully communicates, delivers, transmits, or causes to be communicated, delivered, or transmitted, or attempts to communicate, deliver, transmit or cause to be communicated, delivered, or transmitted the same to any person not entitled to receive it, or willfully retains the same and fails to deliver it to the officer or employee of the United States entitled to receive it;
(2) intentionally accesses a computer without authorization or exceeds authorized access, and thereby obtains–
(A) information contained in a financial record of a financial institution, or of a card issuer as defined in section 1602(n) of title 15, or contained in a file of a consumer reporting agency on a consumer, as such terms are defined in the Fair Credit Reporting Act (15 U.S.C. 1681 et seq.);
(B) information from any department or agency of the United States; or
(C) information from any protected computer if the conduct involved an interstate or foreign communication;
(3) intentionally, without authorization to access any nonpublic computer of a department or agency of the United States, accesses such a computer of that department or agency that is exclusively for the use of the Government of the United States or, in the case of a computer not exclusively for such use, is used by or for the Government of the United States and such conduct affects that use by or for the Government of the United States;
(4) knowingly and with intent to defraud, accesses a protected computer without authorization, or exceeds authorized access, and by means of such conduct furthers the intended fraud and obtains anything of value, unless the object of the fraud and the thing obtained consists only of the use of the computer and the value of such use is not more than $ 5,000 in any one-year period;
(1) The United States Secret Service shall, in addition to any other agency having such authority, have the authority to investigate offenses under this section.
(2) The Federal Bureau of Investigation shall have primary authority to investigate offenses under subsection (a)(1) for any cases involving espionage, foreign counterintelligence, information protected against unauthorized disclosure for reasons of national defense or foreign relations, or Restricted Data, as that term is defined in section

11y of the Atomic Energy Act of 1954 (42 U.S.C. 2014 (y)), except for offenses affecting the duties of the United States Secret Service pursuant to section 3056 (a) of this title.

A federal law enforcement cyber-investigator (FBI or USSS) who is contacted by a corporation on an intrusion, etc., impacting the organization, will use Title 18 USC 1030 as the legal authority to open a case and start an investigation on possible violation of the law. Subpoenas or warrants that may be required in the investigation will be requested through a federal prosecutor who has received cybercrime training or is a designated cybercrime prosecutor for the United States Department of Justice (DOJ). If specialized support is required for federal prosecution, the DOJ has an organization available to provide assistance, the Computer Crime and Intellectual Property Section (CCIPS), which has specially trained prosecutors and resources.[4]

At the state level, state law enforcement organizations (NY State Police, NC Bureau of Investigations, etc.) have dedicated cybercrime units that are tasked with investigating cybercrimes that impact the state.[5] At the local or city level, major metropolitan police departments (NYPD, LAPD, etc.) have specialized cybercrime units that investigate cybercrime impacting the city.[6]

Corporate cyber-investigators can facilitate a relationship with law enforcement simply by calling the local federal, state, and local cyber-investigators using information found on their websites and asking for an in-person meeting. These officers are usually happy to have the opportunity to discuss the type of business in which the corporation is involved, the type of information that is maintained, how long logs are maintained, the criticality of the information, and how the corporation can assist law enforcement in the event of an incident. Another venue to meet law enforcement cyber-investigators is through the local chapter of the High Technology Crime Investigation Association (www.htcia.org). The corporate cyber-investigator can receive information on the type of information that would be required during an incident, with whom the law enforcement authorities would probably need to speak, and how both organizations can work closely to minimize the potential for negative publicity.

In the event of an actual investigation, a law enforcement cyber-investigator will require access to a wide variety of individuals in the organization. Employees who will probably need to be interviewed to assist in the identification of the perpetrators of the cybercrime include IT or system administrators, corporate investigators, and attorneys. The law enforcement cyber-investigator will require information on the Internet Protocol (IP) addresses that are believed to be used by those responsible for the incident, the systems that were impacted, logs for analysis, and a description or copy of the data that was compromised or lost. The officer will typically (determination is made by corporate counsel or attorney on whether information can be provided to law enforcement without legal authority) need to provide legal authority in the form of subpoenas to search and seize corporate information and digital evidence. It is very helpful if corporate cyber-investigators can provide all the information requested early in the incident to facilitate the job of a law enforcement cyber-investigator. The officer will need to meet with prosecutors and judges to receive the required judicial authority to collect information and acquire digital evidence. If not properly acquired, this information may be "tainted" and not usable in prosecution.

10.1.2 Technical Characteristics

The technical characteristics of cybercrime and its impact on an organization are diverse. Depending on the corporation, an organization may not know how to respond to a cybercrime incident. In my experience, having responded to numerous cyber incidents, the vast majority of companies do not have a very well organized incident response plan. There may be a lack of awareness around proper identification and seizure of digital evidence that is crucial for identification, arrest, and prosecution of a cybercriminal.

It is regrettable when law enforcement officers cannot utilize the information with which they are provided because of contamination of digital evidence. The contamination can occur through the sloppy or improper preservation of electronic data with evidentiary value in the corporation. It may involve storing digital information on a hard drive or tape that is placed in a desk without proper access control mechanisms being implemented. It may be that a corporate investigator does not know from where the digital evidence arrived and cannot provide this information to law enforcement officers. Law enforcement also have very strict protocols on chain-of-custody, which, if not followed properly, will lead to the unacceptability of the data that is acquired and any information that is derived from the original evidence (known in law enforcement jargon as "the fruits of a poisonous tree").

To avoid these mistakes, a corporation should plan in advance to technically facilitate the ability of law enforcement cyber-investigators to assist the organization that is victim to cybercrime by implementing the following technical measures:

1. Develop an incident response policy/process for identification, acquisition, preservation, and chain-of-custody of digital evidence. The policy/process must describe how digital evidence will be identified/searched, how it will be preserved, how it will be authenticated (i.e., digital hash), and with whom and where custody of the data will be maintained.
2. Identify who will be the primary point of contact in communication with law enforcement cyber-investigators. If it is going to be a member of the corporate investigations staff, ensure that the appointed investigator(s) has the authority to provide law enforcement officers with the information that they require (usually in consultation with corporate general counsel or attorney). Cyber investigations can move very quickly, and law enforcement authorities will require data as fast as possible to maintain momentum in what could be a very dynamic investigation.
3. Acquire equipment (hardware and software) that will be required to identify, acquire, and preserve digital evidence. The equipment must be tested and validated by the corporation to ensure that it will perform as advertised. It is critical that validation take place before an incident. The corporation should not wait until an incident to determine if the equipment functions.

File system investigations are more thoroughly covered in Chapter 8, but the minimum equipment that a corporation should acquire is as follows:

   a. Removable storage media: Large storage digital media formatted with FAT 32 file system. The FAT 32 file system is recommended because it the most universally compatible file system and can be mounted and read by all flavors of Windows, Unix/Linux, and Macintosh.
   b. Forensic acquisition software: Choices include, but are not limited to, Accessdata (www.accessdata.com) FTK Imager, Forward Discovery (www.forwarddiscovery.com), Raptor, and EFense (www.e-fense.com) Helix. These are free and easy-to-use applications to acquire and authenticate digital evidence.
   c. Forensic analysis software: Choices include, but are not limited to, Guidance Software (www.guidancesoftware.com) EnCase, and AccessData Forensic Took Kit (FTK). These are the industry leaders and standard of applications for conducting digital investigations on file systems and documenting incident response. Additional applications such as HB Gary (www.hbgary.com) may be planned for use in conducting live memory analysis.
4. Train corporate investigators and identified IT staff in using the equipment that will be utilized for incident response. The corporation should develop a core team that will conduct incident response for the organization. Simulations should be run on a regular schedule to identify any issues that may develop and provide remediation through equipment, training, or staffing. If a good relationship exists with a federal, state, or local law enforcement cyber-investigator who has previously been engaged by the corporation, invite this individual to participate in the simulation exercises. This cooperation will introduce the incident response team to the law enforcement authorities who will respond to an actual incident. Especially beneficial will be the insight that a law enforcement cyber-investigator can provide the team on requirements that law enforcement has to assist in identifying a perpetrator.

10.1.3 Investigator Role

The role of the corporate cyber-investigator and their engagement with law enforcement are critical. It cannot be overemphasized that corporate cyber-investigators should establish contact with federal, state, and local law enforcement cyber-investigators at the earliest opportunity possible. It can never be determined if a potential future investigation will require federal, state, or local law enforcement action, and thus it is important to establish relationships with all these agencies.

This contact ideally will result in a mutual understanding and respect for each organization's (corporate and law enforcement) goals and responsibilities. The corporate cyber-investigator will want to know whom to contact, when to contact them, and importantly, what are the law enforcement requirements when contact is made and law enforcement cyber-investigators respond to the organization.

A corporate cyber-investigator can meet law enforcement cyber-investigators in their local area by joining groups such as the High Technology Crime Investigators Association.[7] This organization is designed to encourage, promote, aid, and effect the voluntary interchange of data, information, experience, ideas, and knowledge about methods, processes, and techniques relating to investigations and security in advanced technologies among its membership.

The interaction between corporate and law enforcement roles in a cyber investigation cannot be minimized. Both need to be well trained and flexible to respond to threats in a very dynamic and changing landscape. Corporate cyber-investigators do not usually have training on rules of evidence and other legal requirements that law enforcement officers must adhere to when conducting an investigation. Law enforcement investigators do not normally have training on business application information flow. Frequent contact outside an investigation context will create awareness of training needs on both sides that may be addressed before an actual investigation.

10.2 Investigative Approach

10.2.1 Polices and Procedures

Key to a successful cybercrime investigation is having polices and procedures that are followed by the corporate cyber-investigator. The corporate cyber-investigator's primary responsibility is to minimize the threat to the company data. In certain unique and exigent circumstances, this may require that critical systems be "shut down" to avoid further data loss. Within this context, polices and procedures define how this activity will occur and hopefully ensure that the process is repeatable in the event that the activity needs to be recreated for law enforcement or judicial officials.

To assist in the development of polices and procedures, a criticality matrix should be produced that identifies and classifies information systems which contain sensitive information. The established process must provide information on the techniques that will be utilized and how the integrity of the data from these sensitive systems will be maintained. Depending on the system maintaining the information, the systems may be running a variety of operating systems, and different techniques (processes) will be needed to acquire the data. It is important that the data mapping take place well before an incident occurs. The data mapping should be conducted on a regular basis to ensure that, if data is moved within the corporation, this information will be updated in the criticality matrix. It is of no use for this information to be available if it is not current and accurate.

10.2.2 Electronic Crime Scene

The electronic crime scene is an elaborate and fascinating place for a corporate cyber-investigator to navigate in search of a cybercriminal. There are usually numerous computing systems and a tremendous amount of data that must be identified and analyzed in the quest to determine what occurred and who is responsible. Interaction with IT personnel from the company is not only necessary; it is mandatory when conducting an investigation. These personnel are intimately familiar with the computing systems of the organization and will know where information resides, who has access to systems, what logs are maintained by systems, and other systems attributes of interest to investigators.

This aspect is where it is important to have forensic equipment that was earlier purchased and tested, with personnel trained on its use. This equipment is utilized by corporate cyber-investigators to identify and acquire the digital evidence that will be important for the identification of the perpetrator. As described in Chapter 6, criminals have become adept at developing and deploying malicious software (malware) that resides in system Random Access Memory (RAM). Malware that resides in RAM is used by criminals to capture and steal sensitive corporate data to include names, passwords, etc. It is extremely difficult to detect and investigate this type of program running on a computing system. A corporate cyber-investigator must be familiar with acquisition techniques to capture malware in RAM. Once the RAM is acquired and preserved, analysis of this data must be conducted to identify if malicious programs exist on the system.

There are a number of different applications that can assist a cyber-investigator in analyzing RAM.[8] These applications, referred to generically as disassemblers, will analyze source code and provide information on the activity that is taking place in the RAM. For example, if what seemed to an unsuspecting user as free download of a friendly screen saver is actually spying on e-banking sessions or copying e-mails to a criminal server, a disassembler can reveal it. For cyber-investigators who do not have the background or training in disassembly language, visually interactive analytic software is a great alternative to a traditional dissassembler.[9] These applications will analyze the contents of captured RAM and provide visual representation of what is occurring inside the system.

Given that the days of conducting digital investigations on a hard drive are becoming more difficult because of the ingenuity of cybercriminals in placing their malicious code in memory, these applications are quickly becoming a requirement for cyber-investigators conducting an incident response.

10.2.3 Communication Patterns

The corporate counsel will most likely want to be involved in all contact or communications with law enforcement officials and outside officials regarding the investigation. They want to ensure that no privileged information is released without the proper paperwork (subpoena, search warrant, etc.) being provided by law enforcement. The legal barriers to communication that can be imposed by corporate or outside counsel can appear to be quite burdensome to a corporate cyber-investigator.

The established process should describe at what point in the workflow the attorneys are contacted and made aware of the investigation. During incident response simulation exercises, it is important to have someone from corporate counsel to participate so they are aware of the processes that take place during an incident and can comment or make changes they feel are warranted before an actual event.

Communication is central to responding to a cyber incident in a corporation. Communication must take place between groups or teams inside the company that have a role in responding to or supporting a cyber investigation. A corporation (primarily the communications department) should have draft templates of announcements to customers and the press for different cyber scenarios that could occur in the organization, that is, scenarios such as a Denial of Service (DoS) attack, intrusions, or loss of Personal Identifiable Information (PII). These templates may be updated with the investigation-specific and pertinent information when an incident occurs. This advanced preparation will make it much easier to respond to customer/client/regulatory or media inquires when an incident occurs.

The communication with law enforcement typically follows the pattern of a complaint being transmitted to the authorities through a phone call made by attorneys or investigators in the corporation. The officer receiving the complaint will request information on what occurred, when it occurred, who the suspects are, etc. As cyber cases are technologically complex, there may be some confusion from the officer taking the complaint on what office to refer the complaint (that is why it is extremely important to have established contacts; otherwise, the complaint may take some time to be routed to the correct department). The law enforcement officer in the cybercrime unit (if there is one) will receive information that has been transmitted by the corporation and determine whether there is a violation of the law. Depending on which agency is contacted, there may not be the available resources to provide the law enforcement assistance that the corporation requires. Small local law enforcement agencies may not have the personnel with the background or training to investigate large cyber intrusions cases and it may be necessary for the corporation to contact state or federal authorities.

Federal law enforcement officers have the greatest amount of resources, but there is a higher threshold for their involvement. Because of resource constraints, federal law enforcement typically only become involved in high loss or high publicity investigations. The high volume of cases that federal law enforcement officers are responsible for managing means these cases tend to take many weeks and months to investigate. It may sometimes be advisable for a corporation to conduct their own internal investigation to determine what occurred to "lock" systems down and prevent further damage or compromise of information systems on the network.

10.3 Case Studies

10.3.1 Defense Industry Case Study

A defense industry corporation's File Transfer Protocol (FTP) Internet site was compromised by cybercriminals without detection by the company. The cybercriminals placed malicious software (malware) on the Demilitarized Zone (DMZ) computing systems of the corporation. The cybercriminals then used the compromised site to acquire additional "footholds" inside the company and intercept network traffic to include userid and passwords of employees. The corporation security staff eventually identified the compromise when an IT administrator detected employee userid and passwords leaving the company in clear text via an FTP session.

Through frequent interaction with federal, state, and local law enforcement, the corporate investigators in this case knew that the FBI handles most large-scale intrusion cases, especially if they involve what appears to be espionage against the DOD. In addition, they knew that, of the law enforcement contacts they had so far made in their region, the FBI agents were better able to investigate because they had more training and resources than the state and local agencies with whom they had made contact. They also learned from prior conversation with state and local law enforcement officers that, once an IP is identified and the IP is outside their state or local area, then they need to contact other state or local law enforcement agencies with jurisdiction over the location of the IP address for support, and in turn this requires a lot of paperwork and resources that they may not have available. It is easier for the FBI or other federal agencies to conduct investigations across state lines.

Because the corporate victim was in the defense industry, they also had established contact with another agency that conducts cyber investigations: the Defense Criminal Investigative Service (DCIS). They had learned that DCIS conducts investigations that cross more than one military service, for instance, if a hacker hacks into a U.S. Army computing systems and then uses that system to break into a U.S. Air Force computing system.

Through DCIS, the investigators knew that each of the military services has their own investigative agencies: the U.S. Navy (Naval Criminal Investigative Service) (NCIS), U.S. Air Force (Office of Special Investigations) (AFOSI), and U.S. Army (Criminal Investigation Division) (CID). They conduct investigations that impact their particular military service but do not have jurisdiction over civilians. If civilians are involved, they work the case with the FBI as the FBI has arrest authority over civilians and the military investigative agencies do not. Given the complexity of the potential communication within the military domains combined with the probability that the perpetrator was nonmilitary, the investigators decided to make first contact with the FBI.

Corporate cyber-investigators used established incident response procedures to isolate the compromised system and identify the additional systems that were also compromised by the cybercriminals. They called an FBI agent with whom they had previously discussed the possibility of such a case and requested law enforcement support. They notified the FBI agent that they would like to file a complaint against the perpetrator, and this gave the FBI agent the jurisdiction to become involved in the investigation. Once the FBI became officially involved, they made requests for information using subpoenas.

FTP and system logs were collected that provided information on where the cybercriminals' last point of attack "hop" was located. The investigation of the IP addressed determined that it was a foreign IP address. Corporate cyber investigators coordinated with their management and legal staff and notified established federal law enforcement cyber-investigators of the incident. The IP address information was provided pursuant to a subpoena that the authorities provided to the corporation. The compromised systems, which had been pulled offline and forensically imaged, were provided to the federal law enforcement cyber-investigators for analysis. Additionally, the FBI requested and were provided with log records that had also been identified and preserved for the law enforcement investigators. The federal law enforcement cyber-investigators were able to use this information to establish the point of origin. This data was passed to the foreign law enforcement counterparts who identified additional "hops" that were being used by the cybercriminals.

The close cooperation between the corporate cyber-investigators and law enforcement was very important in stopping the cyber-attack and identifying where the perpetrators were coming from to commit their criminal activity. The investigation was also successful because, thanks to the established relationship, both the corporation and the law enforcement officials knew what the expectations were and what would be required for the authorities to identify the perpetrator.

10.3.2 Health Care Industry Case Study

A health care company employee inadvertently placed client Personal Identifiable Information (PII) on a website that was accessible on the Internet. The PII was subsequently downloaded by unknown individuals without the corporation's knowledge. The health care company, upon realizing the serious breach of their policy (i.e., not to have PII accessible on the Internet), immediately shut down the site and removed the data from the site. An internal investigation revealed that a number of individuals, across the globe, had downloaded the PII.

The company, not having a plan or process to manage this type of incident, went into crisis mode. The corporation contracted with a local cyber-investigator to assist in identifying the individuals who had accessed and downloaded the PII. The cyber-investigators determined, based on the IP addresses that were provided by the health care company, that the download of the data was from several overseas countries.

Because of the international aspects of this case, international cooperation was required. The local private cyber-investigator was a member of an organization called the International Association of Computer Investigative Specialists (IACIS) that is composed of current and former law enforcement officers and which has a tremendous network of individuals who can be contacted to request support, either through formal law enforcement channels or corporate contacts. The investigator sent an e-mail to the mailing list for IACIS members. In the e-mail, he identified himself as a private investigator working on a corporate investigation and requested assistance to gather evidence in the countries where the IP addresses that downloaded the data were located. He quickly received responses from several individuals who were either current law enforcement officers in that country who also had private investigator (PI) licenses to do civil work during off-duty hours, or former law enforcement cyber-investigators who engage in private forensics work. The local investigator quickly checked some references and contracted with PIs in the countries of interest.

The international PIs were provided with the IP addresses in their region and asked to identify specific individuals who had the IP addressed during the date and time of the downloading of the data. Using their own contacts at the international Internet Service Providers, the international PIs were able to provide the health care company with contact information for the owners of the IP addresses. The health care company contacted the IP address owners, and the IP address owners cooperated with the local private cyber-investigators. He led them through a preestablished, checklist approach to identify the current location of the downloaded PII. The checklist requested such information as the following:

1. What systems the PII had been located on to include name and IP addresses of the systems
2. The name of the file, extension, and data fields
3. The IP addresses that had downloaded the data and the type of operating systems that were used to download the data
4. The date and time that the data was downloaded from the company
5. What other identifying information including the file name and the IP addresses of both the health care company and the foreign system was captured by logs in other security systems such as intrusion detection systems and firewalls

By these efforts, the complete information flow taken by the inadvertently exposed PII was identified. The companies accidentally in possession of the data agreed to return the data and to provide assurance to the health care company that they had not provided the data to anyone else. The health care company legal counsel determined that the data was not exposed to malicious interests. Hence, costly and potentially embarrassing notification to clients and regulators was not necessary.

10.3.3 Financial Industry Case Study

Numerous customers of a financial services company reported that their funds were being moved/transferred without their authorization to different institutions. An investigation by corporate cyber-investigators determined that the personal computing systems of customers had been compromised by cybercriminals. The cybercriminals had compromised the personal computing systems of the financial services company customers, installed malicious software (malware), and stolen Personally Identifiable Information (PII), which included account numbers and passwords. The cybercriminals used the PII to access their victim's accounts and steal funds.

The corporate cyber-investigators followed proper policy and process in acquiring, preserving, and analyzing the data from the victim computing systems. This investigation allowed them to formally establish that the loss of PII was not occurring at the financial services company but on the customer's personal computing systems.

All counterfeit cases (which would include cases that pertain to the compromise of credit card data used to make fake credit cards) also fall under the jurisdiction of the Secret Service. Yet, using the same reasoning that led the defense industry company to choose the FBI, the financial services company cyber-investigators contacted previously established Federal Bureau of Investigations (FBI) cyber-investigator contacts. The organization fell back on contacts that were well established. That is not to say, in those types of cases, it is always more appropriate to call the Secret Service and not the FBI. In fact, it is more important to call a preestablished contact than to try to make a new contact at the time of an investigation. However, it is worth mentioning that organizations who are vulnerable to counterfeiting schemes should also work to build a relationship with the Secret Service, as they may be involved in investigations of the same type of crime. Although the FBI performed admirably for the organization in this case, it nevertheless makes sense for organizations to strategize on relationships with law enforcement based on preexisting jurisdictional boundaries.

The case was referred for both regulatory requirements and the large amount of losses that the financial institution was experiencing. The corporate cyber-investigators used established policies and procedures when acquiring the digital evidence from their customers/victims. The protocols were developed in a manner that would ensure that chain-of-custody was maintained and could be provided to law enforcement by corporate cyber-investigators. The digital evidence was provided to the FBI with the permission of the customers/victims for their own independent analysis. The law enforcement authorities used this and other information (system and application logs) provided by corporate cyber-investigators to determine the origin of the cyber-attack and where the stolen funds were being moved to overseas.

10.3.4 Court Appearances

Testimony by cyber-investigators involved in these types of cases is well documented in federal, state, and military courts. The types of questions that are typically asked concern these points:

1. Background of the cyber-investigator
2. Experience of the cyber-investigator
3. Training of the cyber-investigator
4. Applications or tools used by the cyber-investigator
5. Analysis of the cyber-investigator and how the conclusion was reached

Well-documented planning and due diligence in evidence preservation in each of these areas will ensure that the evidence identified by the cyber-investigator will be admissible in court.

10.4 Issues and Trends

10.4.1 International Issues

The international aspects of cybercrime are important. They matter because a cybercriminal can be anywhere in the world and impact a corporation wherever they may be on the globe. The criminal no longer needs physical access to steal sensitive corporate information from their victims. As such, when an IP address resolves to a foreign entity, it is going to be crucial for law enforcement cyber-investigators to work closely with foreign law enforcement officers to identify the perpetrators.

The majority of nation-states do not have the capability or capacity to investigate cyber. Most countries do not have the personnel, training, or resources to effectively respond to cyber threats. This fact makes it extremely difficult for law enforcement investigators with established capability to identify cybercriminals who are traversing or "looping" through foreign Internet sites in an attempt to circumvent government investigators.

More needs to be done in this area by foreign governments to fill this gap; until that happens, cybercriminals will continue their illegal activity with little concern of being identified and arrested.

The international legal framework that has guided nation-state cooperation on crime is seriously lacking in the cybercrime arena. Cybercrime is incredibly dynamic and changes much faster than the traditional diplomatic or judicial channels that currently exist internationally to address the acquisition and sharing of criminal evidence.

The problems that can arise can be very complex. Nation-states have different requirements on data retention, with data retention being one of the most critical requirements when conducting a cyber investigation. If data is not retained for cyber-investigators to analyze, then it becomes difficult if not impossible to identify the perpetrators of the crime.

Nation-state cooperation in developing a legal framework is vital to investigating cybercrime. If legal assistance is not established, then it makes the job of law enforcement officers throughout the globe extremely difficult.

Cybercrime has a divergent impact on a nation-state that is woefully dependent on who is being victimized. If a nation-state is not aware of loss to cybercrime within their country (consequent to lack of reporting from individuals and corporations), then there may be a feeling that there is not a problem. If there is no problem, then there is not a reason to legislate laws or fund very expensive cybercrime units. This is a false illusion, because cybercrime can and does reach any nation-state that has an Internet connection. It is many times a matter of priorities or awareness that hampers taking action.

There is also a realization by law enforcement agencies across the globe that cybercrime is the crime of now and the future. Cybercrime can be viewed by some law enforcement organizations as a victimless crime because it takes place on the Internet and can be very abstract. In the opinion of some agencies, no visible harm or damage occurs. Physical crime (homicide, robbery, etc.) tends to attract the attention of the media and the public and thus garners support for the funding and resourcing of law enforcement to investigate this type of crime.

Cybercrime is also extremely difficult to investigate because of the international aspects of this violation. If law enforcement organizations are not properly resourced or funded, it becomes challenging to receive assistance from international agencies to investigate crimes across national boundaries.

10.4.2 Inertia and Resistance to Cooperation

Cooperation with law enforcement is vital to identifying and prosecuting cybercriminals. Without cooperation, it is virtually impossible for law enforcement to receive the support they need to investigate cybercriminal activity. Corporate support and involvement will provide much needed information that law enforcement cyber-investigators require to identify trends and patterns and thus identify the resources and funding they require to investigate.

There is a hesitancy to report cybercrime when it affects a corporation. As already discussed, these fears can be alleviated by engagement with law enforcement cyber-investigators before an incident actually materializes.

10.4.3 Conclusion

All corporations, at some point in time, will be impacted by a cyber-attack or intrusion. How they fare through this event will depend on several factors.

Preparation is the key to being successful in identifying and mitigating the damage that these incidents can cause to an organization. It is a responsibility of corporate cyber-investigators to develop a plan for responding to cyber incidents. The plan must provide for law enforcement notification and cooperation. Law enforcement assistance will be required to identify and prosecute cybercriminals. A corporation should not wait until an incident occurs before establishing law enforcement contacts. The plan must then be tested on a regular basis to ensure that it will work as developed. Acquire the equipment and receive the training that is so necessary for success on these tasks. Being prepared will make the difference between success and failure.

Notes

1. See X, X, 20 Indicted in RBS Hacking Case, *Wall Street Journal*, November 20, 2009.
2. See www.fbi.gov and www.secretservice.gov
3. See https://www.x.gov
4. See www.cybercrime.gov
5. See for example, www.statecybercrimeunit.gov
6. See for example, www.citycybercrme.gov
7. See www.htcia.org
8. For example, IDA Pro is a well-known disassembler that will assist a cyber-investigator in determining what activity is occurring in RAM. See www.hex-rays.com
9. An free example of such an application is HBGary Responder Field Edition (www.hbgary.com).

Chapter 11
Technology Malpractice

Paul Rohmeyer

Paul Rohmeyer has more than 20 years experience in Information Technology management and consulting. He is a faculty member at Stevens Institute of Technology's Howe School of Technology Management, where he teaches and conducts research on IT risk management and business resiliency. Rohmeyer frequently publishes on technology management issues and was a contributing author to the book *Guarding Your Business, A Management Approach to Security*. In addition to his academic career, he consults on Technology Investigation, Technology Management, Project Management, Information Security, and IT Audit. Past positions include Director of Strategic Business Intelligence with AXA Financial Services, Director of IT Architecture Planning for Bellcore, and information systems audit and IT management positions with Citicorp and American Home Products Corporation. Rohmeyer holds a BA in Economics from Rutgers University, a MBA in Finance from St. Joseph's University, and MS and PhD degrees in Information Management from Stevens Institute of Technology. He holds the PMP (Project Management Professional), NSA IAM (Information Assurance Methodology), and CGEIT (Certified in the Governance of Enterprise IT) credentials.

11.1 Investigation Characteristics

Technology malpractice is not yet a household phrase, but given the increasing number of circumstances in which it applies and the public's increasing familiarity with the scenarios that provoke its investigation, it may well soon be. There are many types of situations that provoke an investigation into the practices an organization uses to manage its technology: these include information systems audit and risk assessment as well as all types of cybersecurity forensic investigations that have been discussed in the previous chapters.

Security breaches are often identified in the course of an information systems audit or a network security risk assessment. Even in cases where a breach is known to occur, a cybersecurity incident investigation team's first steps will be similar to those of an audit or risk assessment team. Findings range from purely technical discoveries of previously unknown threat-enablers such as "zero-day" viruses to obvious neglect of any security strategy on the part of the breached enterprise (see Fig. 11.1).

The term zero-day refers to the number of days information about a given systems vulnerability has been available to the general Internet community concerned with cybersecurity events.[1] For example, assume a hacker created a new type of malware and used it for the first time to invade the desktops in a targeted corporate enterprise. Also assume that the security staff at the corporation identified this malware and reported it to their antivirus software vendor. A week later, that vendor includes a capability to detect the new malware in using its software and publishes a description of it to warn the rest of their clients of its dangers. The day after the vendor announcement

P. Rohmeyer (✉)
Howe School of Technology Management, Stevens Institute of Technology, Castle Point on Hudson, Hoboken, NJ 07030, USA

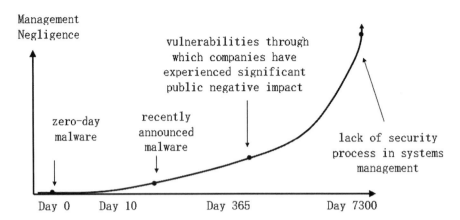

Fig. 11.1 Relationship between vulnerability awareness and accountable management neglect if vulnerability exists

is day 2. The time between the point at which the hacker wrote the software and the day the vendor published it is day 1. So, a zero-day attack is one that happens before vendors or users even know they are vulnerable.

At the other end of the spectrum are attacks that happen because the victim does not pay any attention to security at all. At this end of the spectrum is a company that is completely unaware that security professionals have been publishing best practices in securing cyber assets since the 1970s.[2] These attacks happen to companies who fall victim to attack simply because they do not manage security well or at all.

In the middle are attacks that have happened in the past to other companies, of which security professionals are generally aware, but for some reason, despite relatively sound management practices, did not adequately protect against or detect. The extent to which management may be in neglect for such lack of defense is the extent to which a reasonable person may believe that they are at risk from the given threat.

This chapter is concerned with findings at the extreme right-hand side of the curve in Fig. 11.1. It is investigations into situations wherein security management did not take advantage of expertise that has been available for 20 or more years on security management practices. Were this situation to be a finding in an information security audit, the lack of management strategy for security would usually be escalated to upper management. Upper management would likely close the audit finding by a due diligence measure such as reorganizing the security function. Were this situation to be a finding in an information security risk assessment, the artifacts of poor management, such as inaccurate technology inventory, would likely be remediated via project work by existing management. The project work would serve to reduce the negative impact to the enterprise identified in the risk assessment. However, in the event of a security breach investigation, the lack of security management is not an internal affair. A negative finding of cybersecurity management can become the subject of a lawsuit charging the breached enterprise with *technology malpractice*.[3]

Technology malpractice investigations are motivated by suspicion of management neglect of security issues. For example, a customer of an online retailer may experience negative impact because their credit card information is being stolen from an online retailer website. They may suspect that the reason for the breach was poor security at the retail company.[4]

Other typical cases are those brought by the U.S. Federal Trade Commission in response to large-scale data breaches.[5] There is an assumption in some organizations that poor technology management costs less than competent technology management. For this reason, poor technology management has been labeled an unfair business practice by the FTC. Although there may be debate over whether this assumption is correct, that fact is irrelevant to the conclusion that management neglect of security gives one company competitive advantage over another. It most certainly often exposes consumers to harm, and so for that reason, the FTC cases set an important precedent.

Cases that are likely to end up requiring investigation into technology management are characterized by differences in opinion in the degree to which management is accountable for security monitoring. While no one doubts that management is responsible for protection strategies, there is only nominal awareness that data breaches are preventable. The defendant often speaks of the data breach in the same manner as someone would speak of a natural disaster such as a flood or hurricane. The plaintiff places it in the same category as a flaw in packaging that impacts secure product delivery.

Yet the prosecutors of these cases understand that it is unnecessary to specify whether poor management is the result of neglect or incompetence. Perception by a judge on the level to which negligence was intentional may affect the size of a settlement, but management motivation to provide security is generally independent from the proof that low security standards was a factor contributing to harm to the plaintiff.

11.2 Investigative Approach

A technology malpractice investigation may begin with a security breach. Internal to an enterprise, the investigation should follow the approach described by Leibolt in Chapter 2. However, where internal security expertise does not exist, enterprise management will most likely follow the approach of the case study in Chapter 3, and engage a private sector investigation firm. Regardless of whether an investigation is internal or external, technology malpractice investigations will start the same way. As Liebolt describes in Chapter 2, "... It is human nature for people to think that their network or system has not really been compromised. .....Additionally, people may be afraid that they could be in trouble and are not likely to provide any self-incriminating information." As Valentine describes in Chapter 3, "... It is statistically likely that the investigation team will have a difficult time getting accurate information about the network." In these situations, the cybersecurity investigation initially follows the same general activity you would see in an audit or risk assessment. Data flow through the network is critically analyzed and mapped onto network control points. Where network documentation is inaccurate or nonexistent, it must be created. Systems that store, retain, or transmit the data that was compromised are reviewed for vulnerabilities. Those assumed to be responsible for operational integrity are interviewed, and interview results are validated by comparison with each other as well as actual systems configurations.

By using skills borrowed from the audit or risk assessment side of the information security profession, the investigator eventually figures out how management expected the data to be protected, if at all, as well as whether the management strategy worked. If you think of management controls as a series of top-down levels starting with the highest level of management within the firm, and ending with the lowest, or staff, it is possible to identify the controls themselves with the company management who executes them.

For example, Fig. 11.2 lists evidence of cybersecurity management controls in descending order, from those that are expected to be maintained at the highest levels of management to those which are expected to be maintained by staff. At each level, the evidence of controls should be consistent with those at every other level. Each level of documentation should contain pointers to those above and below it. Where it is an organizational priority to maintain this evidence of management control, investigation into technology malpractice will be easy, and actual malpractice found will be minimal, if any.

On the other hand, in discussing encounters with accountable management, Valentine says, "Even more commonplace are situations where no one maintains ownership over network assets at all. Instead of Mr. Corey and Mr. Gibbs accusing the other of being responsible for the failure, investigators will often find that *no one* maintains responsibility over the affected assets, and that no documentation exists to make any kind determination either way." Investigators conclude that neither can actually be held responsible for the failure, given the way that their job functions are defined. In this situation, it is obvious that there is no cohesive and consistent chain of evidence showing how data is to be protected by whom within the organization. This is where the investigation of technology malpractice will follow a different route than the incident investigation itself.

Once it has been determined that an investigation of technology malpractice needs to happen, it will start with the top. Many organizations claim to have a high-level sponsor for their security program. The investigator must identify what person or persons within the organization have the authority to establish an information security program, and then see if there is any evidence that any one or group of

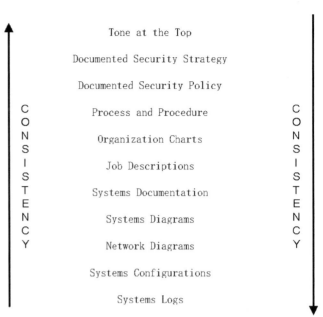

Fig. 11.2 Levels of security program evidence

them have done so. In some cases, a security program sponsor is too low on the reporting chain to have the security program objectives bind staff that handles information, and this creates an inconsistency between accountability for security and authority to establish controls.

Once it has been established that the security program has authority, the investigator will look for evidence that the scope of the security program covers the information in scope of the data breach. There should be a documented security strategy that includes an information classification which clearly identifies the data and the organizational strategy for ensuring that all data flow containing that information is addressed within the security program. The security program itself should include documented security policy and processes that reflect the security strategy, as well as comply with any and all application laws and regulations for handling each type of classified data. Those processes must be supervised by managers whose job descriptions state that they are accountable for their correct implementation of security process. Those managers must support process implementation with technology and operations designed to prevent, detect, and recover from harm to data confidentiality, integrity, and availability.

In the absence of this set of coherent and consistent set of documentation, shared cross-functionally by all who handle information in the scope of the breach, it is very hard for management to show that they have been duly diligent in protecting the information in scope. Even with this documentation, there must be artifacts that demonstrate that the management strategy is actually followed. These should be metrics by each domain of management responsibility. As you cannot manage what you cannot measure, each level of management responsible for a "level" of security management must demonstrate that they have a way of knowing that their part of the security process is working correctly. For example, the technical staff responsible for log collection must show that logs are routinely collected and archived, corrupt and missing logs are detected, investigated, and restored, and that logs are analyzed, either manually or automatically, to detect harm to configuration or data at higher levels. Those responsible for supervising this staff member should have aggregate metrics showing that the lower-level metrics were accurately collected and routinely reviewed. At the highest level, the CEO should also have aggregate evidence across all organizations that handle data which shows that the overall security strategy is effectively working.

An investigator in a technology malpractice investigation is not necessarily looking for evidence that the security program is not working, or somehow broken. Rather, he or she is looking for evidence that it is working from the point of view of a reasonable and informed observer. As organizational management may not have previously understood that all internal documentation must be consistent or contain pointers to each other to be easily investigated, an investigator should request a copy of all documentation that is related to information security from all levels of management. He or she should, so far as possible, map all the technology, process, and procedure in the documents to the information in the scope of the breach, and identify gaps in responsibility for controls.

As with any investigation, there is a point at which it becomes an iterative process. The investigator should bring control accountability gaps to the attention of the organization under scrutiny to see if there is some documented activity that will provide evidence that a given control is in place and actively managed. Examples of such supplemental evidence may be e-mail threads, meeting minutes, and/or statistics generated from automatically generated alerts and reports. An investigator will piece all this together in an effort to fully understand *how security is supposed to work*.

An investigator may find great evidence of management controls at both the top of the organization but then find that the evidence trail lags the closer they get to the bottom. Conversely, an investigator may find great evidence of management controls in technology operations, but find that the evidence trail lacks attention at higher levels in the organization. More often than not, evidence of technology malpractice is found closer to the middle. The investigator works simultaneously from both the bottom and the top, trying to make the documentation and metrics trail meet in the middle, focusing on the information flow identified in the breach/incident. It is common to find a mid-level manager who dropped a ball for reasons of his or her supervisor's lack of priority for security, or find security inconsistently implemented in different departments that have different supervisors who did not talk to each other.

Where an organization has made no effort to implement security, reporting technology malpractice results is easy, and the investigation conclusion is that the organization was negligent. However, where there has been any attempt at all to run a comprehensive security program, and yet there remain critical gaps in information protection, the investigator is in the unfortunate position of showing management that they have failed in this effort. In this case, it is helpful to rely on comparison of the management strategy in the organization under scrutiny with industry standards for information security management such as ISO 27002 [6] and NIST 800-33.[7]

11.3 Case Study

A recent case that was widely reported concerns the ChoicePoint data breach. As reported, ChoicePoint was accused by the U.S. Federal Trade Commission (FTC) of "failing to implement a comprehensive security program protecting consumers' sensitive information."[8] Furthermore, the FTC charged the failure led directly to a data breach that compromised thousands of consumers.

The term "security program" is quite broad and may be interpreted to included dimensions of personnel, organizational processes, and technologies. In a 2006 case ChoicePoint data breach case, the FTC defined a security program in the course of a stipulated final judgement and order for civil penalties, permanent injunction, and other equitable relief. It was an order that ChoicePoint be permanently restrained and enjoined from "Failing to establish and implement, and thereafter maintain, a comprehensive information security program that is reasonably designed to protect the security, confidentiality, and integrity of personal information collected from or about consumers. Such program, the content and implementation of which must be fully documented in writing, shall contain administrative, technical, and physical safeguards appropriate to Defendant's size and complexity, the nature and scope of Defendant's activities, and the sensitivity of the personal."[9]

As part of the settlement for the 2006 case, ChoicePoint implemented a variety of controls, including a monitoring system, presumably designed to detect future data breaches. However, in 2009, the FTC asserted that a decision by ChoicePoint to disable a specific access monitoring tool for a period of four (4) months allowed an anonymous individual to access the data and conduct unauthorized searches. The FTC claimed if the monitoring tool was working, the organization would have detected the breach sooner and minimized its impact. The failure also was considered by the FCC as a violation of the 2006 court order requiring ChoicePoint to implement an information security program. The 2009 settlement included reference to the program as follows: "The FTC further alleges that this reveals that Defendant had failed, for a 4-month period, to establish and implement, and thereafter maintain, a comprehensive information security program that is reasonably designed to protect the security, confidentiality, and integrity of personal information collected from or about consumers."

The 2009 ChoicePoint case was settled, with ChoicePoint paying a $275,000 fine and agreeing to implement stricter information security program standards. Although there have been no documented results of the internal ChoicePoint investigation that led them to settle rather than argue the case, it is instructive to consider how such a forensic investigation into security program management might proceed. The fact that the monitoring tool was specifically identified in the settlement meant that a forensic investigation into these issues resulted in a legal opinion that the tool was implemented as part of a security program envisioned in the 2006 stipulation and should have played a role in preventing the 2009 breach. So an investigation into this issue would surely focus on data gathering regarding the monitoring tool. Both parties would be interested in determining when the tool was implemented, when it was disabled, who disabled it, when it was reactivated, and who reactivated it. To show that the tools were being used as part of the overall security program, all these activities would have to be supported by top-level management, be documented in a well-defined process, and have evidence of oversight and metrics review by technology management. There would also most likely be interest to recover logs generated while the tool was active to show that it, at least at one time, was able to identify attempted attacks.

Furthermore, the investigation into the detection process as a subset of an information security program would have extended beyond the monitoring tool to include the personnel who interacted with it in the context of the organizational structure of the security program. Therefore, there should be some examination of the personnel charged with the engineering, deployment, and maintenance of the tool, as well as those charged with day-to-day monitoring and response, including evidence of their training program, management evaluations of their competency, and potentially investigation of how they responded to past incidents. This result suggests the FTC perhaps could have pursued investigation into process negligence – a failure of personnel oversight in the execution of a security program, as well as failure of the technology itself. Forensic evidence that revealed a management inability to adequately respond to attacks despite the existence of the working monitoring tools would strengthen the FTC case.

ChoicePoint did not admit any facts with respect to the FTC's allegations that the monitoring tool would have detected the security breach, nor that the security program was lacking. Nevertheless, they would perhaps not have needed to settle had they been able to prove that they had complied with the FTC's 2006 order that they had a working information security program designed to detect such breeches. As they could not make this case, they paid the fine and reaffirmed their 2006 commitment to establish and maintain a security program.

11.4 Issues and Trends

It is no accident that cases such as the ChoicePoint case do not come to trial; this may happen because standards of due care with respect to security are becoming so well known that once the facts of a case become obvious to internal lawyers, they see no point in pursuing argument. Unfortunately, that means there is little by way of case law in actual court cases, and the way of the future may be dictated via interpretation of settlement decrees. Moreover, as responsibility for technology management becomes more distributed both within and across organizations, there will emerge even more situations in which organizations that had not considered themselves negligent may nevertheless be considered as such by an independent technology malpractice investigator. Two such scenarios are where management uses managed security service providers and where businesses utilize cloud services.

11.4.1 Managed Security Service Provider (MSSP)

Many organizations outsource the operational monitoring of information security devices, particularly in the detection arena. Commonly referred to as Managed Security Service Providers (MSSP), these firms continuously receive activity logs from various security devices (i.e., sensors) and evaluate the logs using a combination of automated and manual techniques in the hope of alerting the customer to potential attacks or attempted attacks. Once notified, the customer is typically responsible for the ensuing investigation. But what happens if the MSSP fails to identify an actual attack? Potential causes of ineffective detection include equipment failures of the security sensor, communications channel, MSSP data consolidation process, MSSP data analysis process, and perhaps oversight or incompetence on the part of MSSP personnel. Failure at any point of the monitoring process could result in undetected incidents and, therefore, damage to the client. As illustrated in the ChoicePoint case, failure to detect an incident has consequences. The FTC pursued charges in the ChoicePoint case, while the subscriber to an MSSP service who is damaged by a breach may seek civil damages from a provider who they accuse of failing to detect an incident that caused them harm.

Specific failures that would benefit from forensics investigations include validating the configuration of the sensor and the communications line from client to MSSP. The management and maintenance of the sensor device could be verified as well, such as verification of timely updates to attack signatures and even software patches. The next step would be validation of integrity throughout the process, namely, evidence the logs are continuously transmitted, unaltered, from sensor to MSSP.

The outsourcing arrangement itself may add to the complexity of the investigation, as some MSSP contracts include provisions simply for monitoring, while others include payment for maintenance of the localized sensor device and associated communications infrastructure.

11.4.2 Cloud Computing

The move toward service outsourcing in the technology space is culminating in "cloud computing." Cloud has quickly become a popular euphemism for "hide the nuts and bolts from the business." The word "cloud" evokes an image of benign existence, free from the messy details business technologists have struggled to manage for decades.

However, as the cloud masks the technical architecture and processes, the capabilities for investigations become severely restricted, essentially the result of technical realities as successive layers of abstraction mask fundamental technical processes, making "traditional" forensic investigations extremely challenging if not, in some cases, impossible.

In the case of outsourced cloud architectures and services, technical limitations are compounded by increasingly restrictive service level agreements that blunt any reasonable level of technical investigation. Unfortunately, organizations investigating computer misuse will simply be unable to conduct their own detective work "behind the cloud." Instead, the emerging vehicle for gathering technical data from cloud (or other service) providers may prove to be the subpoena. And as time passes while requesting, granting, and executing such orders, hard drives are being overwritten, memory on RAM chips is fading, and personnel at the service provider are changing shifts.

One answer could be seeking specific provisions for forensics investigations in agreements with external cloud providers. Such agreements could at least force the provider to declare a "forensic investigation service level" so subscribers understand what that will and will not easily get if they need to pursue an investigation. Agreed-upon principles for forensic support should ideally become a standard request for organizations placing any amount of sensitive information in the clouds.

11.4.3 Accountability

Although neglect has always been cause for common law tort cases, neglect with respect to technology management strategy is increasingly easy to prove. Documented international standards for security management and operation provide clear guidelines for expert testimony as to how an enterprise should manage security, as well as what types of methods, tools, and procedures they should use to implement security process.[10] Even gray areas such as managed security and cloud services are rapidly being assimilated by modern cybersecurity experts into standards documents.[11] All types of cyberforensics investigators should be cognizant of information security management standards, because these parameters will be increasingly important to future judgments concerning management accountability.

Notes

1. Etymology of the term zero-day.
2. For a history of information security professional practices, see Bayuk, J.L., *Stepping Through the InfoSec Program*, Information Systems Audit and Control Association, 2007.
3. This term was coined to apply to lawyers who do not protect client data by Calloway, Jim, *Malpractice or Ethical Violations with Your Computer*, Oklahoma Bar Association, Law Practice Tips, 2009. (See http://www.okbar.org/members/map/articles/malpractice.htm).
4. For example, class action fallout form the Heartland Payment Systems case includes Cooper v. Heartland Payment Systems, USDC NJ Trenton and Financial Institution Class Representatives v. heartland Payment Systems USDC Southern District of Texas Houston Division. http://www.bankinfosecurity.com/articles.php?art_id=1181
5. See Wolf, Christopher, *Proskauer on Privacy*, Practicing Law Institute, 2008.
6. *Information Security Management Standards: 27001/27002*, International Standards Organization, 2006. See www.iso.org
7. Bowen, Pauline, Joan Hash, Mark Wilson, *Information Security Handbook: A Guide for Managers*, National Institute of Standards and Technology, Special Publication 800-100, October, 2006. The NIST series for security professionals is available at: http://csrc.nist.gov/publications/PubsSPs.html
8. Unites States District Court, Northern District of Georgia, Atlanta Division, Civil Action No. 1:06-cv-198-JTC, FTC File No. 052-3069, see http://www.ftc.gov/opa/2009/10/choicepoint.shtm
9. Ibid., http://www.ftc.gov/os/caselist/choicepoint/0523069stip.pdf
10. See ISO 27001/2 and NIST reference above, as well as ISACA CoBIT (www.isaga.org), PCI DSS at https://www.pcisecuritystandards.org
11. See for example, Cloud Security Alliance, *Security Guidance for Critical Areas of Focus in Cloud Computing*, 2009, see www.cloudsecurityalliance.org. An Information Systems Audit and Control Association, *Cloud Computing: Business Benefits with Security, Governance and Assurance Perspectives*, 2009, see www.isaca.org

Glossary

ACL: Access Control List; used to specify a set of computer users and associated permissions to access programs or data within a system

Anti-reversing capabilities: Subroutines, modules, or other bit patterns embedded in malware that are intended to thwart investigation attempts

Applet: A small single-purpose web service often used for system-to-system communication

Application layer: Network traffic that contains programs and data as opposed to network transmission instructions

Audit: Process whereby external subject matter experts analyze management control processes with respect to objectives, test whether controls are effectively implemented, and assess process effectiveness

Backdoor: A program that allows unauthorized access to a computer via network connections which are unknown to the authorized users or owners of the computer

Behavioral analysis: Study of characteristics that software exhibits as it interacts with its environment

Bot: Derived from the word "robot," and used in a variety of Internet contexts; in this book usually refers a program that runs in the background on a personal computer of an unsuspecting user, having been installed by malware

Botnet: A collection of bots that received instructions from the same "master" program

Data breach: Situation in which information subject to confidentiality requirements is exposed to systems or individuals who have no reason to access it

CD: Compact disk

CERT: Computer Emergency Response Team

CIRT: Computer Incident Response Team

Cloud computing: Computer service that is Internet accessible and does not require a customer to own hardware other than a personal computer

Code analysis: Study of the bits that comprise the code of a software specimen

Cross-site scripting: A method of injecting scripts, or programs, into a web browser that are unnoticed by the user, and which usually perform malicious actions

Configuration: Values for variables and parameter setting read by programs and used by programs in logic that determines the course of a program through the alternative functions

Control points: Steps in a procedure, a program execution, or a management process where data available at the time is used as the basis for a decision on whether to allow a subsequent activity

Cyberforensics: Incident investigations wherein significant evidence is determined to be stored, transmitted, or managed using computers

Data loss prevention: Technologies that identify data based on pattern matching technology and logs or blocks attempts to transport such data outside a system boundary

Defense in depth: A method of planning security architecture that ensures the result will provide technology access controls in at least two distinct technology categories to protect each system access point

Due diligence: A legal term referring to management's responsibility to perform fact-based reasoning to support decision making

Escalation: Management process whereby incidents that cannot be resolved by operations staff are referred to appropriate management for resolution

Exfiltration: Method by which malware exports data from an infected host

Faraday cage: A metallic enclosure that prevents the entry or escape of an electromagnetic (EM) field

Finding: A situation that describes a management control weakness: a documented finding will often include a description of the situation, criteria according to which the situation has been determined to be a weakness, and the potential impact to the organization of neglecting to remediate the situation

Footprint: With reference to a software component used to indicate the physical characteristics of a file such as its size and the file names as well as the operating system's resource utilization; these characteristics help to uniquely identify the various software components encountered during the investigative process

Forensics: Activity concerned with the preparation of evidence for use in legal argument

Hacker: Slang for an individual who identifies methods of obtaining unauthorized access to systems that are configured to limit access to authorized use

IDS: Intrusion Detection System

Information pathways: The sequence of devices on a network through which data passes in the course of being manipulated by computer programs

Insider: Person familiar with technology and processes within a system or enterprise

LFI: Local File Inclusion, or an attack wherein the perpetrator modifies user-executable application files locally stored on a compromised server

Live analysis: Forensics processes that rely on data gathered from computer operating memory at a given point in time, including running processes, lists of open files, and network activity in flight on running computers

Malware: Malicious software

Memory: Computer storage that contains software instructions either currently or recently executed

Mobile devices: Personal digital assistants and other computers that are small enough to be hand-carried and communicate via networks

Mount points: Operating system file indexes that provide local pointers that programs on a computer follow to access shares on other computers or other remote storage devices such as SAN or NAS

Network intelligence: Information concerning network topology, connectivity, and usage

NAS: Network Attached Storage

OS: Operating System

Packet capture: A data collection technique wherein network data transmissions are copied to electronic file stores in real time

PDA: Personal Digital Assistants, hand-carried devices that are used to store contacts, calendars, and tasks, such as blackberries, iphones

Pen-test: See penetration test

Penetration test: A systems security assessment technique wherein the tester imitates the behavior of an advesary and attempts to exploit system vulnerabilities with malicious code or conduct

PII: Personally Identifiable Information

RAID: Redundant Array of Independent Disks

RSA: Name of a company that produces two factor authentication tokens

Registry: A file in a Microsoft operating system that holds configuration information

Remediation: Activity intended to correct control weaknesses

Rootkit: Malware that changes the operating system to the extent that it changes the results of administrative operating system commands

SAN: Storage Area Network

Script: Software program written in a programming language that is interpreted at run time and so does not need to be compiled

Script kiddie: Slang for a hacker who does not know how to program so has to use programs written by others

SecurID: Brand name of RSA two-factor authentication token

Security architecture: The methods, tools, and processes that provide support for system security features

SIEM: Security Incident and Event Manager

Signature: Set of technical measurements corresponding to a program's systems characteristics or behavior

Signature-based: Technology that relies on measurable technical aspects of a target to identify it

Slices: Partitions of digital media

Sniffer: Generic name for a program that reads network traffic

Static analysis: Forensics operations that work with data stored in end-user-accessible formats on disk drives

Technology malfeasance: Negligence in management techniques to meet information security requirements

Threat landscape: A method of cataloguing the activities that have potential to negatively impact a given system

USB: Universal Serial Bus

Volatility: The state of being changeable and transient

WORM: Write Once Read Many, this acronym refers to electronic media that is designed to accept only one image, such as a file copy, and provides evidence of lack of integrity if attempts are made to alter the data stored on it

Zero Day: Modifier for the word threat or attack, meaning that the vulnerability that is used by the threat agent is not known to potential victims

Index

Note: The letters 'f', "n" and 't' refers to figures, notes and tables respectively.

A

AccessData® Enterprise, 9, 12
AccessData Forensic Took Kit (FTK), 108, 132
Accounting forensics
   case study, 55–57
      U.S. Securities and Exchange Commission (SEC) publication, 56f
   investigation characteristics, 53–54
      FINRA, 54
      sample testing, 54
      Statement of Auditing Standards No. 99 (SAS 99), 54
   investigative approach, 54–55
      business applications and balance sheet, 54
      senior leader in finance, help of, 54
      "smoke-screen" approach, 55
      trace transactions of interest to investigation, 54
   issues and trends, 57
Accounting fraud, *see* Accounting forensics; Data breach response and risk mitigation, interactive analytics
ACL, *see* Complex access control lists (ACL)
Acme Corp, 38–42
   See also Large-scale data breaches
Acxiom Corporation, 55–56
AFOSI, *see* Air Force Office of Special Investigations (AFOSI)
Agresta, A., 117–128
Agresta, T., 5
Air Force Office of Special Investigations (AFOSI), 5, 129, 135
All service-level agreements (SLA), 112
aMAC address, 41
Anti-forensics, 116
Antifraud programs, 55

"Anti-reversing capabilities," 60–61
Applet, 9, 13–15, 26 n5
Artifact, 11, 14, 16, 21, 26 n8, 114, 120, 142, 144
Audit, 1–2, 10–11, 18, 21, 49–50, 53–55, 57, 117, 141–143
Automated behavioral analysis websites, 82 n19
Autoruns, 65, 65f, 82 n10

B

Bad clusters, 110
Barney, 112–113, 114t
Barrios, R., 5
   software expert and forensics consultant, 5
Barrios, R. M., 5, 103–116
Bayuk, J., 1–6
   CGEIT, 1
   CISA, 1
   CISM, 1
   CISSP, 1
   security software engineer at AT&T Bell Laboratories, 1
Beacon Trojan, 93–95
Behavioral analysis, 15, 61, 63, 65–67, 70, 81, 82 n19, 82 n21, 97
BinText, 68, 74, 82 n26
Bot
   IRC, 21
   malware, 25
   software, 15–16
Botnet, 24
Building an Automated Behavioral Analysis Environment paper, 82 n21
Bureau of Alcohol, Tobacco and Firearms (ATF), 3

C

California Database Security Breach Notification Act (SB 1386), 18
CaptureBAT, 64, 64f, 82 n6
Carrier, B., 26 n27, 115, 116 n3, 116 n8
CART, *see* Computer Analysis and Response Teams (CART)
Case study, accounting forensics, 55–57
    U.S. Securities and Exchange Commission (SEC) publication, 56f
Case study, corporate cyberforensics, 19
    complex in many dimensions, 19
    environment, 19
    extended analysis, 21–22
        evidence-gathering tools, 22
        "password-free" access, 21
        unallocated space, 22
        web portal scenario, 22
    incident, 19
    initial investigation, 19–21
        local file inclusion (LFI) vulnerability, 21
        memory images, 19, 21
        remote Linux/UNIX incident response in port-restricted environments, 20f
    investigation conclusions, 22
        appropriate cleanup measures, 22
        investigators' primary goals, 22
    simplified web farm network diagram, 20f
    technical/functional/legal/economical/political dimensions, 19
Case study, cybercrime and law enforcement cooperation, 135–137
    court appearances, 137
    defense industry, 135–136
    financial industry, 137
    health care industry, 136–137
Case study, data breach response and risk mitigation, interactive analytics, 120–128
    analytics repository storing analytical assets, 127f
    background, 120–121
    connecting the Dots to identify cybercrime suspects, 123–125
    connecting to data and profiling network traffic, 121–123
    connecting to important data sources, 121f
    geospatial map of suspected cybercriminals, 127f
    identifying individuals, accessed many user accounts, 125f
    individual accessing 19 different user accounts, 126f
    integrating other sources of data, 125–128
    interactive analytic tool, 121
    investigator bringing in data "on demand," 124f
    linkages between user account IP and source IP addresses, 122f
    linking to government watch list, 126f
    new data available for profiling, 124
    profiling login activity using interactive table views, 122f
    user account access (cell) from specific source IP addresses, matrix chart, 123f
Case study, insider threat
    action, 49–50
    outcome, 50
    situation, 49
Case study, large-scale data breaches
    account data compromise, 38
    Acme Corp management, 38–42
    company profile, 38
    forensic work, 40
    investigation, 38–39
    investigation control points, 39
    investigative procedure, 39
    network analysis, 39–40
    scoping exercise, 40
    wireless vulnerability, 40–41
Case study, malicious software
    behavioral analysis steps, 70–73
    BinText extracted clear-text strings embedded in malicious executable, 74f
    code analysis steps, 73–78
    "E-mail address" field, 76
    initial analysis steps, 70
    OllyDbg, extracting clear-text strings embedded in malicious executable, 74f
    OllyDbg, searching memory contents of running executable, 75f
    overwriting the specimen's hardcoded characteristics, hidden options screen, 77f
    specimen comparing first letters, typed as input to first letter of string "test," 76f
Case study, network forensics
    covert channels, advanced data leakage, and command shells, 95–99
        backdoor, 99f
        behavioral analysis reveals malware on network, 97f

extra-large "DNS" session, 98
incident analysis, 98
isolated sessions, 96f
nonstandard network traffic on port 53, 98
requirements, 95–97
resolution, 98–99
value of port agnostic traffic inspection, 97f
"drive by," 91–95
detection and response, 92–93
incident analysis, 93–94
insider tip post on Google site, 90f
pinpointing user, 91f
reconstructed event in NetWitness investigator, 91
requirements, 91–92
resolution, 94–95
spike in dynamic DNS activity, 93f
suspicious service type, 94f
unknown traffic types and Beacon Trojan, 95f
Case study, Random Access Memory (RAM), 111–115
background, 111–112
investigation process, 112–114
result of data analysis, 114t
Case study, technology malpractice
case study, 2009 ChoicePoint, 145–146
Categories of Common Malware Traits, 82 n2
CCIPS, *see* Computer Crime and Intellectual Property Section (CCIPS)
Centrifuge Systems, 117
CenturionGuard, 62, 82 n3
Certified Ethical Hacker (C|EH), 7
Certified Forensics Analyst (GCFA), 7
Certified Incident Handler (GCIH), 7
Certified Information Security Auditor (CISA), 1, 85
Certified Information Security Manager (CISM), 1, 85
Certified Information Systems Security Professional (CISSP), 1, 7, 45, 59, 85
Certified in the Governance of Enterprise IT (CGEIT), 1, 141
Certified Penetration Tester (GPEN), 7
CGEIT, *see* Certified in the Governance of Enterprise IT (CGEIT)
Chain of custody, 8, 29–30, 42, 48–50, 120, 132, 137
CIRT, *see* Computer Incident Response Team (CIRT)
CISA, *see* Certified Information Security Auditor (CISA)
CISM, *see* Certified Information Security Manager (CISM)

CISSP, *see* Certified Information Systems Security Professional (CISSP)
Clausing, Jim, 67
Cloud providers, external, 147
Cloud Service Delivery Models, 25
Clusters
additional, 110–111
bad, 110
Code analysis, 61, 67–69, 73–74, 76, 81, 82 n15, 82 n37
See also Malicious software
Command and control, 15, 24, 60, 63, 66, 93, 95, 98, 100
Commercial sandbox analysis software, 15–16
Common Point of Purchase (CPP), 38
Communications Assistance for Law Enforcement Act (CALEA), 7
Complex access control lists (ACL), 8, 15, 18–19, 23, 26 n22, 42
Computer Analysis and Response Teams (CART), 2
Computer Crime and Intellectual Property Section (CCIPS), 131
Computer-enabled fraud, 2
Computer forensics, 1, 6 n5, 7, 29–31, 34, 48–49, 115, 116 n6
Computer Incident Response Team (CIRT), 31, 92–94
Computer-on-computer crime, 2
Computer Online Forensic Evidence Extractor (COFEE), 13
Computer surveillance, 48–49
Coroner's Toolkit, 26 n27
Corporate cyberforensics investigations
approach, 8–18
See also Investigative approach in IT
case study, *see* Case study, corporate cyberforensics
characteristics, 7–8
ACL, 8
administration, 8
complexity of corporate IT environments, 8
cooperation from management, 8
different operating systems, 8
operating systems, 7–8
VLANs, 8
issues and trends
complex investigations, 23
compromise systems, use of, 23–24
considerations for future, 24–25
cyberforensics in corporate environment, 23–24

Corporate cyberforensics investigations (*cont.*)
    internal network space, reason for, 23
    investigators, traits of, 25
    kinds of cases, 24
Correlation, 16, 22, 38, 86–87
Counterintelligence, 1, 130
CPP, *see* Common Point of Purchase (CPP)
"Cracking" passwords, approaches to
  brute force attack, 17
  commercial/free tools, 18
  dictionary attack, 17
  IM, 18
  IRC, 18
  John the Ripper, 17
  simple/complex passwords, 17
Criminal forensics methods, 113
Cross-site scripting (XSS) code, 18
Cyber attack, 118, 121, 128, 136–138
    anatomy of, 50–51
Cybercrime and law enforcement cooperation
  case studies, 135–137
    court appearances, 137
    defense industry, 135–136
    financial industry, 137
    health care industry, 136–137
  investigation characteristics, 129–133
    corporate cyber-investigators, 131
    dynamics of cybercrime, 129
    forensic acquisition software, 132
    forensic analysis software, 132
    High Technology Crime Investigation
      Association, 131
    investigator's role, 132–133
    minimum equipment for corporation, 132
    organizational characteristics, 129–131
    organized crime (OC), 129
    planning and preparedness, 130
    technical characteristics, 131–132
    technical measures to be implemented, 132
  investigative approach, 133–135
    communication patterns, 134–135
    electronic crime scene, 133–134
    polices and procedures, 133
    RAM, 133–134
  issues and trends, 137–138
    inertia and resistance to cooperation, 138
    international issues, 137–138
Cyberforensics
  framework, 3–5, 4f

  history of, 1–3
    AT&T prosecution of *The Mentor*, 2
    computer-enabled fraud, 2
    The Cuckoo's Egg, 2
    cybercrime and cybercriminals, 2
    cyberforensics investigators, 1
    digital evidence/investigations, 1–2
    investigations of physical crimes, 2
    law enforcement investigations of cybercrime, 1
    U.S. military and intelligence agencies,
      pioneers, 1
  investigations, 1, 5, 7–27, 31, 147
Cybersecurity investigation
  case study, 5
  investigation characteristics, 5
  investigative approach, 5
  issues and trends, 5
Cyber surveillance, 47–49
  computer surveillance, 48–49
    data harvesting surveillance, 48
    e-mail attachment surveillance, 48
    mobile phone picture surveillance, 48–49
    print job surveillance, 48
    universal serial bus surveillance, 48
    web-based e-mail account surveillance, 48
  network surveillance, 48
Cyber threat groups, evolution of, 45, 51

D

Dan Farmer, 20, 26 n27
DarkSpy, 81, 83 n46
Data analysis, 5, 12, 113, 114t, 118, 147
Data breach response and risk mitigation, interactive
    analytics
  case study, 120–128
    analytics repository storing analytical assets,
      127f
    background, 120–121
    connecting the Dots to identify cybercrime
      suspects, 123–125
    connecting to data and profiling network traffic,
      121–123
    connecting to important data sources, 121f
    geospatial map of suspected cybercriminals,
      127f
    identifying individuals, accessed many user
      accounts, 125f
    individual accessing 19 different user accounts,
      126f

integrating other sources of data, 125–128
  interactive analytic tool, 121
  investigator bringing in data "on demand," 124f
  linkages between user account IP and source IP addresses, 122f
  linking to government watch list, 126f
  new data available for profiling, 124
  profiling login activity using interactive table views, 122f
  user account access (cell) from specific source IP addresses, matrix chart, 123f
  investigation characteristics, 117–119
  anomalous communication patterns, 118
  IA, combination of techniques, 119
  primary goals of forensic investigator, 119
  investigative approach, 119–120
  collaboration in digital forensics, 120
  collaborative analysis, 120
  "360-degree view" of cyber-activity, 120
  interactive data visualization, 119
  unified data views, 119–120
  issues and trends, 128
  collaboration and knowledge sharing, 128
  next-generation business intelligence technology, 128
Data-gathering techniques, 3
Data harvesting surveillance, 48
Data-mining techniques, 48, 55–56
Daubert, 115
"Dbindex," 14
DCIS, see Defense Criminal Investigative Service (DCIS)
Debuggers, 15, 81
Decryption methods, 9
Defense Criminal Investigative Service (DCIS), 135
Defense industry case study, 135–136
"360-Degree view" of cyber-activity, 120
Deliberately hidden data
  hidden in computer, 109–110
    additional clusters, 110–111
    bad clusters, 110
    slack space, 110
  hidden within file, 111
    embedding, 111
    watermarking and fingerprinting, 111
Denial of Service (DoS), 45, 100, 107, 112, 134
Department of Homeland Security (DHS), 29, 117–118
Digital forensics/live/static analysis tools, use of, 12

Disassemblers, 15, 81, 134
Disgruntlement, 46, 51
DLLs, see Dynamically linked libraries (DLLs)
DoS, see Denial of Service (DoS)
Drug Enforcement Administration (DEA), 3
Due diligence, 1, 46–48, 53, 57, 137, 142
Dynamically linked libraries (DLLs), 18, 67, 69, 78, 79f
Dynamic analysis, 69
DynLogger, 68, 82 n30

E
e-discovery, 9, 24, 26 n4, 88, 109, 115–116, 116 n9
e-fense's Helix3 Pro and Live Response tools, 13
Ehuan, A., 5, 129–139
Electronically Stored Information (ESI), 26 n4, 115
Electronic discovery (or e-discovery), 9, 24, 26 n4, 88, 109, 115–116, 116 n9
Electronic evidence, 30
E-mail Attachment Surveillance, 48
Embedded strings, 68, 74, 78
Embedding, 68, 111
Encase® Enterprise Edition, 12, 18, 88, 108, 132
Enterprise
  AccessData® Enterprise, 12
  CGEIT, 141
  data protection efforts, 46
  Encase® Enterprise Edition, 18
  Enterprise Edition, 12
  enterprise security investigations, 5, 12
  environment, 19
  investigator, 12
  mainstream security operations process within, 99–100
  process within, 99
  with technology malpractice, 142
  transnational criminal, 46, 51
  -wide network forensics, 101
Enterprise Security for the Executive, Setting the Tone from the Top, 1
Entry Point, 36, 50, 67
ESI, see Electronically Stored Information (ESI)
Evidence-gathering techniques, 48
Exfiltration, 46, 60, 95, 98, 100
Expanded database of PEiD-compatible signatures, 82 n38
Exploitation techniques, 46

F

FAT (File Allocation Table), 107–108, 132
Federal Bureau of Investigation (FBI), 2–3, 5, 6 n11, 29, 45, 129–130, 135, 137, 139 n2
Fergus, D., 5, 117–128
File system table, 68
Financial Industry Regulatory Authority (FINRA), 54
Footprint, 12, 26 n9–26 n10, 42, 62, 109, 116
"Forensic Examiners Database Scalpel," 18
Forensic images, 29
Forensic interviews, 47
"Forensic-script," 14
Forensics investigation, 15, 18, 26 n11, 42, 89, 112
Forensic Toolkit®, 18, 112
Forward Discovery, 129, 132
Fred, 111–114, 114t
Free ssdeep utility, "fuzzy" hashing capabilities, 82 n35
F-Response®, 14
FTK, see AccessData Forensic Took Kit (FTK)
Full packet capture, 86, 92, 98–98, 101 n1

G

GIAC Security Expert (GSE), 59
GID, see Group identifier (GID)
GMER, 81, 82 n44
"Golden weeks," 11
Graduate Certificate in Computer Forensics (GCCF), 7
GREP, 36, 112
Group identifier (GID), 106
GS Tool, 16
Guidance Software (R), 9, 12, 108, 132
"Guide to Integrating Forensic Techniques into Incident Response," 99

H

Hacktivism, 3
Hash, 15–18, 20, 70, 132
HB Gary's Responder, 18
Health care industry case study, 136–137
    checklist, 136
Hex-Rays Decompiler, 69, 82 n33
Hidden data (deliberately)
    in computer, 109–110
        additional clusters, 110–111
        bad clusters, 110
        slack space, 110
    within file, 111
        embedding, 111
        watermarking and fingerprinting, 111
HideOD, 81, 83 n50
HideToolz, 81, 83 n52
High Technology Crime Investigation Association, 131
Hoglund, G., 18, 26 n20
Honeyd, 66, 82 n16
Honeypot tools, 66
    See also Honeyd

I

IA, see Interactive analytics (IA)
IaaS, see Infrastructure as a Service (IaaS)
IACIS, see International Association of Computer Investigative Specialists (IACIS)
IceSword, 81, 83 n47
IDA Pro, 69, 82 n31, 139 n8
Identity theft, 3, 5
IDS, see Intrusion detection systems (IDS)
IDS/IPS called snort developed by SOURCEfire®, 16
i-list, 108
IM, see Instant messaging (IM)
Immigration and Naturalization Service (INS), 3
Import Table, 67–68, 78, 79f
ImpREC, 80, 82 n42
Incident response
    CIRT, 31
    "Guide to Integrating Forensic Techniques into Incident Response," 99
    ProDiscover(R), 12
    remote Linux/UNIX in port-restricted environments, 20
    The Value of Physical Memory for Incident Response (Greg Hoglund), 18
Information Security Management Standards: 27001/27002, International Standards Organization, 2006, 147, 148 n6
Informix®, 18
Infrastructure as a Service (IaaS), 25
Insider threat
    case study
        action, 49–50
        outcome, 50
        situation, 49
    investigation characteristics, 45–46
        exploitation techniques, 46
        state sponsored threat, 46
        transnational criminal enterprises, 46

investigative approach
    cyber surveillance, 47–49
    due diligence, 46–47
    forensic interviews, 47
  issues and trends
    anatomy of cyber attack, 50–51
    emerging and key capabilities for
      cyberforensics, 50–51
    evolution of cyber threat groups, 51
Insider trading, 55–57, 90
InstallWatch, 65, 82 n9
Instant messaging (IM), 18, 69
Intekras, 117
Intellectual property, 3, 7, 24t, 45–46, 91,
  111, 131
Interactive analytics (IA), 5, 51, 117–128
  See also Data breach response and risk mitigation,
    interactive analytics
Internal Revenue Service (IRS), 3
International Association of Computer Investigative
  Specialists (IACIS), 136
International Organization on Computer Evidence
  (IOCE), 3
Internet protocol (IP), 19, 23, 26 n26, 41, 49, 64, 66,
  68, 72, 87, 89–92, 95, 100, 119–124, 131,
  135–136, 138
Internet Relay Chat (IRC), 18
INTERPOL, 3
Introduction to Malware Analysis, 82 n36
Intrusion detection systems (IDS), 8, 10, 16–17, 19,
  22, 26 n7, 27 n28, 32, 87, 89, 100, 119, 136
Intrusion prevention systems (IPS), 10, 16, 26 n7, 32
i-number, 108
Investigation characteristics, accounting forensics,
  53–54
  FINRA, 54
  sample testing, 54
  Statement of Auditing Standards No. 99 (SAS 99),
    54
Investigation characteristics, cybercrime and law
  enforcement cooperation, 129–133
  corporate cyber-investigators, 131
  dynamics of cybercrime, 129
  forensic acquisition software, 132
  forensic analysis software, 132
  High Technology Crime Investigation Association,
    131
  investigator's role, 132–133
  minimum equipment for corporation, 132

organizational characteristics, 129–131
organized crime (OC), 129
planning and preparedness, 130
technical characteristics, 131–132
technical measures to be implemented, 132
Investigation characteristics, data breach response and
  risk mitigation, 117–119
  anomalous communication patterns, 118
  IA, combination of techniques, 119
Investigation characteristics, insider threat, 45–46
  exploitation techniques, 46
  state sponsored threat, 46
  transnational criminal enterprises, 46
Investigation characteristics, large-scale data
  breaches, 29–34
  attack difficulty, 33, 33f
  breach discovery methods by percent of breaches
    in 2008, 32
  challenges with large data breaches, 33–34
  Computer Incident Response Team (CIRT), 31
  control points, 34
  digital evidence, 31
  evidence preservation, 31
  legal counsel, 34
  malware customization, 33f
  number of records compromised per year in
    breaches, 30f
  Personnel working, 32
  phenomena of non-ownership, 32
  procedures designed to safeguard evidence, 29–30
  transference of asset ownership, 32
  types of cybercrimes, 30
Investigation characteristics, malicious software
  common malware characteristics, *see* Malware,
    common characteristics
  dual-phased analysis, behavioral/code, 61, 61f
  malware analysis as part of the forensic
    investigation, 59–60
Investigation characteristics,
  network forensics, 85–86
    advances in analytic technology and security
      practice, 87–88
      improving effectiveness of SOC, 87
      investigatory support, 88
      situational awareness, 88
  definitive insight into actions and behaviors, 86
  JavaScript obfuscation depicted in Wireshark, 88f
  network forensics metadata, 87f
  "patient zero" in designer malware attack, 87

Investigation characteristics, network forensics (*cont.*)
   reconstruction of network events, 86
   session reconstruction, example of, 86f
   users, devices, and applications, 86–87
Investigation characteristics, RAM, 103–104
   detailed timeline and observations, 104
   "live" investigative environment, 103
   seizing volatile data of electronic device, 104
Investigation characteristics, technology malpractice, 141–143
   inaccurate technology inventory, 142
   vulnerability awareness and accountable management neglect, relationship, 142f
Investigative approach, accounting forensics, 54–55
   business applications and balance sheet, 54
   senior leader in finance, help of, 54
   "smoke-screen" approach, 55
   trace transactions of interest to investigation, 54
Investigative approach, cybercrime, 133–135
   communication patterns, 134–135
   electronic crime scene, 133–134
   polices and procedures, 133
   RAM, 133–134
Investigative approach, data breach response and risk mitigation, 119–120
   collaboration in digital forensics, 120
   collaborative analysis, 120
   "360-degree view" of cyber-activity, 120
   interactive data visualization, 119
   unified data views, 119–120
Investigative approach, malicious software
   behavioral analysis, 63–67
      automated behavioral analysis, 66–67
      Autoruns, 65, 65f
      CaptureBAT, 64, 64f
      honeypot tools, Honeyd, 66
      identifying important changes to the system, 65
      InstallWatch, 65
      interacting with malware, 66
      malware, interacting with, 66
      "Mini Fake DNS" Python script, 66
      monitoring the network, 65–66
      Netcat, 66
      process monitor display, 64, 64f, 71f
      real-time monitoring of system, 63–65
      Regshot, 65, 70f
      SpyMe Tools, 65
      TCP port 25, 73
      TCP port 25, specimen attempted to connect to, 73f
      victim's msnsettings.dat file, 72f
      Wireshark captured attempt to resolve hostname of SMTP server, 72f
   code analysis, 67–69
      BinText, 68
      dynamically linked libraries (DLLs), 67f
      DynLogger, 68
      embedded strings, 68
      executable's instructions, 68–69
      Hex-Rays Decompiler, 69
      IDA Pro, 69
      KaKeeware Application Monitor, 68
      Kerberos, 68f
      OllyDbg, 69
      PEiD, 67
      PE Tools, 67
      references to external functions, 68
      stepping through the executable, 67f
      structure of the executable file, 67
      TextScan, 68
      xPELister, 67f
   creating analysis report, 69
      behavioral and code analysis findings, 69
      characteristics, 69
      dependencies, 69
      identification, 69
      incident recommendations, 69
      summary, 69
      supporting figures, 69
   malware analysis laboratory, 61–63
   See also Malware analysis laboratory
Investigative approach in IT, 8–18
   ability to think similar to hackers, 11
   Access Data®, 9
   access to user computer systems, 9
   anomalies or suspicious activity in network traffic
      AT&T-developed tool (GS Tool), 16
      NetWitness® Investigator, 16
      SilentRunner™, 16
   applications and operating system programs
      log parsing tools, 16
      preserving these logs, 16
   combination of vendor software and script utilities, 14
   Commercial sandbox analysis software, 15–16
   Computer Online Forensic Evidence Extractor (COFEE), 13

Index

"cracking" passwords, approaches to
    brute force attack, 17
    commercial/free tools, 18
    dictionary attack, 17
    instant messaging (IM), 18
    Internet Relay Chat (IRC), 18
    John the Ripper, 17
    simple/complex passwords, 17
cross-site scripting (XSS) code, 18
"dbindex," 14
digital forensics/live/static analysis tools, use of, 12
digital forensics tools, 12
e-discovery, 9
e-fense's Helix3 Pro and Live Response tools, 13
factors, determining "best forensics practices," 9
"forensic-script," 14
goals, 10
"golden weeks," 11
Guidance Software (R), 9
IDS/IPS called snort developed by SOURCEfire®, 16
"just re-image the system" approach, 10
"malware analysis," 15
MANDIANT, 9
Microsoft's older Windows OnLine Forensics (WOLF), 13
"modify, access, and create" (MAC), 13
occasions where tools cannot be used, 14
    "jump server" Linux/UNIX environments, 14
penetration testing, 11
PII, 18
possible scenarios, 12
remote vendor forensics tools
    advantages/disadvantages, 13
script tools
    advantages/disadvantages, 13–14
security protocol, 11
self-incriminating information, 9
sources of potential evidence, steps, 10
Stealthy investigative techniques, 14
Technology Pathways, 9
time needed, factors determining, 10–11
volatility of data, 14
ways for hackers to gain access to systems
    "jsmith" account, 17
web defacement or retrieval of noncritical information, 11
web farms, 12
web portal, 9

Investigative approach, insider threat
    cyber surveillance, 47–49
    due diligence, 46–47
    forensic interviews, 47
Investigative approach, network forensics, 88–91
    input developed from existing security technology sources, 89–90
        sourcefire defense center, 89
    input received from someone in the organization, 90–91
    sample placement of network forensics devices, 89f
    sample sourcefire defense center event, 89f
Investigative approach, RAM and file systems revelations, 105–111
    analysis approach, 109
    data acquisition
        Guidance Software's Encase or Access Data's FTK, 108
        PCI or PCMICA cards, 108
        steps in the acquisition process, 108–109
    deliberately hidden data
        hidden in computer, 109–110
        hidden within a file, 111
    file systems
        FAT (File Allocation Table), 107
        file slack space within a cluster, 107f
        NTSF (New Technology File System), 107–108
        Unix File systems (Ordinary Files, Special Files, Directories, and Links), 108
        windows file systems, 107–108
    general data acquisition, 105–114
        Unix vs. Windows, 105
        volatile data items, 105
        volatile data vs. nonvolatile data, 105
    virtual memory
        RAM, 106
        SWAP File, 107
Investigative approach, technology malpractice, 143–145
    documented security policy and processes, 144
    information security program, 143
    iterative process, 145
    levels of security program evidence, 144, 144f
    shared cross-functionally, 144
IOCE, see International Organization on Computer Evidence (IOCE)
I-PingU, 103, 111
IPS, see Intrusion prevention systems (IPS)

IRC, *see* Internet Relay Chat (IRC)
IRC bot, 15, 21, 26 n17
ISO 27002, 145

J
Joy riders, 3
"jsmith" account, 17
Jump servers, 14–15, 19, 26 n16
"Just re-image the system" approach, 10

K
KaKeeware Application Monitor, 68, 82 n29
Kenston, J., 91
Kerberos, 68f, 82 n28
Key staff, 7, 9, 11, 36
　key stakeholders, 5
King Chuen Tang, 55
Koslowski, D., 53–54

L
Large-scale data breaches
　case study
　　account data compromise, 38
　　Acme Corp management, 38–42
　　company profile, 38
　　forensic work, 40
　　investigation, 38–39
　　investigation control points, 39
　　investigative procedure, 39
　　network analysis, 39–40
　　scoping exercise, 40
　　wireless vulnerability, 40–41
　investigation approach, 34
　　accurately scope evidence and acquisition, 37
　　detect and manage misinformation, 37
　　goals for investigation, 35
　　GREP, 36
　　information flow and data discovery exercise, 36
　　leverage fraud data, 37–38
　　network discovery, 36
　　percent of "unknown unknowns" in 2004–2007 forensic caseload, 35f
　　set investigation control points, 34–35
　　SuperScan/Nmap/Nessus, 36
　　unknown unknowns, managing, 35–36, 35f
　investigation characteristics, 29–34
　　attack difficulty, 33, 33f
　　breach discovery methods by percent of breaches in 2008, 32
　　challenges with large data breaches, 33–34
　　Computer Incident Response Team (CIRT), 31
　　control points, 34
　　digital evidence, 31
　　evidence preservation, 31
　　legal counsel, 34
　　malware customization, 33f
　　number of records compromised per year in breaches, 30f
　　personnel working, 32
　　phenomena of non-ownership, 32
　　procedures designed to safeguard evidence, 29–30
　　transference of asset ownership, 32
　　types of cybercrimes, 30
　issues and trends, 42–43
Law enforcement, *see* Cybercrime and law enforcement cooperation
Legislation, 18, 53
Leibolt, G., 5, 7–27, 143
　senior technical director at AT&T, 5
Ligh, Michael, 81, 83 n49
Lightweight Directory Access Protocol (LDAP), 8, 19, 26 n2
Linux LVM, 14, 26 n14
Litchfield, D., 18, 26 n22
Live analysis, 12–14
"Live," definition, 104
"Live" investigative environment, 103
LVM, 14, 26 n14

M
Mailpot, 73, 73f, 82 n37
Malicious software
　case study
　　behavioral analysis steps, 70–73
　　BinText extracted clear-text strings embedded in malicious executable, 74f
　　code analysis steps, 73–78
　　"E-mail address" field, 76
　　initial analysis steps, 70
　　OllyDbg, extracting clear-text strings embedded in malicious executable, 74f
　　OllyDbg, searching memory contents of running executable, 75f
　　overwriting the specimen's hardcoded characteristics, hidden options screen, 77f
　　specimen comparing first letters, typed as input to first letter of string "test," 76f

investigation characteristics
    dual-phased analysis, behavioral/code, 61, 61f
    malware analysis, 59–60
    malware characteristics, *see* Malware, common characteristics
investigative approach
    behavioral analysis, 63–67
    code analysis, 67–69
    creating the analysis report, 69
    malware analysis laboratory, s*ee* Malware analysis laboratory
    See also Investigative approach for malicious software
issues and trends
    anti-virtualization defenses, 81
    GMER, 81
    Olly Advanced, 81
    OllyDbg plugins HideOD, 81
    other anti-analysis trends, 81–82
    packed malware, 78–80
    RKDetector, 81
    RootkitRevealer, 81
    Structured Exception Handling (SEH), 81
    VMware, 81
    Volatility Framework, 81
Malware analysis laboratory, 61–63
    isolating malware laboratory, 62–63
        issue of "downstream liability," 62–63
    lab set up, 61
    virtualization software, options for, 61–62, 62f
        drawback, 62
        instant snapshots, 62
        VMware Workstation Snapshot, 63f
Malware, common characteristics, 60–61
    categories of traits
        capabilities, 60
        command and control, 60
        exfiltration, 60
        infection, 60
        propagation, 60
        self-defense, 60
Managed Security Service Provider (MSSP), 146–147
MANDIANT, 9, 12, 18
    Intelligent Response™, 12
MANDIANT's Memoryze, 18
McBride, T., 5, 53–57
Memory
    analysis, 18, 94, 132
    dumps, 12, 67
    images, 21
    live memory analysis, 132
    MANDIANT's Memoryze, 18
    map of debugged process, 75
    map window, 75
    "paged out" (swap) memory, 15
    RAM, *see* Random Access Memory (RAM)
    ROM, 106
    "swapped" or "paged" memory, 18
    system address space, or OS memory, 106
    virtual memory
        RAM, 106
        SWAP file, 107
    volatile memory, 108–109
Microsoft's older Windows OnLine Forensics (WOLF), 13, 148 n5
Microsoft SQL Server®, 18
Microsoft TechNet, *Interoperability and Migration Guide*, 116 n4
"Mini Fake DNS" Python script, 66, 82 n14
Mobile phone picture surveillance, 48–49
"Modify, access, and create" (MAC), 13, 26 n11
MSSP, *see* Managed Security Service Provider (MSSP)
Musashi, M., 12, 26 n9
MySQL, 18

N

National Aeronautics and Space Administration (NASA), 3
National Cyber-Security Month, 117
National Software Assurance Repository (NSAR), 103
Nation-state
    cooperation, 138
    divergent impact of cybercrime, 138
Nessus, 36
Netcat, 19, 21, 66, 73, 82 n18
NetWitness® Investigator, 16, 91, 91, 92, 94, 101
Network-Attached Storage (NAS), 8, 26 n1
Network forensics
    best freeware tools, 101 n2
    case studies, 91–99
        covert channels, advanced data leakage, and command shells, 96–100
        "drive by," 91–94
    future trends, 99–101
        network forensics as mainstream process, 99–100

Network forensics (cont.)
  rise of antiforensics techniques, 100–101
  "situational awareness," 98–100
  investigation characteristics, see Investigation characteristics, network forensics
  investigative approach, see Investigative approach, network forensics
  tools, 16
Network investigation, see Network forensics
Network surveillance, 48–49
Network traffic, anomalies or suspicious activity
  AT&T-developed tool (GS Tool), 16
  NetWitness® Investigator, 16
  SilentRunner™, 16
New Technology File System (NTSF), 107–108
NIST 800-33, 145
Nmap, 36
NTSF, see New Technology File System (NTSF)

O

OllyDbg, 69, 82 n32
  advanced, 81, 83 n51
  plugins HideOD, 81
Operating system (OS), 3, 5, 7–8, 13–14, 16–19, 26 n1, 40, 51, 61, 67, 105–107, 109–110, 133, 136, n12
Oracle®, 18, 26 n22
Organized crime (OC), 42–43, 129
Original copy, 109

P

Packed malware, 78–80
  bypassing the packer's protection, 80
  comparison to unpacked executable, fewer readable strings in packed file, 79f
  LordPE can "dump" the original executable from RAM to a file, 80f
  packed executable often stores very few external DLL references in its import table, which can be viewed with tools such as PEiD, 79f
  packing, 78
    executable complicating analysis process, 78f
    PEiD can identify many common packers based on its signature database, 80f
  "UPX" or "Themida," 80
"Packerid.py" script, 80, 82 n40
Packet analysis, 16, 78, 80
Packet capture, 101 n1
Packing
  definition, 78, 78f
  techniques, 16
  unpacking code, 78, 80–81
PCI or PCMICA cards, 108
"Pefile" Python module, 80, 82 n39
PE Header, 18, 67–68, 80
PEiD, 67, 79–80, 82 n23, 82 n38
Penetration testing, 7, 11
Persistent cross-site scripting (XSS), 18, 26 n23
Personally identifiable information (PII), 18, 22, 45, 134, 136–137
PE Tools, 67, 80, 82 n24
Physical crime, 1–2, 138
PII, see Personally Identifiable Information (PII)
PIN Entry Devices (PEDs), 40
Platform as a Service (PaaS), 25
Point of Sale (POS), 40–42
Ponzi scheme fraud, 57
Portal, 9–10, 12, 16, 19, 21–22, 24
Print Job Surveillance, 48
Private investigators, 25, 113, 115, 120, 136
Procedures
  CIRT procedure, 31
  cybercrime and law enforcement cooperation, 129
  large-scale data breaches, 39
    procedures designed to safeguard evidence, 29–30
  multi-team procedures, 8
  network forensics tools and, 90
  traditional forensics procedures, 8
  U.S. Federal Rules of Civil Procedure, 115
Process Monitor, 34, 63, 65, 70, 71f, 82 n5
ProDiscover(R) Incident Response, 12
Propagation, 60
PsExec, 13, 26 n13

R

RAM, see Random Access Memory (RAM)
Random Access Memory (RAM), 60–61, 68, 78, 80, 104–107, 109–111, 113, 115, 133–134, 139 n8, 147
  case study, 111–115
    background, 111–112
    investigation process, 112–114
    result of data analysis, 114t
  investigation characteristics, 103–104
    detailed timeline and observations, 104
    "live" investigative environment, 103
    seizing volatile data of electronic device, 104

investigative approach, 105–111
issues
　usage of standards, 115
trends
　anti-forensics, tools, 116
　e-discovery, 115
　ESI, 115
Read Only Memory (ROM), 106
Reborn PCI Card, 62, 82 n4
RedSeal, 36
Redundant Array of Independent Disks (RAID), 8, 14, 26 n1
Regshot, 65, 70, 70f, 82 n7
Regulation, 19, 53, 144
Remote vendor forensics tools
　advantages/disadvantages, 13
Reverse Engineer Malware (GREM), 7
RKDetector, 81, 82 n43
Rohmeyer, P., 5, 141–147
　industry professor of technology management, 5
　management consultant, 5
ROM, see Read Only Memory (ROM)
RootkitRevealer, 81, 83 n45

S
Salt, 17, 26 n19
"Sample," 17, 39, 54–55, 69, 82 n1, 89f
Sandbox environment, 15, 26 n18
Sarbanes-Oxley Act of 2002 (SOX), 19, 53–54
Savvis, 59
Schwartz, E., 5, 85–101
　law enforcement and corporate investigator, 5
"Script kiddie," 9, 26 n6
Script tools
　advantages/disadvantages, 13–14
Securities and Exchange Commission (SEC), 53–55, 56f, 90
Security architecture, 1, 88
"Security program," 86, 143–146, 144f
Security protocol, 11
Self-defense, 60
Self-incriminating information, 9, 143
Service Set Identifier (SSID), 41
SIEM, see Specialized Log Manager or Security Incident and Event Manager (SIEM) appliances
Signori, Y., 5, 103–116
SilentRunner™, 16

Sims, S., 5, 45–51
　Federal Bureau of Investigation Agent, 5
SkyBox, 36
Slack space, 107, 110, 116
SmartSniff, 65, 82 n12
"Smoke-screen" approach, 55
Sniffer, 9–10, 15–16, 23, 25, 27 n28, 51, 65–66, 72
Social engineering techniques, 3
Software as a Service (SaaS), 25
Solaris ZFS file system, 14
The Solaris ZFS file system, 14
SOURCEfire®, 16
Specialized Log Manager or Security Incident and Event Manager (SIEM) appliances, 16
"Specimen," 82 n1
　See also "Sample"
SpyMe Tools, 65, 82 n8
Stanley, M., 53
Statement of Auditing Standards No. 99 (SAS 99), 55
State sponsored threat, 46
"Static" analysis tools, 12
Static linking, 68
Steganography, 111
Stepping through executable, 68
Stevens Institute of Technology, 1, 141
Stoll, C., 2
　The Cuckoo's Egg, 2
Storage Area Network (SAN), 8, 14, 26 n1, 59
Structured Exception Handling (SEH), 81
SuperScan, 36
SWAP file, 106–107
Sybase®, 18
System address space, or OS memory, 106
System programs, applications and operating
　log parsing tools, 16
　preserving these logs, 16

T
Tcpdump, 16, 65, 82 n13
TCP port 25, 73
　specimen attempted to connect to, 73f
Techniques
　antiforensics techniques, 100–101
　computer exploitation and data exfiltration techniques, 46

Techniques (*cont.*)
  computer forensics techniques, 1
  cyber-investigative techniques, 3, 45
  data-gathering techniques, 3
  data mining, 55–56, 101
  evidence-gathering techniques, 48
  exploitation techniques, 46
  packing techniques, 16
  social engineering techniques, 3
Technology
  malfeasance, 45, 49
  management, 4–5, 141–142, 146–147
  pathways, 9
Technology malpractice, 142
  case study, 2009 ChoicePoint, 145–146
  investigation characteristics, 141–143
    inaccurate technology inventory, 142
    vulnerability awareness and accountable management neglect, relationship, 142f
  investigative approach, 143–145
    documented security policy and processes, 144
    information security program, 143
    iterative process, 145
    levels of security program evidence, 144, 144f
    shared cross-functionally, 144
  issues and trends
    accountability, 147
    cloud computing, 147
    MSSP, 146–147
Telemetry, 89, 99
Tempur-pedic International, Inc. (Tempur), 55
Terrorism
  anti-, 128
  counter-, 128
TextScan, 68, 82 n27
Three "A's" – Accounting, Auditing, and Asking, 54
Title 18 United States Code 1030 Fraud and Related Activity in Connection with Computers (Title 18 USC 1030), 130–131
Truman, 15, 67, 82 n20
Tyco, 53

U
UID, *see* User identifier (UID)
United States Department of Justice (DOJ), 131
United States Secret Service (USSS), 39, 130
Universal Serial Bus Surveillance, 48
Unix File systems (Ordinary/Special Files/Directories/Links), 108

Unix *vs.* Windows, 105–106
  daemon *vs.* service, 105
  GID, 106
  multiple users, 105
  process hierarchy, 105
  security, 105–106
  UID, 106
Unknown unknowns, 35–36
"UPX" or "Themida," 78, 80
U.S. Air Force Office of Special Investigations (AFOSI), 5, 129, 135
U.S. Army Criminal Investigation Division (CID), 135
U. S. Customs Service, 3
User identifier (UID), 106
U.S. Federal Trade Commission (FTC), 142, 145–147, 148 n8
U.S. Navy (Naval Criminal Investigative Service (NCIS)), 135
U. S. Postal Inspection Service, 3
U.S. Secret Service (USSS), 3, 39, 41, 130

V
Valentine, J., 5
  law enforcement veteran, 5
Valentine, J. A., 29–43, 143
The Value of Physical Memory for Incident Response (Hoglund)
  challenges, 18
Verizon Business, 29–30, 43
Virtual LAN (VLAN), 8, 26 n3
Virtual memory
  RAM, 106
    "main memory," 106
    ROM (Read Only Memory), 106
  SWAP File, 107
"Virtual" operating systems, 26 n26
Virtual systems, 25, 61–62
VLAN (Virtual LAN), 26 n3
VMware, 62, 63f, 81
Volatile data
  items, 105
  vs. nonvolatile data, 105
Volatile memory, 108–109
  creating image of, 109
Volatility Framework, 81, 83 n48
Volatility scripts for malware analysis (Ligh), 83 n49
Vulnerability, 11–12, 21–22, 27 n32, 40–41, 50, 60, 99, 118, 141–142, 142f

W

Watermarking and fingerprinting, 16, 111
Web-based E-mail Account Surveillance, 48
Web defacement or retrieval of noncritical information, 11
Web farms, 12, 19
Web portal, 9, 12, 16, 19, 21–22, 24, 26 n24
What to Include in a Malware Analysis Report, 82 n34
Wietse Venema, 6 n18, 20, 26 n27
Windows file systems, 107–108
Windows Management Instrumentation (WMI), 13, 26 n12

Wireless access points (WAPs), 40–41
Wireshark, 16, 65, 72, 82 n11, 87, 88f

X

XPELister, 67f, 82 n22

Z

Zeltser, L., 5, 59–83
  director of leading security consulting practice, 5
Zero-day, 141, 148 n1
  viruses, 141